THE LEGACY OF SLAVERY AT HARVARD

THE LEGACY

of SLAVERY *at*

HARVARD

REPORT AND RECOMMENDATIONS

OF THE

PRESIDENTIAL COMMITTEE

Harvard University Press

Cambridge, Massachusetts & London, England   2022

This publication was funded in part by the Presidential Initiative
on Harvard and the Legacy of Slavery.

Any proceeds will benefit the Royall House and
Slave Quarters in Medford, Massachusetts.

Frontispiece: "A Prospect of the Colledges in Cambridge in New England,"
Engraving attributed to John Harris after William Burgis, 1726.
Massachusetts Historical Society.

Cataloging-in-Publication Data available from the Library of Congress
ISBN: 978-0-674-29240-6 (alk. paper)

Dedicated in memory of Paul Farmer (1959–2022),
our beloved colleague and committee member

CONTENTS

PREFACE

For the fortunate institution of higher education, there are signal moments when teaching, research, and service converge, creating a powerful current that speeds change and progress. The Report of the Committee on Harvard & the Legacy of Slavery catalogs truths long obscured: that enslaved people worked on our campus; that the labor of enslaved people enriched donors and, ultimately, the institution; that members of our faculty promoted ideas that gave scholarly legitimacy to concepts of racial superiority; and that the University continued discriminatory practices long after the Thirteenth Amendment was ratified in 1865. The report also recommends, with clarity and conviction, how Harvard ought to marshal its intellectual, reputational, and financial resources to address the persistent corrosive effects of slavery and its legacy.

When the report was released in April 2022, I could not have anticipated the number of positive and heartfelt responses I would receive as president, not just from members of the University community but also from individuals across the country. Honesty and humanity, as well as a deeper understanding of Harvard, were welcome even as they ushered in feelings of disappointment and indignation. Our willingness to understand how we as a community might redress—through teaching, research, and service—our legacies with slavery was hailed as a turning point for the University. Our commitment of $100 million and our establishment of a committee devoted to implementation signaled the ongoing need for careful attention, focused leadership, and dedicated resources in the years to come.

Beginning to fulfill our moral responsibility is an act of service not only to our community but also to our society. It is a sad commentary on the state of our Union that efforts to expand knowledge of Harvard's past were undertaken in parallel with drives in thirty-six states to suppress teaching about race and slavery. Education in this area of American history is essential to understanding our democracy—and to confronting and addressing persistent inequity. Negative responses to the release of the report, though rare, were sobering reminders of the ignorance and racism that are still part of our national life. None of us can afford to be complacent if we hope to address injustices that limit us all.

The University owes a debt of gratitude to Dean Tomiko Brown-Nagin for leading our effort and for giving us the opportunity to confront the truth and its consequences—and to take action. Hers was a selfless act of belief in the power of institutions to make a difference in the lives of individuals, and she and the members of the committee devoted themselves to their task with unflagging energy, even in the midst of a pandemic. Yet they would be the first to say that they could not have done it alone. Though the pages that follow are the result of the committee's two and a half years of extraordinary effort, many years of tireless work across and beyond the University preceded them, and this volume would not exist without the insistence and patience of countless members of our community. We are indebted, as well and as always, to Ruth Simmons, who, in 2004, launched a landmark effort as president of Brown University to, in her words, "investigate and discuss an uncomfortable piece of the University's—and our nation's—history."

I am honored to share this volume on behalf of our community, and especially those members whose contributions were unknown for so long, so that it may persist to the resounding benefit of generations to come.

Lawrence S. Bacow
President, Harvard University
June 2022

Evelynn M. Hammonds
Chair of the Department of the History of Science, Barbara
Gutmann Rosenkrantz Professor of the History of Science, and
professor of African and African American studies, Faculty of Arts
and Sciences; professor in the Department of Social and Behavioral
Sciences, Harvard T. H. Chan School of Public Health

Nancy F. Koehn
James E. Robison Professor of Business Administration,
Harvard Business School

Meira Levinson
Professor of education, Harvard Graduate School of Education

Tiya Miles
Michael Garvey Professor of History, Faculty of Arts and Sciences;
Radcliffe Alumnae Professor, Radcliffe Institute for Advanced Study

Martha Minow
300th Anniversary University Professor, Harvard Law School

Maya Sen
Professor of public policy, Harvard Kennedy School

Daniel Albert Smith
Lecturer on ministry studies, Harvard Divinity School

David R. Williams
Chair of the Department of Social and Behavioral Sciences and
Florence Sprague Norman and Laura Smart Norman Professor
of Public Health, Harvard T. H. Chan School of Public Health;
professor of African and African American studies, Faculty of
Arts and Sciences

William Julius Wilson
Lewis P. and Linda L. Geyser University Professor Emeritus,
Harvard Kennedy School and Faculty of Arts and Sciences

THE LEGACY OF SLAVERY AT HARVARD

This hand-drawn sketch from the records of a 1644 meeting of the Harvard
Board of Overseers is the first rendering of the Harvard seal: a shield
containing three open books that spell out the Latin word *Veritas*, or truth.
The seal was officially adopted by the Corporation during Harvard's bicenten-
nial in 1843, after being rediscovered in the archives by then-President
Josiah Quincy. College Books, 1636–1827/Harvard University Archives

ONE

Introduction

HARVARD'S MOTTO, *Veritas*, inscribed on gates, doorways, and sculptures all over campus, demands of us truth.[1] This report, prepared by the Presidential Committee on Harvard & the Legacy of Slavery, advances our quest for truth through scholarship about the University's historic ties to slavery—direct, financial, and intellectual.

Through research in the Harvard University Archives and in several Harvard libraries, including the Houghton Library and the Radcliffe Institute's Schlesinger Library on the History of Women in America, as well as in collections of the Massachusetts Historical Society, the Boston Athenaeum, the American Philosophical Society, the University of Michigan Library, and the New York Public Library Schomburg Center for Research in Black Culture, among other repositories, this report documents now incontestable truths: During the seventeenth and eighteenth centuries, the sale and trafficking of human beings—in slavery—and the industries rooted in the labor of enslaved women, men, and children were pervasive around the world, comprised a vital part of the New England economy, and powerfully shaped Harvard University. Harvard leaders, faculty, staff, and benefactors enslaved people, some of whom labored at the University;[2] accrued wealth through the slave trade and slave labor; and defended the institution of slavery.[3]

In documenting these truths, this report builds on the groundbreaking work of researchers at Harvard and other universities: In recent years, scholars have documented extensive relationships between American institutions of higher education and slavery.[4] Indeed, a consortium of more than eighty institutions of higher education, called Universities Studying Slavery and based at the University of Virginia, is engaged in this work.[5] We now officially and publicly—and with a steadfast commitment to truth, and to repair—add Harvard University to the long and growing list of American institutions of higher education, located in both the North and the South, that are entangled with the history of slavery and its legacies.[6]

A Community Reckoning with Slavery and Its Legacies

The findings of this committee—summarized in this introduction and detailed in the pages that follow—not only reveal a chasm between the Harvard of the past and of the present but also point toward the work we must still undertake to live up to our highest ideals. Today, Harvard University enrolls a racially diverse student body;[7] champions race-conscious admissions policies in our courts of law;[8] supports "inclusive excellence;"[9] employs a faculty that includes renowned scholars of African descent and a celebrated department of African and African American studies;[10] hosts a Native American Program that supports Native students and distinguished Native American faculty;[11] and embraces reckoning with its past. Yet legacies of slavery persist, and our community, working together, has the opportunity to shape a better future.

Harvard's 29th president, Lawrence S. Bacow, established the Presidential Initiative on Harvard & the Legacy of Slavery in 2019, appointed a committee representative of all the University's schools, and charged this group with diving deep into our history and its relationship to the present. President Bacow asked the committee to "give additional dimension to our understanding of the impact of slavery" at Harvard. This work, he said, should "have a strong grounding in rigorous research and critical perspectives" that "will inform . . . our understanding of facts," as well as "how we might address the ramifications of what we learn." President Bacow also asked the committee to "concentrate on connections, impact, and contributions that are specific to our Harvard community" and "provide opportunities to convene academic events, activities, and conversations that will encourage our broader University community to think seriously and rigorously about the continuing impact and legacy of slavery in 2019 and beyond."[12]

This charge built on earlier work. In 2016, Drew Gilpin Faust, the University's 28th president, publicly acknowledged that "Harvard was directly complicit in America's system of racial bondage from the College's earliest days in the seventeenth century until slavery in Massachusetts ended in 1783, and Harvard continued to be indirectly involved through extensive financial and other ties to the slave South up to the time of emancipation."[13] She established a committee on the University and slavery[14] that, with the aid of the researcher Caitlin Galante DeAngelis (PhD 2014), conducted a preliminary investigation upon which this report builds. These initial efforts included, in 2016, a public ceremony in which then-President Faust and the late civil rights leader US Congressman John Lewis unveiled a plaque affixed to Wadsworth House in Harvard Yard that acknowledges the unfree labor of four enslaved people—Titus, Venus, Juba, and Bilhah—who lived there and worked for two Harvard presidents and their families.[15] A 2017 conference at the Radcliffe Institute for Advanced Study, organized at Faust's suggestion with the support of then–Radcliffe Dean Lizabeth Cohen, brought together prominent thinkers about universities and slavery from around the country.[16]

The work of excavating and confronting the truths that this committee now discloses has been, and continues to be, a community-wide endeavor. Whereas prior histories of Harvard scarcely mentioned the University's ties to slavery,[17] Harvard scholars and students have worked assiduously in recent years to reveal painful truths. Beginning in 2007, Laird Bell Professor of History Sven Beckert and his undergraduate students began investigating Harvard's ties to slavery in a multiyear series of research seminars, releasing a report on their findings in 2011.[18] At Harvard Law School in 2008, Royall Professor of Law Janet Halley explored the history of slave-owning colonial benefactor Isaac Royall Jr.,[19] sharing knowledge that helped spur student protests decrying the Law School's shield, which featured the Royall family crest.[20] Martha Minow, 300th Anniversary University Professor and then-dean of Harvard Law School, established a committee that recommended the retiring of the shield.[21] In 2017, Harvard Law School dedicated a memorial on the School's campus to the enslaved people whose labor generated Royall's wealth.[22] In 2020, Harvard Medical School students petitioned against the "Oliver Wendell Holmes" academic society because of namesake Oliver Wendell Holmes Sr.'s role in the expulsion of Black students in 1850 and his promotion of so-called race science.[23] Upon the recommendation of a faculty subcommittee and with the approval of Dean George Q. Daley, the society was renamed for William Augustus Hinton (SB 1905; MD 1912), a clinical professor of bacteriology and immunology at HMS and the first Black full professor at Harvard.[24]

Moreover, as this committee conducted its work, many Harvard alumni engaged with it, including some with family connections to slavery and others who were present on campus during the era of segregation, bearing witness to parts of the history documented in this report. With support from the Presidential Initiative, Harvard students from multiple schools and departments also aided and augmented our efforts through research and the production of poetry and dramatic art.[25]

And as Harvard embarks on reparative efforts to address the University's entanglements with slavery, discussed below, the committee hopes and expects that our community will continue to participate in this reckoning.

Slavery in the North

Context is vital to understanding the complicity of American institutions, including institutions of higher education such as Harvard, with slavery. This context reframes what many believe about slavery, and it belies a common myth.

The story most often told about American slavery focuses on large plantations in the South, forced agricultural labor, and brutal auctions where enslaved people were sold "down the river." New England is not, in general, a part of this narrative.[26] The Commonwealth of Massachusetts and the City of Boston are, rather, remembered as the birthplace of the American Revolution, and they are typically associated with the *anti*slavery moment. Massachusetts is thought to have been a hotbed of opposition to slavery, and so it was at critical junctures. The Commonwealth can rightly claim noted abolitionists like William Lloyd Garrison, Frederick Douglass, David Walker, and US Senator Charles Sumner (AB 1830; LLB 1833) along with courageous soldiers who fought for the Union during the Civil War—including the famed 54th Massachusetts Volunteer Infantry Regiment, commanded by the Harvard alumnus Robert Gould Shaw (Class of 1860; posthumous AB 1873).

This conventional telling—focused on the region's celebrated roles in the Revolutionary War, the abolitionist struggle, and the preservation of American nationhood during the Civil War—makes valor, social consciousness, and liberty the through lines in New England's history. Resistance to tyranny in service of American democracy is an integral part of the region's cultural identity. But history is rarely, if ever, so neat and linear; and reality complicates this incomplete, if popular, narrative.[27]

In fact, slavery thrived in New England from its beginnings, and was a vital element of the colonial economy. Colonists first enslaved and sold Indigenous people, and they dispossessed and massacred Native peoples through war.[28] They also enslaved Africans and played a key role in the Atlantic slave trade, building a thriving economy based on "an economic alliance with the sugar islands of the West Indies."[29] This trade involved the provision of food, fuel, and lumber produced in New England to plantations of the Caribbean, where those goods were exchanged for tobacco, coffee, and sugar produced by enslaved Africans—or for enslaved people themselves.[30] "This effectively made Boston a slave society," according to a leading historian of the region, "but one where most of the enslaved toiled elsewhere, sustaining the illusion of Boston in New England as an inclusive republic devoted to the common good."[31] By 1700, New Englanders had made at least nineteen voyages to Africa and then to the West Indies, the chief route of the slave trade, as well as many more voyages between Massachusetts Bay and the Caribbean.[32]

The Massachusetts Bay Colony's Body of Liberties, written in 1641, made such exchanges lawful. The first legal code governing slavery in

British North America, it prohibited "bond-slavery," "unless it be of lawfull captives, taken in just warrs, and such strangers as willingly sell themselves, or are solde to us," leading one historian to note, "the word 'unless' has seldom carried more baggage."[33] Even as it paid homage to the Magna Carta, the Body of Liberties permitted the buying, selling, and trading of Indigenous people and Africans. Slavery would not officially end in Massachusetts until 1783.

So, too, was slavery integral to Harvard. Over nearly 150 years, from the University's founding in 1636 until the Massachusetts Supreme Judicial Court found slavery unlawful in 1783, Harvard presidents and other leaders, as well as its faculty and staff, enslaved more than seventy individuals, some of whom labored on campus.[34] Enslaved men and women served Harvard presidents and professors and fed and cared for Harvard students. Moreover, throughout this period and well into the nineteenth century, the University and its donors benefited from extensive financial ties to slavery. These profitable financial relationships included, most notably, the beneficence of donors who accumulated their wealth through slave trading; from the labor of enslaved people on plantations in the Caribbean islands and in the American South; and from the Northern textile manufacturing industry, supplied with cotton grown by enslaved people held in bondage. The University also profited from its own financial investments, which included loans to Caribbean sugar planters, rum distillers, and plantation suppliers along with investments in cotton manufacturing.[35] The balance of the University's financial ties shifted over time; with the development of industrial capitalism in the late eighteenth and early nineteenth centuries, the plantation economy evolved, and cotton began to take center stage. Northern textile industrialists interacted with the institution of slavery through the cotton trade; enslaved laborers produced the cotton that was the engine of textile production and, therefore, of the region's economy. Senator Sumner called this vital economic link between the industrial North and the slaveholding South an "unhallowed alliance between the lords of the lash and the lords of the loom."[36]

Harvard's donors in this period—and their wealth—were vital to the University's growth. They allowed the University to hire faculty, support students, develop its infrastructure, and, ultimately, begin to establish itself as a national institution.[37] Still today, early Harvard benefactors who accumulated their wealth through slavery are memorialized throughout campus in statues, buildings, student houses, and endowed professorships—and indeed in other educational, civic, and cultural organizations across Massachusetts. These individuals' involvement as critical players in the University's early development, and the commemorations of their contributions still visible in the campus landscape, are an important part of the history with which we must now reckon.

Slavery and Its Legacies before and after the Civil War

During the antebellum era, well after the end of slavery in Massachusetts, and even after the Thirteenth Amendment to the US Constitution conferred emancipation nationwide in 1865, vestiges—or legacies—of the system lingered. Legacies of slavery such as exclusion, segregation, and discrimination against Blacks in employment, voting, housing, healthcare, public accommodations, criminal punishment, and education, among other areas, persisted in the South as well as the North.[38] Notwithstanding the Commonwealth's Revolutionary War heritage as birthplace of the colonists' struggle for liberty, its celebrated antislavery activists, and its many brave Union veterans of the Civil War,[39] racial inequality flourished in Massachusetts—and at Harvard—as Blacks struggled for equal opportunity and full citizenship.[40]

Slavery and Antislavery before the Civil War

In the years before the Civil War, the color line held at Harvard despite a false start toward Black access. In 1850, Harvard's medical school admitted three Black students but, after a group of white students and alumni objected, the School's dean, Oliver Wendell Holmes Sr., expelled them.[41] The episode crystallized opposition to Black students on campus, which outweighed the views of a vocal contingent of white classmates who supported the admission of the three African American students.[42] Over a hundred years would pass before these more welcoming attitudes toward Blacks would prevail and open the door to significant Black enrollment.

The passage of the Fugitive Slave Act of 1850, requiring the return of enslaved people to their owners, even if slaves had escaped to free states, turned more white Northerners against slavery and its cruelties.[43] Yet support for antislavery efforts remained anemic at Harvard, even amid the rise of abolitionist sentiment in the Commonwealth. In some cases, University leadership even attempted to suppress abolitionist sentiment.

Within the context of increasing political rancor and social division on and off campus, a small but vocal group of Harvard affiliates pressed the abolitionist cause. In addition to Charles Sumner, outspoken abolitionist voices included Wendell Phillips (AB 1831; LLB 1834), founder of the New England Antislavery Society; John Gorham Palfrey (AB 1815; dean and faculty member, 1830–1839; overseer, 1828–1831, 1852–1855), the first dean of the Divinity School; and several other faculty members, among them cofounders of the Cambridge Anti-Slavery Society.[44] Richard Henry Dana Jr. (AB 1837; LLB 1839; lecturer 1866–1868; overseer, 1865–1877) cofounded the antislavery Free Soil party and represented Anthony Burns, a fugitive slave who had been arrested in Boston. In a turn of events decried by many Northerners, a Massachusetts judge, himself a Harvard alumnus and lecturer, ordered Burns returned to slavery in Virginia.[45] Because of such controversies, the Fugitive Slave Act became a catalyst of the Civil War, and by the time war began in 1861, the University officially supported the Union. Many Harvard men fought and died for the Union, and their sacrifices are commemorated on campus in Memorial Hall; some also fought and died for the Confederacy.[46]

Intellectual Leadership

Harvard's ties to the legacies of slavery also include, prominently, its intellectual production—its scholarly leadership and the influential output of some members of its faculty. In the nineteenth century, Harvard had begun to amass human anatomical specimens, including the bodies of enslaved people, that would, in the hands of the University's prominent scientific authorities, become central to the promotion of so-called race science at Harvard and other American institutions.[47] Charles William Eliot—Harvard's longest-serving president—and several prominent faculty members promoted eugenics, the concept of selective reproduction premised on innate differences in moral character, health, and intelligence among races.[48] These were ideas of the sort that had long been deployed to justify racial segregation and which would in the nineteenth and twentieth centuries cement profound racial inequities in the United States and underpin Nazi Germany's extermination of "undesirable" populations.[49] In addition to research in the University's extensive collections of human remains, Eliot authorized anthropometric measurements of Harvard's own student-athletes.[50] Many of the records and artifacts of this era remain in the University's collections today.[51]

Vestiges of Slavery after the Civil War

The decades after the Civil War, during the period of Reconstruction when debates raged about whether and how to support the Black American quest for equality, are especially germane to understanding legacies of slavery in American institutions of higher education. The US Constitution changed, reflecting the nation's formal break with slavery and commitment to equal citizenship rights regardless of race. The Fourteenth Amendment, conferring equal protection and due process of law, and the Fifteenth Amendment, prohibiting discrimination against males in voting, were enacted and ratified.[52] Within this context, reformers conceived policies and social supports to lift the formerly enslaved and their descendants. But it fell to the nation's institutions, its leadership, and its people to safeguard—or not—citizens' rights and to implement these policies.[53]

Around the same time, Harvard itself aspired to transform: it sought to enlarge its infrastructure, expand its student body, and recruit new faculty. Samuel Eliot Morison, a noted historian of the University, explained that during the period from 1869 into the twentieth century, the University resolved "to expand with the country."[54] Harvard's leaders, particularly Presidents Charles William Eliot and Abbott Lawrence Lowell, argued that Harvard should become a "true" national university that would serve as a "unifying influence."[55] They viewed the recruitment of students from "varied" backgrounds and a "large area" of the country as a linchpin of these ambitions.[56]

Hence, two developments critical to understanding this moment of promise and peril occurred at once: the fate of African Americans hung in the balance; and Harvard, already well-known, sought to grow, evolve, and build a yet greater national reputation. The University, as a prominent institution of higher education, held influence in a sphere deemed particularly critical to racial uplift. Because so many considered education "a liberating force," legislative and philanthropic efforts to create opportunity for African Americans often emphasized schooling.[57] Massachusetts was already a leader in this area; in addition to its many universities, the state had led the movement to establish taxpayer-supported "common schools" at the elementary and secondary levels.[58]

Nevertheless, in Massachusetts and in every corner of the nation, African Americans encountered roadblocks to achieving social mobility through education. White opposition to racially "mixed" schools, born of racist attitudes about Black ability and character promoted by slaveholders as well as intellectuals at Harvard and elsewhere, blocked equal access to education.[59] Segregated, under-resourced, and often inferior elementary and secondary schools became the norm for African Americans. In this, too, Massachusetts led the way.

Harvard alumni played prominent roles on both sides of the struggle over school segregation. One critically important chapter in that struggle, which would have dire nationwide consequences for Blacks into the twentieth century, had occurred in Boston before the Civil War. In *Roberts v. City of Boston*, an 1850 decision, the Commonwealth helped normalize segregated schools. In that case—filed by Charles Sumner on behalf of a five-year-old Black girl—the Massachusetts Supreme Judicial Court held that racial segregation in the city's schools did not offend the law.[60] Judge Lemuel Shaw (AB 1800; overseer, 1831–1853; fellow, 1834–1861) authored the opinion for the court. "[T]he good of both classes of school will be best promoted, by maintaining the separate primary schools for colored and for white children," he wrote.[61] Advocacy by the local Black community with important support from Sumner led the Commonwealth to ban segregated schools in 1855, the first such law in the United States.[62] Nevertheless, decades later, in 1896, the US Supreme Court cited *Roberts* as authority when it held in *Plessy v. Ferguson* that racially "separate but equal" facilities did not violate the Fourteenth Amendment to the Constitution.[63]

In higher education, Blacks also found themselves in separate and unequal schools. It was left to historically Black colleges and universities (HBCUs), supported by the federal government beginning in 1865 and often founded by Black self-help organizations and religious societies, to provide a measure of opportunity.[64] But from the start, HBCUs were sorely underfunded, a reality that hobbled school leaders as they sought to fulfill the HBCUs' mission of racial uplift through postsecondary school access.[65]

Predominantly white universities did not fill the breach. In keeping with prevailing racial attitudes and the relegation of African Americans to poorly resourced HBCUs of uneven quality, Harvard—like all but a few white universities—did little to support the African American quest for advancement.[66]

In the decades following the Civil War, at Harvard and other white universities, Blacks still faced discrimination, or plain indifference. Notwithstanding Harvard's rhetorical commitment in the war's wake to recruit a nationally representative student body that would model political collegiality, the University's sights remained set on a white "upper crust." Harvard prized the admission of academically able Anglo-Saxon students from elite backgrounds—including wealthy white sons of the South—and it restricted the enrollment of so-called "outsiders."[67] Despite access to civic organizations in major cities that could identify a pool of able Black students, the college enrolled meager numbers of African Americans.[68] During the five decades between 1890 and 1940, approximately 160 Blacks attended Harvard College, or an average of about three per year, thirty per decade.[69] The pattern of low enrollment of Blacks also held true at Radcliffe College,[70] founded in 1879 as the "women's annex" to all-male Harvard.[71] Radcliffe did consistently enroll more Black women than its Seven Sisters peers.[72] Yet the women educated at Radcliffe overwhelmingly were white, and Black women were denied campus housing.[73]

Those Blacks who did manage to enter Harvard's gates during the nineteenth and early-to-mid-twentieth century excelled academically, earning equal or better academic records than most white students,[74] but encountered slavery's legacies on campus. Two examples illustrate the segregation and marginalization that the few Black Harvard students faced.[75] First, Harvard President Abbott Lawrence Lowell's signature innovation—a residential college experience for first years that was meant to build community—excluded the handful of Black Harvard students.[76] Lowell's exclusionary policy was eventually overturned by the University's governing boards following press attention and pressure from students, alumni, and activists.[77] Second, Black Harvard athletes, whose talents sometimes earned them respect and recognition from other students on campus, encountered discrimination and exclusion in intercollegiate play, and Harvard administrators sometimes bowed to it.[78] Yet Black students generally could and did participate in campus clubs and activities—illustrating a "half-opened door," as one author termed the Ivy League experience of African Americans and, for a time, Jewish and other students from disfavored white ethnic backgrounds.[79]

The University's history is complex, and its record of exclusion— not only along lines of race but also ethnicity, gender, and other categories—is clear and damaging. Yet this report does not explore the entirety of that difficult history; nor does it discuss at length the significance of Indigenous history to Harvard's evolution, beyond colonial era dispossession and enslavement. This report focuses specifically on Harvard's involvement with slavery and its legacies, from the colonial period into the twentieth century, which is distinct in both degree and kind. Harvard's very existence depended upon the expropriation of land and labor—land acquired through dispossession of Native territories and labor extracted from enslaved people, including Native Americans and Africans brought to the Americas by force. And, long after the official end of slavery, intellectual clout of influential Harvard leaders and distinguished faculty would be a powerful force justifying the continued subjugation of Black Americans.

Hence, the truth—*Veritas*—is that for hundreds of years, both before and after the Civil War, racial subjugation, exclusion, and discrimination were ordinary elements of life off and on the Harvard campus, in New England as well as in the American South. Abolitionist affiliates of the University did take a stand against human bondage, and others fought for racial reform after slavery. The willingness of these Harvard affiliates to speak out and act against racial oppression is rightly noted and celebrated.[80] But these exceptional individuals do not reflect the full scope of the University's history. The nation's oldest institution of higher education—"America's de facto national university," as a noted historian described it—helped to perpetuate the era's racial oppression and exploitation.[81]

A Legacy of African American Resistance

This report uncovers Harvard's complicity with slavery and its legacies, and in so doing, also recognizes as a part of the University's history enslaved people of African and Native descent whose contributions have been overlooked. These individuals include Titus, Venus, Juba, and Bilhah, whose service in bondage to Presidents Wadsworth and Holyoke and their families supported their leadership of the University and enabled their lives as scholars.[82] It also includes Cuba, once owned by Penelope Royall Vassall—sister of the slaveholding benefactor of Harvard Law School—as well as Darby Vassall, the son of Cuba and her husband, Anthony (Tony). Darby Vassall went on to play an important role in Boston's free Black community, and his life and activism illustrate a critically important theme embedded in this report: Black resilience, agency, and achievement in the face of persistent discrimination.

The theme of Black resilience, agency, and achievement is especially relevant to this report's discussion of late nineteenth- and twentieth-century vestiges of slavery at Harvard. During the era of segregation, small numbers of African American students arrived on campus. Despite the oftentimes inhospitable learning environment, these Black Harvardians made vital contributions to the nationwide struggle *against* slavery's legacies. A few examples make the point.

W. E. B. Du Bois, a graduate of Harvard College (1890) and the first African American to earn a PhD from Harvard (1895), made towering intellectual contributions even as he experienced racism on and off campus. Building on work he had first explored as a Harvard student, Du Bois, as a faculty member at HBCUs—first at Fisk University, the

"Negro Harvard," and then at Atlanta University—described and analyzed the persistent problem of the American "color line."[83] Moreover, Du Bois and the Black Harvard graduate William Monroe Trotter (AB 1895; AM 1896) cofounded the Niagara Movement, the precursor to the nation's oldest civil rights organization, the NAACP.[84]

Charles Hamilton Houston (LLB 1922; SJD 1923), the first African American editor of the *Harvard Law Review,* went on to become the vice-dean of Howard Law School[85] and special counsel to the NAACP. A brilliant lawyer who was called "the man who killed Jim Crow," Houston laid the legal groundwork for the reshaping of American law and society during the Civil Rights Movement.[86]

And Eva Beatrice Dykes, the first summa cum laude graduate of Howard University, completed a master's degree and, in 1921, earned a PhD from Radcliffe—the first African American woman to complete the requirements for a doctorate in the United States and one of three Black women in the country to complete a PhD that year. A daughter of enslaved people, Dykes went on to an illustrious career as a professor of English at historically Black colleges, first at Howard and then at Oakwood University.[87] But when she first sought admission to graduate studies at Radcliffe College,[88] administrators were unimpressed by her credential earned at the historically Black Howard, and they required a do-over; Dykes, like some other HBCU graduates who enrolled at Harvard and Radcliffe, was forced to earn a second bachelor's degree. She did, graduating magna cum laude and Phi Beta Kappa in 1917.[89]

The efforts of these African Americans, with support from white allies, including some at Harvard,[90] gave rise to *Brown v. Board of Education,* the landmark 1954 US Supreme Court decision that outlawed state-sponsored school segregation and was "nothing short of a reconsecration of American ideals."[91] *Brown* and the Civil Rights Movement prepared the way for passage of the Civil Rights Act of 1964 and the Voting Rights Act of 1965, groundbreaking legislation that barred discrimination in key American institutions and helped create the more equitable world in which we live today.[92]

These individuals, too, represent Harvard. They are important actors in the University's history and in the making of a more perfect

American union; and they must be made visible in this report. Through struggles against racial oppression and for human freedom, these graduates created legacies of professional leadership and civic engagement, and they made profound legal and social changes. The achievements of Black graduates of Harvard illustrate the entwining of the nation's racial progress and access to a Harvard, and a Radcliffe, education.

Summary of the Report's Key Findings

This account of the University's entanglements with slavery and its legacies focuses on "connections, impact, and contributions" in the following categories: ownership of enslaved people; presence of enslaved people on campus; financial ties to slavery; intellectual leadership; and vestiges of slavery and resistance to racial oppression during the early twentieth century. For purposes of this report, the activities of Harvard leadership, faculty, staff, students, and donors represent "the University."

Our findings are as follows:

- Slavery—of Indigenous and of African people—was an integral part of life in Massachusetts and at Harvard during the colonial era.

- Between the University's founding in 1636 and the end of slavery in the Commonwealth in 1783, Harvard faculty, staff, and leaders enslaved more than seventy individuals, whose names are listed in Appendix A.

- Some of the enslaved worked and lived on campus, where they cared for Harvard presidents and professors and fed generations of Harvard students.

- Through connections to multiple donors, the University had extensive financial ties to, and profited from, slavery during the seventeenth, eighteenth, and nineteenth centuries.

- These financial ties include donors who accumulated their wealth through slave trading; from the labor of enslaved people on plantations in the Caribbean islands and the American South;

from the sale of supplies to such plantations and trade in goods they produced; and from the textile manufacturing industry in the North, supplied with cotton grown by enslaved people held in bondage in the American South. During the first half of the nineteenth century, more than a third of the money donated or promised to Harvard by private individuals came from just five men who made their fortunes from slavery and slave-produced commodities.

- These donors helped the University build a national reputation, hire faculty, support students, grow its collections, expand its physical footprint, and develop its infrastructure.

- The University today memorializes benefactors with ties to slavery across campus through statues, buildings, professorships, student houses, and the like.[93]

- While some Harvard affiliates fought against human bondage, on several occasions Harvard leaders, including members of the Harvard Corporation, sought to moderate or suppress antislavery politics on campus and among prominent Harvard affiliates.

- From the mid-nineteenth century well into the twentieth, Harvard presidents and several prominent professors, including Louis Agassiz, promoted "race science" and eugenics and conducted abusive "research," including the photographing of enslaved and subjugated human beings. These theories and practices were rooted in racial hierarchies of the sort marshaled by proponents of slavery and would produce devastating consequences in the nineteenth and twentieth centuries. Records and artifacts documenting many of these activities remain among the University's collections.

- Research to advance eugenic theories also took place on campus: Dudley Allen Sargent, director of the Hemenway Gymnasium from 1879 until 1919, implemented a "physical education" program that involved intrusive physical examinations, anthropometric measurements, and the photographing of unclothed Harvard and Radcliffe students. Archives documenting Sargent's activities remain among the University's collections.

• Among Harvard's vast museum collections are the remains of thousands of individuals. Many of these human remains are thought to belong to Indigenous people, and at least fifteen are individuals of African descent who may have been enslaved, two of whom also had Indigenous ancestry. President Bacow has established a Steering Committee on Human Remains in Harvard Museum Collections to address this finding.[94]

• Legacies of slavery persisted at Harvard, and throughout American society, after the Constitution and laws officially proscribed human bondage. Such legacies, including racial segregation, exclusion, and discrimination, were a part of campus life well into the twentieth century.

• Many esteemed Black graduates of Harvard and of Radcliffe aided the nation and their communities through activism, teaching, legal advocacy, and community service devoted to the eradication of racism and to equal opportunity.

• The achievements of Black graduates of Harvard and of Radcliffe illustrate the entwining of the nation's racial progress and access to a Harvard, and a Radcliffe, education.

These findings are discussed at greater length in the sections that follow, along with additional historical context and several individual case studies that, while not comprehensive, serve to illustrate both the nature and the extent of Harvard's ties to slavery and its legacies. The final section of this report describes the committee's recommendations for reparative action.

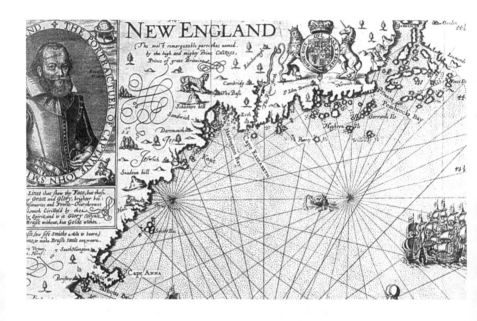

In 1614, Captain John Smith explored the coastline of what he would be the first to call New England. He predicted that the sea would be the region's greatest source of wealth. John Smith, Map of the Coast of New England (1616) / Harvard Fine Arts Library, Digital Images & Slides Collection

TWO

Slavery in New England and at Harvard

HARVARD UNIVERSITY'S early history is inseparable from that of colonial New England and, thus, from the system of slavery. Harvard was important to the region's politics, society, and economy, and as slavery formed the basis of New England's economic life, so it shaped Harvard.[1]

Leading historians agree that the colonial economy thrived based on "an economic alliance with the sugar islands of the West Indies."[2] This trade involved the provision of food, fuel, and lumber produced in New England to plantations of the Caribbean, where those goods were exchanged for tobacco, coffee, and sugar produced by enslaved Africans—or for enslaved people themselves.[3] "This effectively made Boston a slave society," according to one historian, "but one where most of the enslaved toiled elsewhere, sustaining the illusion of Boston in New England as an inclusive republic devoted to the common good."[4] Yet slavery was not absent from New England.

By 1700, New Englanders had made at least nineteen voyages to Africa and then to the West Indies, the chief route of the slave trade, as well as many more voyages between Massachusetts Bay and the Caribbean.[5] The Massachusetts Bay Colony's Body of Liberties, written in 1641, made slavery and the slave trade lawful. The first legal code governing slavery in British North America, it prohibited "bond-slavery," "unless it be of lawfull captives, taken in just warrs, and such strangers as willingly sell themselves, or are solde to us," leading one historian to note, "the word 'unless' has seldom carried more baggage."[6] Even as it paid homage to the Magna Carta, the Body of Liberties permitted the buying, selling, and trading of Indigenous people and Africans. Slavery would not officially end in Massachusetts until 1783.

Indigenous Slavery and African Slavery

Slavery in New England began when early colonists enslaved and sold Indigenous people while dispossessing these Native peoples of the land on which they had lived for generations.[7]

In 1636, the year Harvard was founded, merchants at Marblehead built and rigged a ship, 120 tons and very fast, called *Desire*. That summer, the *Desire* set sail carrying seventeen Pequot War prisoners who were to be sold as slaves in Bermuda on the instructions of John Winthrop.[8] A towering figure in early colonial history who served several terms as Governor and Lieutenant Governor of the Massachusetts Bay Colony, Winthrop was a member of the original "Comittee as to ye colledg at New Toune"—that is, Harvard.[9] Winthrop himself enslaved the wife of a Pequot sachem and her two children in what he seems to have regarded as an act of Christian benevolence, reciprocity for her protection of two captured English girls during the conflict.[10]

Two years later, on February 26, 1638, the *Desire* returned to Boston Harbor carrying cotton, tobacco, salt, and an unspecified number of enslaved Africans who had been purchased on Providence Island. The *Desire* was among the first American slave ships.[11] It is possible that the man known to us only as "The Moor"—who was enslaved by Harvard's first schoolmaster, Nathaniel Eaton, and in that capacity served Harvard's earliest students—arrived in New England aboard the *Desire*.[12]

Not long after, in the early 1640s, a Bermuda minister named Patrick Copeland, grateful for Winthrop's "remembrance of us in sending 12 New England Indians to us," began recruiting the children of wealthy Caribbean plantation owners to attend Harvard.[13] As one historian has noted, "education, like the flag, follows trade"—and many sons of West

Indian planters indeed followed trade to the Massachusetts Bay Colony and Harvard.[14]

Harvard also benefited from land grants by the General Court (the colonial legislature) in 1653:

> For the incouragement of Harvard Colledge and the society thereof, and for the more comfortable maintenance and provicon for the psident, ffellowes, and students thereof in time to come, this Court doth graunt unto the said society and corporation, for the ends aforesaid, two thousand acres of land wth in this jurisdiccion, not formerly graunted to any other, to be taken up in two or three places, where it may be found convenient; and to this end it is desired that the said corporation of the college doe appoint some persons in theire behalfe to finde out the places where such land may be freely taken, and to make retourne as soone as they may, that the Court may more pticularly and expressly confirme the same.[15]

The Harvard treasurer Thomas Danforth personally selected four tracts in Rhode Island and Connecticut, territory from which the Pequot had been driven.[16]

One aspect of the original mission of Harvard College was to educate (and convert) Native students alongside white classmates.[17] In the 1640s, the fledgling Colony was in the throes of an economic crisis, and the College was on the edge of collapse: Christianizing Indigenous people opened up vital new avenues of financial support. Devoted Puritans in England lined up to support the mission, and Parliament opened its coffers to aid the colonization effort by "civilizing" Natives.[18] The Charter of 1650, which has governed Harvard with few interruptions for more than 350 years, committed the institution to "the education of the English and Indian youth."[19] The Indian College building—Harvard's first made of brick—was constructed in 1655. Ultimately, however, Harvard enrolled only five Native students in this era, and only Caleb Cheeshahteaumuck (AB 1665) received a degree during his lifetime.[20] (Joel Iacoombs also completed the requirements of the AB degree but died in 1665 before he formally graduated. Harvard University posthumously presented Iacoombs's degree to the Wampanoag community in 2011.[21]) By 1670, the Indian College building had been given over to the College's printing press, and in 1690, it was dismantled, and its bricks were used to construct a new building for the use of white scholars.[22]

As the colony grew, slavery—now primarily, but not exclusively, African slavery—remained central. In the colonial era, the system that W. E. B. Du Bois would eloquently describe more than two centuries later was just beginning to take shape:

> The giant forces of water and steam were harnessed to do the world's work, and the black workers of America bent at the bottom of a growing pyramid of commerce and industry; and they not only could not be spared, if this new economic organization was to expand, but rather they became the cause of new political demands and alignments, of new dreams of power and visions of empire. . . . Black labor became the foundation stone not only of the Southern social structure, but of Northern manufacture and commerce, of the English factory system, of European commerce, of buying and selling on a world-wide scale; new cities were built on the results of black labor.[23]

The number of enslaved women, men, and children in Massachusetts, itself a small colony of some 33,000 inhabitants according to a 1675 census,[24] remained relatively low until the end of the seventeenth century, and enslaved people formed part of a larger world of unfree labor that also included indentured white servants.[25] In 1676, colonial administrator Edmund Randolph wrote that there were "not above 200 slaves in the colony, and those are brought from Guinea and Madagascar."[26] Four years later, Governor Simon Bradstreet told the Lords of the Committee for Trade and Foreign Plantations that "there are a very few blacks borne here, I think not above [five] or six at the most in a year."[27] Unlike white indentured servants, who eventually left their unfree status behind, these enslaved Africans faced lifetimes of uncompensated labor, both for themselves and for their descendants.

The enslaved population of Massachusetts rose quickly after the British Parliament's revocation of the Royal African Company's mono-

The residence of Harvard's president, known as Elmwood, has a long and complicated history. Its ownership by the University, however, is relatively recent—the house was left to Harvard in 1933 by Arthur Kingsley Porter, a faculty member, and the University took possession in 1962.

Formerly the home of famous poets and diplomats and once a hospital for the Continental Army during the Revolutionary War, the building is listed on the National Register of Historic Places. It was also a site of enslavement.

The original owner of Elmwood, Thomas Oliver, was born on the Caribbean island of Antigua in 1734 to the wealthy slaveholding owners of a sugar plantation.[1] Several years after graduating from Harvard, in 1753, Oliver married Elizabeth Vassall, daughter of a Jamaican plantation owner, and the couple built their home in Cambridge near other members of the Harvard-connected Vassall and Royall families.

In 1774, Oliver was appointed Royal Lieutenant Governor of Massachusetts—a role that carried with it the responsibility of sitting on Harvard's Board of Overseers. It is unclear whether Oliver ever engaged with the College in this role, however, because colonists forced him to abandon his Cambridge home and move into Boston just weeks after he was sworn in.[2] He fled the colony nearly two years later, in March 1776.

We know that Oliver enslaved eleven people at Elmwood—Buff, Cato, Jerry, Jeoffry, Samuel, Mira, Jude, Sarah, Jenny, Violet, and "Young Jerry"—because he petitioned the British government in 1783 for compensation: £480 for eleven "valuable Slaves," the ten enslaved people he left behind plus Samuel, who made the journey with Oliver but was "free by the Laws of England."[3]

poly on English trade with Africa in 1696.[28] It was also at this time that some New Englanders "began to rebel against the growth of actual slavery on New England soil."[29]

Antislavery sentiment was not, however, at the root of resistance in this period.[30] Rather, limited opposition to slavery grew largely out of a concern about the growing presence of Black people and the effect that would have on society, fears that had gained salience in the wake of Bacon's Rebellion in 1677. These concerns culminated in the passage

Harvard has a unique governance structure, with two distinct bodies that, together, perform the role of a more typical board of trustees. These are the Harvard Corporation (officially the President and Fellows of Harvard College) and the Board of Overseers.

Today, the Harvard Corporation is the smaller of the bodies, formed by the president, treasurer, and fellows. Its responsibilities are primarily fiduciary and supervisory in nature, including overseeing annual budgets, capital projects, general finances, and the endowment, and appointing presidents.

The Board of Overseers is composed of alumni. Its responsibilities are tied to the academic life of the University: it advises University leadership and directs the visiting committees to the University, which investigate and report on the schools' execution of their stated goals.

The selection methods and qualifications for these bodies' members have evolved over time (overseers, for example, used to be chosen from local government and clergy), but their important roles have remained constant.

For clarity, throughout this report, members of the Corporation are identified by their individual titles—"president," "treasurer," or "fellow"—and members of the Board of Overseers are identified with the title "overseer."

---

in 1705 of an act "for the Better Preventing of a Spurious and Mixt Issue," which put a prohibitive £4 tax on all slaves imported.[31] The colonial legislature also adopted other measures designed to maintain the racial balance, such as the 1709 "Act to Encourage the Importation of White Servants," which promised payment of forty shillings per white male servant imported into the colony and extended the 1705 import tax to include enslaved Native Americans.[32] Despite such efforts, the number of enslaved people in the Massachusetts Bay Colony rose to 550 by 1708, and in 1720, Governor Samuel Shute wrote that "With respect to slaves either Negros or Indians (but most Negroes) they may be computed at about Two Thousand" alongside an English population of 94,000.[33] By the middle of the eighteenth century, enslaved Black people constituted the main source of bound labor in

Massachusetts, outnumbering indentured servants, apprentices, and Indigenous workers.[34]

Slavery at Harvard

On Harvard's campus, the story was much the same. Over nearly 150 years, from the University's founding in 1636 until the Massachusetts Supreme Judicial Court found slavery unlawful, Harvard presidents and other leaders, as well as its faculty and staff, enslaved more than seventy individuals, some of whom labored on campus.[35] Enslaved men and women served Harvard presidents and professors and fed and cared for Harvard students.

The enslaved man known as "The Moor," who could have arrived aboard the *Desire,* was the first of many enslaved people who would serve Harvard students in the colonial era. Titus, Venus, Juba, and Bilhah, all enslaved people, served Harvard Presidents Benjamin Wadsworth (1725–1737) and Edward Holyoke (1737–1769).[36] Yet more people were enslaved by Harvard's stewards and, in this capacity, likely served Harvard's students and maintained its campus.[37]

The steward was a prominent role in the early years of the College, one that commanded respect and status.[38] Stewards were responsible for feeding the scholars on campus, along with collecting student fees, overseeing staff engaged in student services, and paying many of the College's bills. They also provided lavish feasts for the annual Commencement celebrations. From Harvard's founding, in 1636, through the beginning of the American Revolution, only ten men—five from the same family—held the position.[39] Of these ten, at least three owned enslaved people whose labor maintained the Harvard campus and sustained Harvard students.[40]

Among the Harvard stewards who owned enslaved people, Andrew Bordman (II), steward from 1703 to 1747, stands out for having enslaved at least eight individuals. The documentation of his slaveholding is also characteristic of the period's sparse records, but the picture becomes clear when the evidence is viewed as a whole: First, a deed of sale shows that Bordman paid £40 to buy a man named Cuffe and that his brother-in-law, future Harvard President Benjamin Wadsworth, witnessed the purchase.[41] Separately, in the steward's notebook, Bordman recorded the names of four children born to a woman named Rose: Flora, Jeffrey, Cesar, and Jane, an enslaved woman who died at the age of 22.[42] Jane's tombstone still stands in the Old Burying Ground near Harvard Yard, inscribed "Jane a Negro Servant of Andrew Bordman,"[43] and it is adjacent to a similar memorial of Cicely, a black woman enslaved by the Harvard tutor, fellow, and treasurer William Brattle.[44] We know that Rose and her other children were also enslaved because, according to Massachusetts law at this time, children inherited the status of their mothers: if Jane was enslaved, then so too were her mother and siblings.[45] Two additional people enslaved by Andrew Bordman and his widow, Elizabeth Bordman, appear in extant records: Lucy, "Indian servant of Mr. Bordman," was baptized in 1740.[46] Peter, "negro man servant of Mrs. Elizabeth Bordman," married a woman enslaved in Charlestown in 1758.[47] We cannot know whether the Bordman family owned all eight of these people at the same time. But if Andrew Bordman owned even Rose and her four children all at once, this would have made him one of the largest slaveholders in the colony; in the only surviving tax assessment for the town of Cambridge during this period, from 1749, the largest number of enslaved people recorded in a single household was four.[48] Such was Bordman's reliance on enslaved labor to feed Harvard's students and fulfill his duties as steward.

Other Harvard leaders and faculty members also owned enslaved people in this period. Take, for example, Professor John Winthrop. A direct descendant of the colonial governor of the same name, Winthrop earned his AM from Harvard in 1732 and served as Hollis Professor of Mathematics and Natural Philosophy from 1738 until his death in 1779. He was also a fellow from 1765 to 1779 and served as acting president in 1769 and again from 1773 to 1774.[49] Harvard's Winthrop House is named for Professor Winthrop as well as for his ancestor, the colonial governor.[50]

On a single page of his 1759 Ames Almanack, Winthrop notes the death of his enslaved "negro man George."

13 may, a few minutes before one in y morng [abt hi watr], our poor
George died of a hectic, wch he was thrown into by y measles; havg never
been well since he had yt distemp. He was aged 24 years & one day.[51]

Further down the same page Winthrop recorded that he procured a
replacement:

had a new negro boy, wm I call Scipio. He now measures 3 feet &
11 inches, wtht shoes. By comparg his h^t wth yt of our boys, I jdg him
to be 8 ½ y old.[52]

It is unclear when Winthrop acquired this boy; not all of his notes are
dated. In a subsequent note, this one dated February 6, 1761, Winthrop
provides additional information about his own son's age and height,
the basis for his estimate of Scipio's eight and a half years.[53]

The fact of Winthrop's slaveholding is not new; it is noted in *Sibley's Harvard Graduates,* a compendium of biographical sketches of
colonial-era Harvard alumni. But the story as told in *Sibley's* is sympathetic. The passage on George's death reads: "When [Winthrop's] own
slave boy, George, died of the measles, he was mourned as one of the
family, not as an unfortunate investment." As for Scipio, *Sibley's* reports
he "was watched over like the white children of the family."[54] The truth,
however, is that Scipio and George were undoubtedly purchased to
labor for the Winthrops without compensation.

In 1773, a decade or so after Winthrop purchased Scipio and several
years before the official end of slavery in the Commonwealth, human
bondage captivated an audience at Harvard's Commencement ceremony. Two candidates for the bachelor's degree, Eliphalet Pearson and
Theodore Parsons, participated in a public debate concerning the
legality of slavery. Parsons, then twenty-one years old, took the anti-
slavery position:

To me, I confess, it is a matter of painful astonishment . . . that those
who are so readily disposed to urge the principles of natural equality
in defence of their own Liberties should, with so little reluctance, continue to exert a power by the operation of which they are so flagrantly contradicted. For what less can be said of that exercise of power,

whereby such multitudes of our fellow-men, descendants, my friend from the same common parent with you and me, and between whom and us nature has made no distinction, save what arises from the stronger influence of the sun in the climate whence they originated, are held to groan under the insupportable burden of the most abject slavery.[55]

Defending slavery, Pearson called for the abandonment of "tender sentiment" and a calm return to "the voice of reason." Although he conceded "[t]hat Liberty to all is sweet" he went on to argue that slavery was a benefit to Africans, who had in his view been rescued by slavers: characterizing life in Africa as "an entire subjection to the tyrannizing power of lust and passion," Pearson implored the audience, "reflect, I say, a moment upon the condition of a creature in human shape (for in such a state of degradation one can hardly call him a man), the misery, the wretchedness . . . and compare it with the condition of a slave in this country." He concluded that the slaves' "removal [from Africa] is to be esteemed a favor."[56]

Slavery was not an abstraction to either man, or to the other students and faculty at Harvard. Slavery had, by this time, long been a fact of everyday life in Massachusetts. Parsons's impassioned argument against the institution was about more than overheard tales of abject brutality in the sugarcane fields of the Caribbean, to which New England was economically tied. His father, Reverend Moses Parsons, owned two men and a woman named Violet. Parsons's son later recalled: "When it was generally believed that slavery was unlawful in Massachusetts, [the Reverend] summoned his slaves into his sitting-room, and there, in the presence of his children, declared to them that they were free. The men accepted the gift, or rather the declaration, for gift it was not."[57] Yet Violet, who would have been about eight years older than Parsons, roughly as old as his eldest brother, stayed with the Parsons family until her death at the age of ninety, and is now buried in the Parsons family tomb in Byfield, Massachusetts. John Thornton Kirkland, president of Harvard University, officiated her funeral.[58]

Theodore Parsons became a doctor. Six years after his graduation from Harvard College, at age twenty-eight, he shipped aboard the warship *Bennington* as its surgeon. He disappeared at sea a few days later, and his body was never found.[59] Eliphalet Pearson became Harvard's Hancock Professor of Hebrew and Other Oriental Languages in 1786 and served as president of the University from 1804 to 1806. He died in 1826.[60]

In the nineteenth century, Boston Harbor remained a bustling center of world commerce. Harvard donors were among the many merchants whose ships carried foodstuffs and other raw materials out of New England, which they exchanged for sugar, coffee, tobacco, and, increasingly, cotton to be sold in European and Northern American markets. *Boston Harbor from Constitution Wharf* (1842), Harvard Fine Arts Library, Digital Images & Slides Collection

THREE

The Slavery Economy and Harvard

SLAVERY MAY HAVE ENDED—at least officially—in Massachusetts by 1783, but the ties between Harvard University and slavery continued. Beginning in the colonial period and continuing well into the nineteenth century, the University and its donors benefited from extensive financial ties to slavery.

For roughly a century, Harvard had operated as a lender[1] and derived a substantial portion of its income from investments that included loans to Caribbean sugar planters, rum distillers, and plantation suppliers.[2] After 1830, the University shifted its investments into cotton manufacturing, before diversifying its portfolio to include real estate and railroad stocks—all industries that were, in this era, dependent on the labor of enslaved people and the expropriation of land.

Harvard's financial ties to slavery also take the form of major gifts and bequests from donors who accumulated their wealth through slave trading, from the labor of enslaved people on plantations in the Caribbean islands and in the American South, and from the Northern textile manufacturing industry, supplied with cotton grown by enslaved people held in bondage.

New England and Caribbean Slavery

Harvard's financial ties to slavery are multifaceted, and the economic links between colonial New England and the Caribbean provide critical context to understand such entanglements. Trade between New

England and the West Indies proved so essential to both regions that one seventeenth-century observer declared Boston "the mart town of the West Indies."[3] As early as 1667 the governor of the English colony of Barbados acknowledged that "these colonies cannot in peace prosper, or in war subsist, without a correspondence with" the New England colonies.[4]

While large-scale plantation slavery never took root in New England, for more than a century Boston merchants played an essential role in sustaining the sugar plantation economy of the Caribbean; many of those same merchants were important players in Harvard's early history. New England ships carried enslaved people and critical supplies to the Caribbean islands. They brought back slave-produced commodities like sugar and molasses, most of which was then re-exported throughout the British empire. As early as the 1630s there were already more than twenty ships plying trade between New England and the British Caribbean.[5] As Edmund Burke observed in 1757, New Englanders became "carriers for all the colonies of North America and the West-Indies, and even for some parts of Europe. They may be considered in this respect as the Dutch of America."[6]

Here, too, we begin with Governor John Winthrop. As the historian Wendy Warren has observed, "To understand New England not only by the labor done within its colonies but even more by the commodities that came and went is to understand New England as John Winthrop did, by its place in the world."[7] Winthrop saw the region's profitable trade with the West Indies, in particular, as a gift of God for the benefit both of the Massachusetts Bay Colony's economy and its reputation:

> [I]t pleased the Lord to open to us a trade with Barbados and other Islands in the West Indies, which as it proved gainful, so the commodities we had in exchange there for our cattle and provisions, as sugar, cotton, tobacco, and indigo, were a good help to discharge our engagements in England. And this summer there was so great a drouth [drought], as their potatoes and corn, etc., were burnt up; and divers London ships which rode there were so short of provisions as, if our

vessels had not supplied them, they could not have returned home; which was an observable providence, that whereas many of the London seamen were wont to despise New England as a poor, barren country, should now be relieved by our plenty.[8]

Timber was of particular importance to New England merchants engaged in the triangle trade. Because ships could be built and rigged in New England using only the produce of the region's forests, shipbuilding became a significant facet of its economy.[9] And with so much Atlantic trade focused on slave-grown commodities, Boston merchants soon became central to that industry as well. In 1700, Governor Richard Coote wrote that "more good vessels belong to Boston than to all Scotland and Ireland."[10] Timber from New England was also used to build and rebuild the Caribbean's sugar plantations, whose infrastructure required constant replacement: more than seventy-five hurricanes struck the region between 1700 and 1775.[11]

Trading connections grew stronger throughout the eighteenth century, as Caribbean planters relied on New Englanders to provide the vital supplies required to maintain the plantation complex. New England's fishing industries fed the West Indies sugar plantations, sending "refuse fish"—"salt burnt, spotted, rotten, and carelessly ordered"—to "the *Charib-Islands, Barbadoes, Jamaica*, &c. who feed their *Negroes* with it."[12] Dried cod from New England was "the meat of all the slaves in all the West Indies."[13]

Importantly, these provisions imported from New England allowed West Indian planters to allocate far more land to sugar than would otherwise have been possible, enabling the system to grow. In Barbados, for example, after an unsuccessful attempt in the first decades of the 1600s to produce tobacco, planters turned to sugar as their primary crop; by the 1670s, Barbados produced 65 percent of the sugar sold in England.[14] Initially, sugar was a scarce commodity and commanded very high prices in European markets. In 1647, at which time about half of Barbados's arable land was used for sugar, Massachusetts Governor John Winthrop received a letter stating that planters in the island were "so intent upon planting sugar that they had rather buy foode at very deare rates than produce it by labour, soe infinite is the profitt of sugar workes once accomplished."[15] As other colonies followed Barbados into the market, however, supply increased and prices fell sharply.[16] To remain profitable, planters were forced to devote an ever-greater percentage of land to the crop. By 1767, the share of Barbadian land producing sugar "had risen to 80 percent, which meant that virtually all land useful for agriculture of any kind was devoted to this one crop."[17]

As the amount of land dedicated to sugar production increased, so too did the number of enslaved laborers needed to work it. According to one estimate, the population in the mid-eighteenth century across the Caribbean encompassed approximately 725,000 enslaved people and just over 250,000 whites. In the English colonies to which New England was most closely tied the divide was even more extreme.[18]

In short, New England merchants provided Caribbean sugar plantations with vital supplies, which enabled planters to remain profitable and expand the brutal business of slavery far beyond anything they could have otherwise sustained. In return, New Englanders acquired capital and slave-produced goods that were essential to their trade throughout in the Atlantic world. This cycle was New England's economic bedrock. In 1783, John Adams (AB 1755) wrote: "The Commerce of the West India Islands, is a Part of the American System of Commerce. They can neither do without Us nor We without them."[19]

Harvard Affiliates, Slavery, and the
Slave Trade in the Colonial Era

It is not possible to document here all the many gifts that Harvard received from donors whose wealth was tied up in Caribbean slavery and slave trading, both because of incomplete data and because the precise ways in which donors' profits are connected to sugar production and Caribbean slavery are not always clear or easy to trace. Certain examples stand out, however, and these notable bequests, which proved critical to Harvard's growth and the establishment of its reputation as a prestigious university, warrant specific mention.

Isaac Royall Jr.

Perhaps the most well-known gift to Harvard by a donor involved in slavery is the bequest of Isaac Royall Jr., whose family's sugar plantation on the Caribbean island of Antigua furnished the wealth that endowed the Royall Professorship of Law, Harvard's first chair in law.[20] The plantation proceeds also allowed the Royalls to purchase their Medford, Massachusetts, estate, now a museum and historical site, where Isaac Royall Jr. enslaved at least sixty individuals.[21]

Yet the Royall's wealth and Harvard's first professorship of law are not the whole story. Isaac Royall Jr.'s sister, Penelope Royall Vassall, owned—among other enslaved people—Cuba Vassall and her children. Cuba had been brought to Cambridge by Penelope and Isaac's father, who left Cuba to Penelope when he died. Meanwhile, Penelope's husband, Henry Vassall, had brought another enslaved man, Tony Vassall, to Cambridge from Jamaica. Cuba and Tony married, and Cuba and their children were eventually sold to John Vassall, Henry's nephew and a 1757 graduate of Harvard College. Among the children was Darby Vassall, who is a remarkable figure in his own right. An important player in Boston's free Black community and an early activist for Black rights, his life and activism help to illustrate a critically important theme embedded in this report: Black resilience, agency, and achievement in the face of persistent discrimination.[22]

Samuel Winthrop

The Royalls were just one of many families whose slavery-begotten wealth supported Harvard, both before and long after Isaac Jr.'s bequest.[23]

In 1645, George Downing (AB 1642), a nephew of Governor John Winthrop and a former tutor at Harvard (ca. 1643–1646), toured the British West Indies and delivered sermons in many of the islands' churches. As he headed home to England, he penned a letter to his cousin John Winthrop Jr. encouraging him to migrate to the West Indies to make his fortune growing cash crops with enslaved labor:

> [Colonists in Barbados] have bought this year no lesse than a thousand Negroes; and the more they buie, the better able they are to buye,

for in a year and a halfe they will earne (with gods blessing) as much as they cost.[24]

Downing went on to explain that "Negroes (the life of this place)" were far better than "New England servants" to work West Indian plantations, as white colonists were "noon of the fittest for those parts."[25]

John Jr. did not take Downing's advice, but his younger brother Samuel Winthrop, the governor's youngest son, did, dropping out of Harvard in 1645 and making his way first to Tenerife, in the Canary Islands, and, a year later, to the West Indies. Samuel became one of the first large-scale sugar producers in the British West Indies, eventually owning the rights to one quarter of the island of Barbuda[26] as well as a sugar plantation on Antigua where dozens of enslaved people labored to produce tens of thousands of pounds of sugar a year for export to New England and Europe.[27] He also served as the deputy governor of Antigua from 1667 to 1669.[28] Winthorpes Bay on the north side of the island memorializes the prominence of Samuel and his descendants in its early colonial history.[29]

Although Samuel never returned to New England, he remained deeply connected to the region, and to Harvard in particular. Before leaving Massachusetts Bay in 1645, Samuel, Downing, and two other Harvard graduates had jointly gifted land to the University—the first donation of property by alumni. The parcel, which was planted with apple trees and came to be known as the Fellows Orchard, is today the site of Widener Library.[30]

In an early letter to his father, the governor, Samuel asked to be remembered to family members and to "our most esteemed President, Henry Dunster."[31] Many years later, Samuel would send four of his sons to New England to be educated with the express purpose of eventually enrolling them at Harvard.[32] In correspondence with his brother John Jr., then the governor of Connecticut, Samuel asked for help getting his sons admitted to the College.[33] Ultimately, he could not see these plans through: in 1667, after a French attack on Antigua ruined his plantation and decimated his enslaved labor force, Samuel wrote, "it is now all I have left besides my land & 12 working negroes, wth whoos hard labor I shall not be able to keep my Sonnes in New

England."[34] Despite this setback Samuel's finances eventually recovered, and he died one of the wealthiest men in Antigua.[35]

Harvard Affiliates, Slavery, and the Slave Trade into the Nineteenth Century

Harvard continued to benefit financially from the proceeds of enslaved labor well beyond the end of slavery in Massachusetts. During the first half of the nineteenth century, more than a third of the money donated or promised to Harvard by private individuals came from just five men who made their fortunes from slavery and slave-produced commodities.[36] Four of these men were directly involved in slavery or the slave trade, while the fifth—Peter C. Brooks—became the wealthiest man in New England by insuring New England's merchant ships.[37]

James Perkins bequeathed $20,000 to Harvard for the Perkins Professorship of Astronomy and Mathematics,[38] which the University created in 1842; his business, Perkins and Company, pursued a global strategy that included Caribbean slave trading, western land speculation, and opium trading in China.[39] Perkins and other members of his extended family are also integral to Harvard in other ways. They played a central role in the creation of Massachusetts General Hospital, and the Perkins Room in Massachusetts Hall—the primary conference room used by Harvard's president and other senior leaders—is named for a descendant of this family.

Benjamin Bussey, a sugar, coffee, and cotton merchant, left Harvard an estate valued at $320,000 to be divided among the Divinity School, the Law School, and a school for agriculture. Today, the Arnold Arboretum is located on Bussey's former estate in Jamaica Plain.[40] (By the time Harvard received this bequest, the net value of the trust had increased to roughly $400,000.[41])

John McLean, another merchant, endowed the McLean Professorship of Ancient and Modern History in 1834 and supported Massachusetts General Hospital's department for the care of the insane, the forerunner of McLean Hospital.[42]

Finally, Abbott Lawrence, who owned and operated cotton textile factories in Massachusetts along with a trading firm that marketed and

While the extraction of wealth, directly and indirectly, from the labor of enslaved people is the primary focus of this section of the report, the individual contributions of enslaved people—not only their unfree labor but also their resilience, agency, and achievement in the face of violence and discrimination—are vital to a complete understanding of our past and have for too long been overlooked.

The life of Darby Vassall—also the subject of a virtual exhibition jointly presented by the Museum of African American History in Boston and Nantucket and the Presidential Initiative on Harvard & the Legacy of Slavery—is particularly striking. Born in Cambridge in 1768 and enslaved by John Vassall (AB 1757),[1] Darby was an advocate for equal rights and abolition of slavery throughout his life.

With the outbreak of the Revolutionary War, John Vassall, a Loyalist, left his property—today the Longfellow House National Historic Site—in the care of Darby's parents, Tony and Cuba.[2] Darby, then a small child, was living at the house when General and later President George Washington moved in and made it his headquarters while he oversaw the American colonial forces fighting around Boston. Later in his life, Darby would tell the story of an interaction with the general himself: Washington personally offered Darby work. Darby asked how much he would be paid, and Washington retracted the offer. "General Washington," Darby recalled, "was no gentlemen, to expect a boy to work without wages."[3]

After slavery was made unlawful in Massachusetts in 1783, Darby's parents purchased property just north of Harvard's campus. His father, Tony, operated a stable in what would become the free Black community of Lewisville in Cambridge.[4]

Darby eventually moved to Boston, where he owned property just blocks from the State House, and fought alongside other members of Boston's Black community for equal rights locally and abolition nationally.[5] In 1796, he was a founding member of the African Society, a mutual aid association for Black Bostonians.[6] In 1812, he was one of six signers of a petition to the state legislature requesting funding for the education of Black children;[7] the African School Association named in the petition was a forerunner of the Abiel Smith School, which today houses the Museum of African American History in Boston.[8] Darby also actively supported the New England Anti-Slavery Society with both his time and his money,[9] and he used his personal connections to benefit the Black community. He counted many prominent abolitionists of the day, including Wendell Phillips and William Cooper Nell, among his associates.[10] In 1855, he visited his birthplace, bringing the self-emancipated slave, memoirist, and activist Lunsford Lane along to meet the house's new proprietor, Henry Wadsworth Longfellow—a funder of abolitionist causes.[11]

At the age of ninety-one, Darby again joined his friends and neighbors in Boston's free Black community to petition the Massachusetts legislature, this time demanding legal protections for the Black community against slave-catchers emboldened by the Fugitive Slave Act.[12]

Darby died in 1861 and was buried, at his own request, with his parents' former enslavers in the Vassall family tomb; it is located under Christ Church, near the place of his birth, and within sight of Harvard Yard.[13]

---

distributed the products of his mills, donated $50,000 in 1847—followed by an additional $50,000 at his death in 1855. These gifts established the Lawrence Scientific School, the institutional predecessor of the Graduate School of Applied Science that would also encompass Bussey's agriculture school. The Lawrence Scientific School's most eminent faculty member would be Louis Agassiz, recruited on the recommendation of Lawrence, who also personally paid Agassiz's salary for a time.[43] Eventually, these institutions would evolve into today's John A. Paulson School of Engineering and Applied Sciences.[44]

These donors, among other significant benefactors, are discussed in more detail in the sections that follow. While not comprehensive, these examples illustrate the multifaceted ties between Harvard's major donors and slavery, the slave trade, and the trade in slave-produced goods.

The Perkins Brothers: James, Thomas Handasyd, and Samuel Gardner

When Thomas Nelson Perkins died at his home on October 7, 1937, his friends and colleagues commemorated his contributions as a "servant of Harvard and a leader among Harvard men."[45] Perkins, a graduate of the College (1891) and the Law School (1894), served as a fellow for thirty years (1905–1924 and 1926–1937). He was a prominent lawyer and statesman whose memory would be enshrined "at the very heart and center of the University he loved and served."[46] The Perkins Room in

Massachusetts Hall, for use by the president and senior leaders of the University, was inaugurated on January 6, 1941, in his honor.[47]

Thomas Nelson Perkins was a scion of the wealthy Perkins family, which had, at the time of his death, supported the University for more than a century. The family's wealth originated in the slave economy of the American South and especially the Caribbean, where Thomas Nelson's great-grandfather, Samuel Gardner Perkins,[48] and great uncles, James Perkins and Thomas Handasyd Perkins (Samuel Gardner's brothers), began building their fortune as slave traders in St. Domingue (now Haiti).[49] These three Perkins brothers—James, Thomas Handasyd, and Samuel Gardner—were each significant Harvard donors in their own right, and they bequeathed their estates to descendants who became prominent leaders at the University, among them Elizabeth Cary Agassiz—the first president of Radcliffe College.[50]

The Perkins brothers, active philanthropists, supported Harvard and several other important institutions. James bequeathed $20,000 to the University in 1822 to establish the Perkins Professorship in Astronomy and Mathematics, renamed the Perkins Professorship in Mathematics in 1906,[51] and served as a director of the effort to create the Theological School of Cambridge, now Harvard Divinity School, to which he and Thomas Handasyd both donated.[52] James and Thomas Handasyd also led the effort to create the Massachusetts General Hospital and served in turns as chair of trustees and vice president; Thomas also served as the hospital's second president. As trustees, they were deeply involved in the initial fundraising effort, which raised nearly $150,000, and donated $5,000 each; their brother Samuel Gardner gave a further $100.[53] Thomas Handasyd and Samuel Gardner also supported the creation of the Massachusetts Professorship of Natural History at Harvard, now the Fisher Professorship in Natural History.[54] Beyond Harvard, the Perkins brothers helped to establish several prominent organizations in Greater Boston. James left his mansion on Pearl Street, valued at $40,000, to the Boston Athenaeum, one of the nation's oldest independent libraries and cultural institutions.[55] And the Perkins School for the Blind in Watertown, Massachusetts, is named for the family, specifically Thomas Handasyd, who bequeathed his Boston mansion as a site for the school.[56]

The Perkins brothers' parents and a grandfather were involved in the West Indies trade, so the brothers understood well, as did other New Englanders, the wealth that could be made in the Caribbean. The French colony of St. Domingue promised the opportunity to make a fortune.[57]

In the fall of 1782, long before the brothers became active as philanthropists, a twenty-one-year-old James boarded the merchant ship *Beaver* to Cap Français, modern-day Cap Haitien in the north of Haiti.[58] The city was then a bustling metropolis and the capital of St. Domingue, the "pearl of the Antilles" in the French colonial imagination. It was built upon a rigorous racial hierarchy with a small white planter class at the top and enslaved Africans who worked the island's sugarcane, coffee, and cotton fields at the base;[59] at the height of its economy in this period, St. Domingue imported as many as 40,000 enslaved men, women, and children per year by one estimate, due in part to the high mortality of enslaved people on the island's sugar plantations.[60] Another source estimates a total of 700,000 enslaved people were imported to St. Domingue before the start of the Haitian Revolution in 1791, making it the single greatest exploiter of enslaved people in the Caribbean.[61]

James wrote letters from St. Domingue to family in New England, as did his wife, Sarah Paine Perkins, after she traveled to join him on the island. In November 1789, Sarah Perkins described her new home to a correspondent, lingering over a description of "the sons and daughters of slav'ry" who, she believed,

> have their oppressions & even their wants—but their enjoyments are proportionate & I am very apt to believe that the Cup of Slavery is embittered with less gall than we are wont to imagine—for tho' the task master may lift his whip against them, still their minds are unaffected & they appear as destitute of that smart which is keener than . . . (the anguish of the field) as their fellow mules. I have seen many of them who appeard to be susceptible of the greatest pleasure you can imagine & who were apparently discovering an enthusiastic enjoyment from their wild disorderly gambols, but never was once witness to any thing like that grief of heart, that affliction of the mind, which is the offspring of sensibility.[62]

James joined the firm Wall, Tardy & Co. as a commission agent for American merchants, purchasing colonial products made by enslaved people to ship to New England. When his younger brother Samuel Gardner turned twenty-one, he, too, sailed for St. Domingue.[63] Samuel Gardner later recalled:

> the flourishing state of trade and the prosperity of [St. Domingue's] inhabitants were without a parallel perhaps in the world; for here there were no poor, I may say, either black or white,—for even among the latter those who were slaves were well taken care of, fed and clothed, and well sheltered by their masters, and those that were free were able to get a living without excess labor.[64]

The brothers entered into a partnership with Walter Burling to form Perkins, Burling & Company; the firm traded in the products of slave labor including sugar, molasses, coffee, and cocoa, as well as enslaved people themselves.[65] Thomas Handasyd managed the company's business in Boston, while James and Samuel Gardner lived primarily in St. Domingue. On the island, they visited vessels in the Cap Français harbor to select enslaved women, men, and children for purchase, sometimes boarding ships to choose from among newly arrived Africans, and then selling them to slave owners on the island.[66] They also depended on ship captains and other third parties to sell enslaved captives throughout the Caribbean, especially in Havana, Cuba, and Kingston, Jamaica.[67] The brothers' business correspondence is extensive and documents commercial activities in Cuba, Curaçao, Guadeloupe, Jamaica, Martinique, Puerto Rico, St. Croix, and Trinidad.[68] Other merchants and slave traders sought letters of introduction to the brothers to gain access to the Perkins, Burling & Company network.[69]

In 1791, a rebellion began in the mountains of Cap Français that threatened the slave economy of St. Domingue and, by extension, the Perkins wealth.[70] In December of that year, a business partner wrote to James lamenting "your present situation" and informed him that "one Colonel Murray had in contemplation of sending a small vessel to assist in removing Mrs. Perkins and your family."[71] James and his wife remained in St. Domingue, however, until the burning of Cap Français in 1792 led them and many of the colony's prominent slaveholders to flee to Havana, New Orleans, Baltimore, and New England.[72] James took with him an enslaved man, Mousse,[73] who allegedly helped the family escape.[74] Although Perkins's memoir states that the family freed Mousse, he remained attached to them in New England.[75] Samuel Gardner stayed behind.

James continued to administer the family business, remaining in regular contact with Samuel Gardner regarding activities in St. Domingue, even as the colony was engulfed in war. In May 1792, Samuel Gardner wrote:

> the day after I purchased his Negroes there was not one for sale in the place. Indicott was obliged to wait some time & finally deposit in the hands of a Captain going with N- to Havana a sum of money considerably more than the value of 8 Slaves to get the privilege of carrying that number down in his vessel.[76]

As the situation deteriorated, Samuel Gardner kept James apprised of the difficulty of both acquiring and disposing of new cargoes of slaves.[77] By October 1792, he was reporting on the continued flight of the white population.[78] He returned to New England in 1793, married, and became a partner in his father-in-law's mercantile house of Higginson & Co.[79] Samuel Gardner eventually entered the insurance industry and served as president of the Suffolk Insurance Company of Boston.[80] He would later recall his experience in St. Domingue as he advocated against emancipation in the United States, asking abolitionist women "to contemplate the horrors of degradation which must fall on their own sex throughout the Southern States" if they were to succeed and warning of "misery not only to the innocent whites, but misery and tenfold wretchedness to the slaves themselves; for this would as certainly follow a general rising of the blacks, or an immediate emancipation of them, as effect follows an operating cause."[81]

James and Thomas Handasyd redirected their primary business interest to the opium trade with China[82] and sought to recast themselves as wealthy benefactors through generous gifts and bequests.[83] They were successful in this regard: when Harvard President Josiah Quincy (AB 1790; overseer, 1810–1829; president, 1829–1845) wrote his 1840 history of the University, he described James as among "benefactors of

Harvard College . . . entitled to grateful remembrance."[84] Quincy wrote of James:

> His professional career was commenced in St. Domingo, where he established a commercial house, and conducted a prosperous business until he was compelled to leave the island by the insurrection of the colored population. At the hazard of his life, and with great loss of property, he escaped from St. Domingo, and returned to the United States. Soon after this event, he formed with his brother the commercial house of James and Thomas H. Perkins, which afterwards established a professional reputation second to none in North America. By the amount and discriminating nature of their bounty for the support of learning and the relief of suffering, and by their readiness to aid in every patriotic design, they have rendered their names synonymous with public spirit and benevolence.[85]

Israel Thorndike

In 1818, the Beverly, Massachusetts, merchant and slave trader Israel Thorndike paid $6,500 for a large collection of maps and books from the estate of Cristoph Daniel Ebeling, a professor of Greek and history. This collection, which Thorndike donated to Harvard,[86] contained "one of the most complete and valuable collections of works extant on American history" available at the time,"[87] and came to be the core of the Harvard Map Collection—the "most valuable single collection in existence."[88]

Besides the landmark Ebeling Map Collection gift, Thorndike, together with his son Israel Thorndike Jr., donated $2,100 to Massachusetts General Hospital.[89] In 1815, he served as vice president of A Society for the Promotion of Theological Education in Harvard University, which, with Thorndike's support and that of other wealthy patrons—notably James Perkins, who also served as an officer in the society—established what is now Harvard Divinity School. Thorndike himself donated $500 to that fundraising effort and a further $500 "for the purchase of theological works."[90] He also gave $500 in 1806 to support a natural history professorship and a further $100 in 1820 for a professorship of mineralogy and geology.[91] Like the Perkins brothers, Thorndike's descendants were deeply involved at Harvard too. Augustus

Harvard's economic ties to the slave trade and Caribbean slavery in the colonial era were not just a matter of major benefactors; such ties were also visible on campus, including in financial transactions between individual students and the University.

Some students—often sons of wealthy New England merchants or Caribbean plantation owners—paid their tuition in plantation commodities like sugar, molasses, and cocoa. These goods, produced by enslaved labor, were luxuries of significant value.[1] Lewis Vassall (AB 1728), for example, ostentatiously paid a portion of his tuition with a cask of sugar worth more than the entirety of many of his classmates' dues.[2]

It was advantageous for Harvard to cultivate relationships with families in these lucrative industries, and in many cases, the University would benefit from their patronage for generations.[3]

In Harvard's first century, the school capitalized on its small contingent of ultrawealthy students by making it possible to purchase special privileges and status. Modeled on a similar system in place at Oxford and Cambridge, students willing to "first pay one hundred pounds to the College Treasurer" and then "pay double tuition-money"[4] were granted the distinction of "fellow commoner."[5] (Early on, fellow commoners were also required to present a piece of silver.)

Fellow commoners' privileges included dining at the faculty table, being "excused from going on errands," and having "the title of Masters, and . . . the privilege of wearing their hats as masters do."[6] While records are incomplete, nearly all known fellow commoners at Harvard had ties to slavery. This effectively made students of slave-owning families an elite on campus.

In 1729, John and William Vassall, younger brothers of Lewis, each presented to Harvard a silver tankard with their names and family arms inscribed. These tankards, received as payment for the Vassalls' fellow commoner status, became part of the University's collection of ceremonial silver.[7]

Thorndike was a renowned twentieth-century Harvard Medical School faculty member, and a professorship at the Massachusetts General Hospital bears the family name.[92]

Thorndike's business interests also intersected with those of the Perkins brothers. He built his fortune primarily exporting flour and fish to the sugar plantations of the Caribbean and buying slave-produced goods like coffee, sugar, molasses, and rum to sell in US and European markets. Thorndike traded in enslaved women, men, and children as well, buying slaves in one port to sell at another.[93] In a 1791 letter to the captain of one of their ships, Thorndike and his business partner[94] wrote the following orders:

> Purchase from Five to Fourteen <u>good Negroes</u>, as the price may be, & lay in such food for them as is best suited to preserve their Health & proceed to the Havanna, in the island of Cuba[.] <u>you</u> be <u>very carefull to keep them well secured at all times</u> and on your arival you sell them for the most that can be obtained, & purchase as much Molasses as your <u>Vessel</u> will <u>stow</u>, leaving <u>Room only</u> sufficient to stow the goods you may purchase with your surplus cash, which you vest in Sugar, Cotton or Hides[95]

While such transactions may have been a relatively small part of Thorndike's overall business dealings,[96] it is clear that he engaged in slave trading over the course of many years leading up to the Haitian revolution.[97] Thorndike ultimately shifted—like the Perkins brothers—to the China trade, as well as to investments in New England's textile industry.[98]

Trade in Slave-Produced Goods

John McLean

In his 1840 *The History of Harvard University,* Josiah Quincy wrote that John McLean "disposed of his large estate in a spirit of general benevolence, equally useful, exemplary, and just."[99] From an original bequest of $50,000, left in trust at the time of McLean's death for the support of his widow, the University eventually received $25,000 to endow the McLean Professorship of Ancient and Modern History. Massachusetts General Hospital—the first teaching hospital associated with Harvard Medical School—also received nearly $120,000 from McLean's estate.[100] This gift was monumental: more than a fifth of the total amount of bequests received by the institution in the four decades following its 1811 charter,[101] the gift was equivalent to eight years of the hospital's annual operating expenses at mid-century.[102] For his generosity, the division of the hospital dedicated to the treatment of mental illness was renamed in McLean's honor. McLean Hospital, now an independent Harvard-affiliated hospital in Belmont, Massachusetts, still bears his name.[103]

McLean made his fortune in the slavery-entangled trade with the West Indies that powered the Massachusetts economy from the colony's earliest days. According to Quincy, McLean "prosecuted trade with great skill and success, chiefly with the interior of New England and the West Indies."[104] Like so many Massachusetts merchants, including his father,[105] he shipped lumber from New England to Caribbean plantations. He then purchased sugar produced by enslaved people to sell in Europe and the United States. Between 1793 and 1795 alone, McLean is listed as an owner of ten ships registered in Boston and adjacent Charlestown.[106] A list of spoliation claims submitted to the federal government by US merchants seeking to recoup their losses on cargoes captured by the French in the 1790s notes McLean as an underwriter on eight separate voyages, including shipments of foodstuffs, dry goods, and wood products to the West Indies; cargoes of slave-produced goods, including sugar, coffee, tobacco, and their derivatives, from the West Indies to the United States and Europe; and, in one case, a shipment of slave-produced goods from the American South to Europe.[107]

Benjamin Bussey

In his 1835 will, Benjamin Bussey explained at length his reasoning for leaving a significant portion of his wealth to Harvard University: namely his desire "to advance the prosperity and happiness of our common country." He wrote:

> In a nation whose government is held to be a government of laws, I deem it important to promote that branch of education which lies at the foundation of wise legislation and which tends to ensure a pure and uniform administration of justice and I have considered that in a country whose laws extend equal protection to all religious opinions, that education which tends to disseminate just and rational views on religious subjects is entitled to special patronage and support.[108]

Bussey left half of his estate to Harvard to support theological and legal education and the establishment of a school of agriculture, botany, and other natural sciences.[109] The net value of his bequest, when the University received it in 1861, was just over $400,000—enough to establish Bussey Professorships at Harvard Law School and Harvard Divinity School as well as the Bussey Institution on the property Bussey left to the University, now the Arnold Arboretum, in Jamaica Plain, Boston.[110] In recognition of these gifts, a marble bust of Bussey is displayed in Annenberg Hall, the freshman dining room in Memorial Hall.[111] The Harvard Portrait Collection also contains a likeness captured by the famed American portraitist Gilbert Stuart.[112]

In a brief handwritten memoir composed near the end of his life, Bussey emphasized his humble origins as the son of a poor New England farmer, his service as a quartermaster during the American Revolution, and his work "night & day" to establish himself as a goldsmith in Massachusetts after the war. He devoted less than a paragraph, however, to the period during which he amassed his fortune: he only briefly noted that he "supplied many traders in Prov[idence], New Port, & all ye country round"[113] and did not mention that many of the traders he supplied would have been engaged in the West Indies trade. At this time, the slave trade in Rhode Island—long an important center—was approaching its peak.[114]

In 1790, Bussey tells us, he moved to Boston and worked "as I'd in Dedham, day & night; did a large bus[iness]; owned several ships; engaged in many kinds of merc[antile] adventures" for "ab^t 15 years."[115] Other sources detail these "adventures": records of spoliation claims include multiple vessels owned by Bussey and voyages he underwrote. More than half of these voyages originated in the United States and were bound for the Caribbean with supplies that New England merchants had long provided to island plantations.[116]

Bussey also provisioned the plantation economy in North America. As early as 1789, he invested in a voyage carrying supplies to New Orleans, including flour, building materials, farming implements, and hundreds of yards of "toe cloth"—a rough fabric routinely used to make clothing and bedding for enslaved people. The ship returned north with a cargo of tobacco.[117] By the early nineteenth century, Bussey's business ties spanned the American South,[118] necessitating that Bussey have representatives on the ground. In 1802, his son-in-law traveled to Savannah on his behalf to collect on numerous debts.[119] "Messrs Chapman & Weston" were expected to pay in tobacco,[120] while Ebenezer Jenckes of Louisville, Kentucky, was expected to remit payment in the form of cotton.[121] Such arrangements were typical, and Bussey often shipped such goods—produced by enslaved people in the West Indies and the American South—to Europe, where he sold them and purchased fabrics, dinnerware, and other goods for US markets.[122]

Bussey frequently did business with other Harvard donors, part of a tight-knit community of wealthy Boston merchants and businessmen with ties to the University. Among his French spoliation claims are merchant voyages underwritten or co-owned by Thomas Handasyd and James Perkins, Israel Thorndike, and John McLean, each discussed above.[123] Bussey also invested in the Lawrence Manufacturing Company, owned by Abbott Lawrence, discussed below.[124] And Bussey's attorney, Samuel P. P. Fay (AM 1798; overseer, 1824–1852) is the namesake of Fay House, the principal administrative building of the former Radcliffe College—today the Radcliffe Institute for Advanced Study.[125]

During the latter decades of his life, Bussey's focus shifted to business interests in New England. He owned property across the region, including extensive holdings along Boston's waterfront that city officials repeatedly sought to acquire for city projects. This included land "bounding on yᵉ Mill Creek South of Ann Street and North of the Town dock,"[126] part of what is now the Quincy Market complex, which Josiah Quincy, then mayor of Boston, purchased for the city in 1824.[127] At the time of his death in 1842, Bussey still owned large swaths of the city, a country estate in Roxbury (now Jamaica Plain), a woolen manufactory in Dedham, and extensive property in what is now Maine.[128]

After Bussey's death, it fell to Quincy—by then the president of Harvard—to thank Bussey's widow on behalf of the Corporation.[129] Like his business dealings in life, Bussey's final bequest illustrates not only the links between Harvard and economies of slavery, but also the close ties that bound the Massachusetts elite—merchants, businessmen, and politicians—to one another and to the University.

Edwin F. Atkins

Examples until this point all date to the era in which slavery was legal in the United States, if not in Massachusetts. Yet Harvard connections to slavery persisted even after the end of the Civil War.

In 1899, for example, the Boston-based sugar magnate Edwin F. Atkins granted $2,500 to the Harvard botanist Oakes Ames to begin research on the possible development of new, better strains of sugar-cane through selection and breeding at the Atkins family's Soledad Plantation in Cuba.[130]

Cuba had by the 1830s replaced St. Domingue (Haiti) as the most prominent slave economy of the Caribbean,[131] and the Atkins family had been exporting sugar and molasses from the island since 1838, some thirty years before the beginning of Cuba's gradual abolition of slavery. In 1868, at the beginning of the Ten Years' War, Cuban inde-pendence leaders declared emancipation, and enslaved people who fought on either side were granted their freedom, setting in motion a slow and halting path toward the end of slavery.[132] Meanwhile, during the war, American investors, including the Atkins family, ex-tended credit to Cuban plantation owners. By the end of the nine-teenth century, such investors had acquired most of the plantations in Cuba; Atkins, looking to expand into sugar production, acquired Soledad Plantation in 1884.[133]

Four years earlier, the Spanish government's 1880 abolition law had established an eight-year period during which nominally free formerly enslaved people were labeled apprentices, or *patrocinados,* and com-pelled to continue working for their enslavers.[134] This system was, in effect, slavery by another name. In fact, before Atkins purchased Soledad, the plantation's owners sent a bill of sale to his business part-ners that listed 177 *patrocinados* as slaves, despite their new legal status. When E. Atkins & Company officially acquired the plantation, it came with at least ninety-five formerly enslaved *patrocinados.*[135]

Edwin Atkins's correspondence with his plantation manager imme-diately after he took possession reflects a preoccupation with reducing labor costs in order to compete with other producers.[136] They discussed strategies to retain control of the Black workers,[137] as well as the ex-traction of payment for releasing workers from indentured servitude, apparently including some who were already free by law.[138] By the end of the century, Atkins had expanded the estate from its initial 900 acres to 12,000 acres of land in the hills and mountains of Cienfuegos.[139]

A section of this plantation became a Harvard biological research station at the turn of the twentieth century. In later years, scholars and students would test varieties of sugarcane on the property and develop new ways to eradicate diseases.[140] To provide sustained support for this work, Atkins presented to the University initial payments on an en-dowment fund which, between 1919 and 1925, would come to total nearly $200,000.[141] In 1932, Soledad officially became known as the Atkins Institution of the Arnold Arboretum, Harvard University.[142] Harvard's involvement was suspended in 1961, in the wake of the Cuban revolution, and the site is now managed by the Cuban government as the Cienfuegos Botanical Garden.[143]

Southern Slavery and Northern Textile Manufacturing

Harvard's ties to the Caribbean and to wealthy planters and traders is a critical part of the story of the University's financial involvement with slavery, but it is not the whole story. With the development of industrial capitalism in the late eighteenth and early nineteenth centu-ries, the plantation economy evolved, and cotton began to take center stage. By the middle of the nineteenth century, as the historian Sven Beckert observed, cotton manufacturers and merchants in the United Kingdom "stood at the center of a world-spanning empire," acquiring slave-produced cotton from the Americas for their mills and selling cotton products to "the most distant corners" of the globe.[144] New England and its vast textile mills followed, and Harvard affiliates' deep connections to this lucrative industry—fed with cotton produced by enslaved people primarily in the American South—are another impor-tant part of the University's story.

Abbott Lawrence

In his 1846–1847 annual report to the Board of Overseers, Harvard President Edward Everett shared a "plan of organization for an advanced school" to provide "systematic instruction in those branches of sciences which are more immediately connected with the great industrial interests of the country."[145] Disciplines of instruction included chemistry "in its various applications to the arts of life," engineering, geology, and zoology. The plan was approved in February 1847, but the University lacked the funds necessary to construct new buildings and hire relevant faculty.

This uncertainty quickly resolved: in June 1847, the Boston industrialist Abbott Lawrence announced his donation of $50,000 to "defray the expenditures" necessary for the Scientific School, including "the erection of suitable buildings . . . the purchase of apparatus, furniture," as well as "comfortable support of the professors and other teachers employed."[146] The new school would train Harvard students in "the practical sciences," to prepare "engineers, . . . miners, machinists, and mechanics" for skilled employment in America's rapidly industrializing economy.[147] Everett remarked that Lawrence's "munificent donation" was at that time "the largest sum . . . ever bestowed on a place of education in this country, in one gift, by a living benefactor."[148] The new scientific school was named in Lawrence's honor and, upon his death in 1855, he bequeathed an additional $50,000 "for the further advancement of the said school."[149] Today, Lawrence's gifts support endowed professorships in the Lawrence Scientific School's successor, the Paulson School of Engineering and Applied Sciences.

The founder and namesake of the town of Lawrence, Massachusetts, Lawrence was co-owner of the A & A Lawrence Company, which managed the Lawrence Textile Manufacturing Company, and president of both Atlantic Cotton Mills and Pacific Mills, two major textile factories. He also served in the US Congress and as United States Minister to Great Britain.[150] Lawrence had a personal as well as professional stake in the development of educational institutions that would teach "scientific knowledge as then applied to the practical arts," which he viewed as critical for industry generally and for textile manufacturing specifically. He did not merely donate funds but directed how the money should be utilized.[151] He also personally recommended and, for several years, paid the salary of Louis Agassiz as professor of zoology and geology;[152] as discussed below, Agassiz would play an outsized role in the University's intellectual life and promotion of race science.

Lawrence's descendants would continue to be deeply involved with the University. His nephew, Amos Adams Lawrence, expanded the family business and its philanthropic donations to Harvard and other institutions.[153] Abbott Lawrence's grandson, Abbott Lawrence Lowell, served as president of Harvard from 1909 to 1933 and was heir to not one but two prominent Boston families, the Lowells being another family with considerable wealth derived from textiles, and including notable abolitionists.[154] As president, Abbott Lawrence Lowell would preside over the creation of a residential college system that excluded Black students and be a leader among Harvard faculty who supported eugenics.[155]

The wealth that Abbott Lawrence amassed through textile manufacturing and trade—like the fortunes of other Northern industrialists of the era—was inextricably tied to enslaved labor. Lawrence's mills were staffed by free Northern workers, but they depended upon cotton produced by enslaved people laboring on southern plantations.[156]

Transactions between Northern manufacturers like Lawrence and Southern slaveholders operated through the factorage system. Southern planters relied on factors—commercial agents—to negotiate the sale of commodities, chiefly cotton in the nineteenth century, produced by their enslaved laborers. Factors selected and stored the cotton bales, kept abreast of the price of cotton on the world market, and sold the commodity to various commercial houses. They then transported the raw material on freight trains and ships to the northern United States and across the Atlantic. The cotton they traded was the source of incredible wealth in the global economy.[157] As the historian Walter Johnson has written, the Southern plantation system converted "lashes into labor into bales into dollars into pound sterling," and it made men like Lawrence into wealthy entrepreneurs and philanthropists.[158]

Lawrence had at least two agents in the South, one based in Richmond, Virginia, and one based in New Orleans, Louisiana.[159] He corresponded with both on the cost of cotton on the world market and political events in Europe that could affect commodity prices. William Gray, an agent for Lawrence's Atlantic Cotton Mills, traveled between Boston, Lawrence, and New Orleans as he handled business transactions for the mill. In the course of his work, Gray corresponded with Greenleaf & Hubbard, a firm in New Orleans that traded in cotton from Southern plantations throughout the Mississippi Valley, and that had its own Harvard links.[160]

James Greenleaf

James Greenleaf, co-owner of Greenleaf & Hubbard, was the son of Harvard's second Royall Professor of Law, Simon Greenleaf.[161] He was also a philanthropist and the builder of Greenleaf House, the historic Brattle Street mansion purchased by Radcliffe College in 1905. Greenleaf House served as the residence of Radcliffe College presidents and, more recently, deans of the Radcliffe Institute for Advanced Study.

Greenleaf and his wife, Mary (Longfellow) Greenleaf, sister of Henry Wadsworth Longfellow (faculty, 1836–1854), divided their time between Cambridge and New Orleans, where Greenleaf and his business partner, Daniel Hubbard, operated from Canal Street.[162] The violence of slavery—and the auction block—would have been in full view throughout Greenleaf's personal and professional life.[163] His primary business was the purchase of slave-grown cotton—generally by way of factors—and the sale of it to major Northern mills like Abbott Lawrence's.[164]

Due to the structure of these transactions, it is difficult to determine precisely which plantations supplied Greenleaf & Hubbard,[165] but we do know that among them was Brierfield, owned by Jefferson Davis—the US senator from Mississippi and soon-to-be president of the Confederacy.[166] Also the site of Davis's personal residence, Brierfield stood on Davis Bend, a peninsula in the Mississippi Delta with "rich alluvial soil" and direct access to the cotton market via the river.[167] Greenleaf & Hubbard worked with the firm Payne & Harrison, co-owned by Jacob U. Payne, who was not only a factor and a slave trader[168] but also "the most intimate friend Jefferson Davis ever had"[169] and, according his obituary in the *Washington Post,* "the largest cotton dealer in the world."[170]

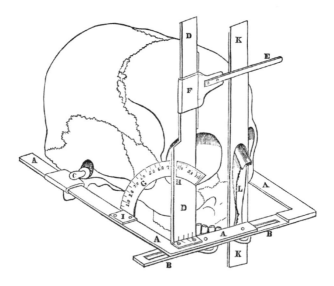

Agassiz, like many race scientists of his era, believed that craniometry, the measurement and dissection of human skulls, could reveal differences in intelligence between the races. During his first trip to the United States, in 1847, he visited prominent anatomist Samuel Morton's skull collection in Philadelphia and spent "four hours in contemplation" of the skulls of Native Americans on display. Samuel Morton, *Crania Americana* (1832) / Image of skull being measured (Philadelphia, PA: J. Dobson, 1832)

FOUR

Harvard, Slavery, and Its Legacies before and after the Civil War

Context: A Nation Torn by Slavery and a Rising University

Well after slavery ended in Massachusetts in 1783, during the antebellum era and even after the Thirteenth Amendment to the US Constitution conferred emancipation nationwide, in 1865, vestiges—or legacies—of the system lingered. Legacies of slavery such as exclusion, segregation, and discrimination against Blacks in employment, voting, housing, healthcare, public accommodations, criminal punishment, and education, among other areas, persisted in the South as well as the North well into the twentieth century.[1] And the hardening of racial categories, advanced by race scientists at Harvard and elsewhere, provided intellectual justification for continued subjugation.

Notwithstanding the Commonwealth's Revolutionary War heritage as birthplace of the colonists' struggle for liberty, its celebrated anti-slavery activists, and its many brave Union veterans of the Civil War,[2] racial inequality flourished in Massachusetts—and at Harvard—as Blacks struggled for equal opportunity and full citizenship.[3]

The decades after the Civil War, during the period of Reconstruction when debates raged about whether and how to support the Black American quest for equality, are especially germane to understanding legacies of slavery in American institutions of higher education. The US Constitution changed, reflecting the nation's formal break with slavery and commitment to equal citizenship rights regardless of race.

The Fourteenth Amendment to the US Constitution, conferring equal protection and due process of law, and the Fifteenth Amendment, prohibiting discrimination against males in voting, were enacted and ratified.[4] Within this context, reformers conceived policies and social supports to uplift the formerly enslaved and their descendants. But it fell to the nation's institutions, its leadership, and its people to safeguard—or not—citizens' rights and implement these policies.[5]

Around the same time, Harvard itself aspired to transform: it sought to enlarge its infrastructure, expand its student body, and recruit new faculty. Samuel Eliot Morison, a noted historian of the University, explained that during the period from 1869 into the twentieth century, the University resolved "to expand with the country."[6] Harvard's leaders, particularly Presidents Charles William Eliot and Abbott Lawrence Lowell, argued that Harvard should become a "true" national university that would serve as a "unifying influence." They viewed the recruitment of students from "varied" backgrounds and a "large area" of the country as a linchpin of these ambitions.[7]

Hence, two developments critical to understanding this moment of promise and peril occurred at once. The fate of African Americans hung in the balance; and Harvard, already well known, sought to grow, evolve, and build a yet greater national reputation. In the end, the University proved unwilling to participate in efforts to promote the welfare of African Americans as it pursued national prominence, whether for the sake of political expediency, because many of its leaders subscribed to the concept of inherent differences among races, or—most likely—a combination of both.

Harvard and Abolitionism

Even as the majority at Harvard accommodated or advanced the era's racial oppression, or tried to protect and promote Harvard's growing reputation as a national institution by keeping it out of the fray, a small but important minority of Harvard faculty, students, and alumni—before and after the Civil War—rejected prevailing social norms and were vocal and active advocates for abolition. These Harvard affiliates spoke out against slavery and racial discrimination, and this counter

Alberta V. Scott, the first Black graduate of Radcliffe College, is memorialized by a marker at her family's home on Union Street in Cambridge.[1] In addition to this distinction, she was only the fourth Black woman to graduate from any college in Massachusetts and the first raised in Massachusetts to graduate from a college in the state.[2]

Scott was born in 1875 in Virginia and moved with her family to Cambridge, Massachusetts, as a child.[3] She attended the Allston School and Cambridge Latin School—both public, coeducational, unsegregated institutions—prior to enrolling at Radcliffe College in 1894.[4] Scott was part of the first class to matriculate after Radcliffe became a degree-granting institution, and she was a member of the German Club and the Idler Club—the College's drama club.[5]

After her graduation, in 1898, Scott dedicated her life to education, teaching first at a predominantly Black elementary school in Indianapolis and then at Booker T. Washington's Tuskegee Institute in Alabama.[6] She believed "it [was] a duty for those young colored people who are so inclined to take every advantage along educational lines which they can easily obtain in New England, and then go South and teach their colored brethren."[7] Her life was cut tragically short by illness, and she died in 1902, at the age of twenty-six.[8]

Scott paved the way for the Black women who followed in her footsteps at Radcliffe, and today she is recognized across campus. The Alberta V. Scott Leadership Academy, a mentorship initiative run by the Association of Black Harvard Women, brings Boston-area high school students together with Harvard College students to foster connection and cultivate leadership skills.[9] And the Greener Scott Scholars Mentorship Program, founded in 2018 by a group of Harvard students, brings together Black undergraduate and graduate students.[10]

history of resistance is also an important element of the story of Harvard's entanglements with slavery.

In the decades leading up to the Civil War, the social and political climate at Harvard largely reflected that of the nation. Northern abolitionists advocated for the end of slavery in the United States; many Southerners in the Harvard community defended slavery, and moderates tried to chart a path between the two that might preserve the union.

Harvard administrators, faculty, staff, and students were vocal participants on all sides of the ongoing national debates. Yet some of the most prominent voices drowned out and sought to suppress antislavery sentiment.

Harvard Affiliates and Abolitionist Organizations in Massachusetts

Notwithstanding pressure to stay away from public abolitionist activities, a review of published lists of supporters of several Massachusetts organizations illustrates the involvement of members of the Harvard community in advocating the abolition of slavery and the protection of the rights of African Americans.

In May of 1836, for example, a group of Cambridge residents, local politicians, and Harvard faculty came together to form the Cambridge Anti-Slavery Society. In addition to Charles Follen and Henry Ware Jr., both of whom are discussed below, the original signers of the group's constitution included two-time acting University President Henry Ware Sr. (1810 and 1828–1829; faculty, 1805–1845), the retired faculty member and former University librarian Sidney Willard (librarian, 1800–1805; faculty, 1807–1831), and seven additional alumni of the University. In all, eleven of the twenty-three original members—nearly half—were Harvard affiliates.[8]

Almost ten years later, the Boston-based abolitionist newspaper the *Liberator* published a list of votes for and against two resolutions passed at that year's New England Anti-Slavery Convention, declaring it "the great fault of the United States Constitution" that it allowed slaveholders to "control the policy and character of the nation" and calling on abolitionists to "agitate for a dissolution of the Union."[9] The diverse group of 250 men and women, both Black and white, who voted on these resolutions included the Harvard graduates and prominent abolitionists Wendell Phillips (AB 1831; LLB 1834) and Edmund Quincy (AB 1827; overseer, 1875–1877)—the latter of whom was the son of then–University President Josiah Quincy. The rolls also included the recording secretary of the Massachusetts Anti-Slavery Society, Henry Willard Williams (MD 1849),[10] who would go on to become a faculty member at the Medical School, serving as the first chair of the Department of Ophthalmology, and the benefactor and namesake of the Henry

Willard Williams Professorship in Ophthalmology at Harvard Medical School.[11]

Perhaps most striking is the prevalence of Harvard affiliates among the active members of the Committee of Vigilance of Boston, often referred to as the Boston Vigilance Committee, which worked through legal channels and in partnership with organizations like the Underground Railroad to assist self-emancipated enslaved people to evade capture after passage of the Fugitive Slave Act in 1850. While membership of the organization was necessarily guarded, in an 1880 memoir, one-fifth of 209 members listed as active between 1850 and 1860 were Harvard graduates. This included the future Harvard faculty members Henry Ingersoll Bowditch (Jackson Professor of Clinical Medicine, 1859–1867), Richard Henry Dana Jr. (lecturer at Harvard Law School, 1866–1868; overseer, 1865–1877), and James Russell Lowell (Smith Professor of the French and Spanish Languages and Literatures and Professor of Belles Lettres, 1855–1886; emeritus, 1886–1891; overseer, 1887–1891).[12]

Joshua Bowen Smith: Black Abolitionist on Campus

One of the most active abolitionists in Harvard's employ in the period before the Civil War was a free Black man, although his abolitionist work was independent of the University. Joshua Bowen Smith founded a catering business in Boston in 1849 and for twenty-five years served gatherings of the local elite. Smith contracted with Harvard to prepare daily meals for students as well as more lavish fare at major celebrations like Commencement;[13] he provided services that had earlier fallen to the stewards and, in some cases, their enslaved workers.[14] Smith invested the proceeds of his work for Harvard and other Boston-area institutions in abolitionist causes.[15] He was directly involved in antislavery efforts as a member of the Underground Railroad[16] and as a member of the executive committee of the Boston Vigilance Committee.[17] Smith was also a cofounder of the New England Freedom Association, which provided basic necessities and legal defense to escaped enslaved people. He sometimes employed waiters and cooks connected to the association, and it is possible that some of the escapees Smith helped evade capture may have prepared food or waited tables for Harvard's students and faculty.[18]

Charles Follen, Henry Ware, and Henry Wadsworth Longfellow: Abolitionist Faculty Members

Members of the Harvard faculty who worked to advance the abolitionist cause often faced particularly significant resistance from the University. In the 1830s, two abolitionist faculty members—Charles Follen (1825–1835), a professor of German, and Henry Ware Jr. (1829–1842; overseer, 1820–1830), a member of the faculty at the Divinity School—faced pressure to curtail their involvement with the newly founded Cambridge Anti-Slavery Society.[19] Follen believed he lost his full-time teaching role at the University because of his abolitionist activities; he resigned rather than accept a demotion to part-time instructor.[20] Ware, according to an 1846 biography written by his brother, was warned by friends and colleagues to limit his involvement with the society, and he eventually resigned from the organization.[21]

Henry Wadsworth Longfellow, Smith Professor of the French and Spanish Languages and Literatures and Belles Lettres (1836–1854), straddled the social and professional networks that divided abolitionists and supporters of slavery.

Throughout his life, Longfellow maintained friendships with prominent abolitionists, including Richard Henry Dana Jr., James Russell Lowell, Ralph Waldo Emerson, and Harriet Beecher Stowe.[22] The firebrand Free Soil Party member and US Senator Charles Sumner (AB 1830; LLB 1834), whom Longfellow supported actively—if mostly in private correspondence—was among his closest friends.[23] Yet so too was Louis Agassiz, the proponent of race science.[24]

Longfellow's most public stand against slavery came in 1842, when he published the volume *Poems on Slavery,* which described the horrors of slavery in painful detail and was popular among white audiences as well as Black.[25] For the most part, however, he expressed his anti-slavery views privately—in his correspondence and his journals.[26] Believing that slavery was "an unrighteous institution,"[27] Longfellow donated to abolitionist causes, too: particularly after the passage of the Fugitive Slave Act, his records show numerous payments in support of escaped slaves, their families, and those who harbored them. He also supported Black schools and churches in the United States, Canada, and Haiti and gave money to purchase enslaved people's freedom.[28]

Longfellow wrote to Sumner that the goal of emancipation should be to place "the black man . . . upon the same footing as the white."[29] And he did so in his home, welcoming members of the Black community as guests. In 1846, the escaped slave Josiah Henson—widely known to be the model for Harriet Beecher Stowe's Uncle Tom—called on Longfellow in Cambridge in search of funds to support a school; Longfellow donated that day and would do so again many times over the next thirty years.[30] At the height of the conflict over the Fugitive Slave Act, Longfellow hosted Lunsford Lane, an escaped slave and abolitionist from North Carolina, and Darby Vassall, the early advocate for free Black rights who was born in bondage at Longfellow's very home in 1769, when it belonged to John Vassall.[31]

John Gorham Palfrey: Abolitionist Dean

The experience of Professor and Divinity School Dean John Gorham Palfrey (faculty, 1830–1839; overseer, 1828–1831, 1852–1855) illustrates both the presence of active abolitionists in the Harvard community and some of the challenges they faced.

Palfrey grew up in Boston, attended Phillips Exeter Academy alongside future Harvard President Jared Sparks (1849–1853), and graduated with a master's degree from Harvard Divinity School in 1818. After more than a decade as the minister of a multiracial congregation at Boston's Brattle Street Church, he returned to Harvard in 1830 as professor of biblical literature and dean of the Divinity School. While one biographer describes the "timidity" of Palfrey's abolitionism during these years—Palfrey joined the nascent Cambridge Anti-Slavery Society in the 1830s but quickly backed away in the face of "public opinion"—Palfrey became more vocal after 1838.[32]

In that year, Palfrey received word from his brothers in Louisiana that his father's health was declining, raising the prospect that Palfrey soon might inherit enslaved people from his father's plantation. He immediately began to investigate how he might legally free any enslaved people who passed to him.[33] At the same time, Palfrey faced pressure from Harvard President Josiah Quincy to postpone an abolitionist public debate, organized by Divinity School students, as Quincy feared a disturbance to campus life. In correspondence, Quincy urged Palfrey to reconsider the event, which Quincy deemed unsuitable for "a seminary of learning, composed of young men, from every quarter of the country; among whom are many whose prejudices, passions, and interests are deeply implicated and affected by these depulsions and who feel very naturally and strongly on the subject."[34] When Palfrey opted not to postpone the debate, Quincy wrote again, objecting to the fact that students from across Harvard had been invited to the event and stating his intention to seek the "advice and action" of the Corporation.[35] Less than two months later—although not in time to prevent the debate—the Corporation adopted a resolution that forbade anyone other than University faculty or staff members "to teach, lecture or preach, or deliver any oration or discourse in any of the schools belonging to the University, or in any Society connected with either of them" without permission.[36] Palfrey resigned from Harvard shortly thereafter, in 1839, and entered politics.

In the ensuing years, Palfrey was elected as the Whig candidate and an abolitionist to the Massachusetts state legislature (1842–1843); appointed secretary of the Commonwealth of Massachusetts (1844–1847); and elected to the United States House of Representatives (1847–1849).[37]

Palfrey's father died in 1843 and, true to his earlier intentions and despite the opposition of his brothers, he hired an agent in New Orleans to seek the bulk of his inheritance in human property. Palfrey then freed the older people among the enslaved he inherited and paid to transport the others—sixteen men, women, and children under the age of thirty who could not legally be manumitted under Louisiana's laws—to the Northeast,[38] where he found paid work for them in homes across Massachusetts and New York.[39]

In 1848 Palfrey, newly affiliated with the abolitionist Free Soil Party, ran for reelection to the US House of Representatives. He lost but remained active in Massachusetts politics, where debate over slavery heated up following the enactment of the Compromise of 1850 and a ruling of the Massachusetts Supreme Judicial Court that the Fugitive Slave Act, a key element of the compromise, must be enforced in the state.[40] These developments helped turn public opinion in the Commonwealth against slavery, and this period marks perhaps the moment of starkest disconnect between Harvard, with its national ambitions, and New England over the question of abolition.[41]

Around this same time, Palfrey's activism again drew the notice of the Harvard community.[42] In March 1850, his longtime friend, Harvard President Jared Sparks (faculty, 1838–1849; president, 1849–1853), made a personal call: Sparks, a moderate who opposed slavery but favored the removal of former slaves from the United States, told Palfrey that his activities on behalf of the Free Soil Party were harming Harvard's reputation—this despite the fact that Palfrey had not worked at the University for more than a decade. Palfrey was outraged by Sparks's request that he moderate his political activities.[43]

Sparks's request appears to have been driven by concerns about how the abolitionist activities of Harvard affiliates like Palfrey were influencing national public opinion of the University. Later in 1850, Sparks received a letter from Caleb Cushing, a Harvard graduate and former US representative from Massachusetts, complaining that "abolitionism and political Free Soilers" were "sheltered and nurtured under the broad wings of the university."[44] This pushback occurred around the same time that Harvard Medical School admitted the Black students Daniel Laing Jr., Isaac H. Snowden, and Martin Robison Delany, only to rescind their admission in the face of protests from white students and families—many of them Southern.[45] (This incident is discussed in greater detail below.) Moreover, in 1851, in response to questions from the Massachusetts legislature—which still provided funding to Harvard in this period—Sparks explained low enrollment by noting that Southerners had been hard to recruit in recent years. Concerns about the recruitment and retention of Southern students were certainly on his and other administrators' minds.[46]

Following Palfrey's failed 1851 run for Governor of Massachusetts[47] and Sparks's 1852 decision to step down as Harvard president and leave the University, Ephraim Peabody, a Harvard Divinity School graduate and pastor of Boston's King's Chapel, wrote to Palfrey to inquire whether he would be interested in being nominated for Sparks's soon-to-be vacant professorship. Peabody, while not an officer of the University, was well connected with prominent Harvard affiliates, several of whom were active members of his parish.[48] The offer came with a caveat: Peabody warned Palfrey that "an active part in the politics of the day beyond what is incumbent on every private citizen, would be thought by the Corporation & by the Public incompatible with an Office in the College."[49]

Palfrey wrote back expressing his interest in the position, not least because he needed a means of supporting his family. He also acknowledged that the University leadership would expect him to show restraint in politics, but he did not commit to remaining on the sidelines.[50] There is no record of any further correspondence on this subject, but Palfrey did not succeed Sparks as the McLean Professor of Ancient and Modern History.

The next year, Sparks himself sought another prominent University position for Palfrey, suggesting to members of the Corporation that Palfrey be considered for the role of treasurer upon the incumbent's retirement. Palfrey did not receive that position either, and in this case, the reasons are on record. Fellow Charles G. Loring (AB 1812; fellow, 1838–1857) advised against nominating Palfrey because of his politics, despite Loring's conviction that Palfrey would be an excellent treasurer:

> The only doubt arises from his <u>peculiar</u> position as <u>a very prominent leader</u> of a political party, against which such inveterate lividity exists among a large portion of the influential members of society at the North, in the Middle States–, & which is unanimously felt at the South.—This would weigh nothing with me, if the appointment were to a private office, in which the public has no interest, nor any right to interfere. But the College is eminently public, & ought to be managed as a <u>national</u> institution–, & it becomes therefore a grave question, how far any office should be filled by a person, who is obnoxious to the [illegible], or ill will of a section of the nation, or any large portion of the people.[51]

Loring went on to imply that he was supported in this view by "the Ch. J."—Lemuel Shaw, then chief justice of the Massachusetts Supreme Judicial Court and another Harvard fellow.[52] While Loring and Shaw were personally opposed to slavery, they took a moderate line in hopes of protecting Harvard as a "national" university.

The events of the 1850s eventually drove Harvard, like every other national institution, to take a stand. In the end, abolitionists were partly vindicated, while political moderates fell out of favor. In 1855, just two years after rejecting Palfrey as treasurer, the Corporation declined to grant an honorary degree to the former treasurer Samuel Atkins Eliot, who had voted for the Fugitive Slave Act while in Congress.[53] In 1859, Harvard granted honorary degrees to the abolitionists Henry Wadsworth Longfellow and Charles Sumner.[54] From 1861 to 1865, Harvard's national stature and the internal divisions that came with it were reflected in the service of Harvard men in the Civil War: 1,358 Harvard men enlisted for the Union, and 136 of them died; another 304 enlisted for the Confederacy, of whom 70 lost their lives.[55] Palfrey ended his career not at Harvard but in politics, appointed the postmaster of Boston in 1861 by President Abraham Lincoln.[56]

Legacies of Slavery in Scholarship: Race Science

By 1850, Harvard Medical School had become a focal point of scientific theories and practices rooted in racial hierarchy, racial exclusion, and discrimination at the University. That same year, as we have seen, the passage of the Fugitive Slave Act of 1850, requiring the return of enslaved people to their owners even if slaves had escaped to free states, turned more white Northerners against slavery and its cruelties. Yet support for antislavery efforts remained anemic at Harvard, even amid the rise of abolitionist sentiment in the Commonwealth. Indeed, at Harvard Medical School, the forces of conformity with the racial status quo, aided by Harvard presidents and leading Harvard faculty members, prevailed against those who dissented.

Harvard Medical School Dean Oliver Wendell Holmes Sr. was at the helm during an 1850 controversy over the abortive admission of the Medical School's first three Black students, and his views on race help contextualize this episode.[57] They also shed light on the group of hugely influential Harvard faculty members whose work in so-called "race science"—the study of racial differences that emphasized the superiority of whites and inferiority of African peoples—would legitimize racist views among generations of scientists, medical researchers, and indeed political leaders. An alumnus of Harvard College (1829) and Harvard Medical School (1836), Holmes was a prominent anatomist and a prolific poet when he became dean in 1847.[58] Among his friends and colleagues were the race science proponents Jeffries Wyman and Louis Agassiz, also hired in 1847 as the University worked to grow its ranks of prominent scientists in the nineteenth century.[59] Holmes, like many scientists of the time, held similar views to Wyman and Agassiz. Holmes at times promoted the idea of innate differences in moral character, health, and intelligence among races.[60] He also defined "the Brahmin caste of New England" to describe himself and his peers, distinguishing between "the common country-boy, whose race has been bred to bodily labor" and the "races of scholars," like himself, who "take to [their] books as a pointer or a setter to his field-work."[61] In an *Atlantic Monthly* essay published in April 1875, Holmes cited, among others, Francis Galton, an English scientist known as the father of eugenics,[62] asserting that "in most cases, crime can be shown to run in the blood."[63]

Such ideas were perhaps related to Holmes's engagement with anatomical racial difference.[64] During the nineteenth century, Harvard had begun to amass human anatomical specimens, some of which were the bodies of enslaved people. Holmes was among the scientists who donated human remains to the Warren Anatomical Museum, including a skull (apparently from Africa): "The obliteration of the cranial sutures that characterize the African is finely shown," he explained.[65] Such racialized collections would, in the hands of the University's prominent medical and scientific authorities, become central to the promotion of race science at Harvard and many American institutions, as discussed in greater detail below.

Oliver Wendell Holmes Sr. and Black Students at Harvard Medical School

On November 2, 1850, Holmes met with Medical School faculty members to consider an inquiry about the admission of two Black students, Daniel Laing Jr. and Isaac H. Snowden, who were well qualified and had the support of members of the American Colonization Society (ACS), which advocated for the removal of free Black Americans to Africa.[66] The day before, Abraham R. Thompson and Joseph Tracy, the former a Medical School alumnus (1826) and both members of the ACS Board of Directors, had written to the Medical School faculty endorsing Laing and Snowden as "two young men of colour, pursuing medical studies . . . for the purpose of practicing in the Republic of Liberia in Africa, where their services are greatly needed."[67] The faculty voted to admit.[68]

Not long thereafter, a third Black applicant sought admission on his own initiative. Martin Robison Delany, who was already a prominent abolitionist, writer, and speaker, visited Dean Holmes in person. Although Delany was not supported by the ACS like Laing and Snowden, he too had the prerequisite medical training, and seventeen white doctors from Allegheny County, Pennsylvania, had endorsed his application. Holmes extended an offer of admission.[69]

Laing, Snowden, and Delany would, however, have a tumultuous and extremely brief tenure at the Medical School. Their reversal of fortune started when ten white students signed a petition asking to be "informed whether colored persons [were] to be admitted as students at another course of lectures."[70] Other resolutions followed. On December 10, 1850, some 60 of Laing, Snowden, and Delany's 116 white colleagues met and, by a slim majority, voted to endorse a resolution stating that the admission of Black students would degrade the quality of their degrees. The signers refused to "be identified as fellow-students, with blacks; whose company we would not keep in the streets, and whose society as associates we would not tolerate in our houses."[71]

The opposition to the Black students was not universal. Another group of students drafted a competing resolution on December 11, cautioning the University against rescinding admission to the three Black students: "As students of science . . . they would feel it a far greater evil, if, in the present state of public feeling, a medical college in Boston could refuse to this unfortunate class any privileges of education, which it is in the power of the profession to bestow."[72]

Nevertheless, Holmes and the faculty determined to exclude the three Black students, deeming them irritants and distractions to the educational environment. In a letter to the sponsors of Laing and Snowden, Holmes and the faculty described this episode as a failed "experiment," which had proved that "the intermixing of different races, on a footing of equality and personal proximity during the course of Lectures, is distasteful to a large portion of the class, and injurious to the interests of the School."[73]

Race Scientists: Louis Agassiz, John Collins Warren, and Jeffries Wyman

This episode took place in the context of the growth of race science at Harvard, which provided an intellectual framework to justify the exclusion and marginalization of Blacks that would endure into the twentieth century. Along with Holmes, those engaging with racial difference at Harvard included John Collins Warren (AB 1797; dean, 1816–1819; faculty, 1809–1856), the son of one of the Medical School's cofounders and himself the first dean of the faculty of medicine, and Holmes's contemporaries Jeffries Wyman (faculty, 1838–1840 and 1847–1874) and Louis Agassiz (hon. 1848; faculty, 1847–1873). No one was as influential in this area as the renowned Swiss-born scientist Agassiz, yet each of these men—Warren, Wyman, and Agassiz—left powerful legacies on Harvard's campus and in the wider world.

Agassiz and Wyman both joined Harvard at a time of institution-building, Agassiz at the new Lawrence Scientific School and Wyman, like Holmes, at the Medical School.[74] Wyman succeeded Warren as a professor of anatomy, but Warren remained active in the University until his death in 1856. These three men, as colleagues and collaborators, were instrumental in the creation of major Harvard institutions.

The Warren Anatomical Museum, now housed within Harvard Medical School's Countway Library, was established when Warren donated his and his father's vast collections of "pathological and other specimens" to Harvard, including human skulls and "phrenological" casts.[75] Wyman led the creation of the Peabody Museum of Archaeology and Ethnology, where he served as inaugural curator. And Agassiz established and served as the first curator of the Museum of Comparative Zoology.[76]

The Agassiz name remains visible across Harvard's campus and the City of Cambridge. Louis, who served as professor of zoology and geology from 1847 to 1873 and as curator of the Museum of Comparative Zoology from its founding in 1862 until 1873,[77] is the most well-known member of the Agassiz family. Yet the memorials that remain are generally named for his wife, Elizabeth Cary Agassiz (for instance, a professorship, a gate in Radcliffe Yard, and Elizabeth Cary Agassiz

House, home of the Harvard College Admissions Visitor Center), or for his son, Alexander Agassiz (namesake of Harvard professorships).

Elizabeth is credited as coauthor of *A Journey in Brazil* (1868), a travelogue about their year-long scientific expedition in the country, discussed below.[78] She also left her own powerful mark at Harvard: in 1879, she was among a group of reformers who founded the Harvard Annex, where women could receive instruction from Harvard faculty. The Annex was soon incorporated as the Society for the Collegiate Instruction of Women, and in 1894, it was chartered as Radcliffe College. Elizabeth served as the first president of Radcliffe College and was a pioneering leader in the history of women's education.[79] Alexander, an engineer and investor in copper mining as well as a scholar of natural history, also worked closely with his father. He handled much of Louis's correspondence in the final years of his life and succeeded Louis as curator of the Museum of Comparative Zoology in 1874.[80] Alexander donated substantial sums to several organizations in the final years of his life, including more than $200,000 to the museum to support research, publications, and the professorships that still bear his name.[81]

Agassiz's Early Career and the Zealy Daguerreotypes

Louis Agassiz's journey to Harvard began when he was invited to deliver the Lowell Institute's Lowell Lectures.[82] While the institute was not affiliated with Harvard, it was a forum that attracted many esteemed Harvard affiliates as lecturers and guests. Agassiz's 1845 invitation came on the recommendation of the German naturalist Alexander von Humboldt, who was able to secure funding for Agassiz's Atlantic crossing through his position as an advisor to the king of Prussia.[83] Agassiz was by then a prominent naturalist, known in Europe's scientific circles for his work on glaciation and the classification of ancient fish species.[84] In this work, he was part of a movement toward classifying flora and fauna according to geographic origin, building upon Carl Linnaeus's universal system of classification.[85] Naturalists of the era were known for their splendid depictions of nature and often went on scientific expeditions in the Americas to collect specimens for their research. Their preoccupation with nature also extended to the classification of humans

Richard T. Greener, the first Black graduate of Harvard College, is memorialized with a marker in Harvard Square.[1] A lawyer and diplomat, Greener was also the first Black faculty member at the University of South Carolina (USC), which installed a statue in his honor in 2018, and he was the only Black professor at any Southern university during the reconstruction era.[2]

Greener was born in 1844 in Philadelphia and was raised in Boston and Cambridge.[3] He worked for a jeweler who later funded his education at Oberlin Collegiate Institute and Phillips Academy at Andover.[4] Following successful stints at these preparatory schools, Greener's employer recommended him to Harvard College. Harvard President Thomas Hill agreed to "seeing the experiment fairly tried," and Greener entered the College at the age of twenty-one.[5]

At Harvard, Greener participated in and won academic competitions,[6] wrote for the *Harvard Advocate,*[7] and belonged to the Pi Eta Society and other clubs.[8] He also lived in a single room in the College House dormitory known to house "the poor and struggling";[9] dined at the Thayer Club, founded by a philanthropist to provide affordable meals to needy students;[10] and overcame racism from his classmates, who spread rumors that he "came direct from the cotton field to college."[11]

Greener graduated in 1870[12] and joined the USC faculty.[13] He also enrolled as a student at the USC law school.[14] Over the course of a long and distinguished career, Greener would become the dean of Howard University Law School[15] and serve as US consul in Russia.[16]

"into a single natural hierarchy of difference and similarity," organized under the rubric of race.[86]

The field of anthropology emerged in this context to study diversity among human groups as a function of visible racial difference.[87] Medical scientists contributed to the field's growth by investigating relationships among racial typology, geography, and disease. Phrenology, which related the shape and size of the cranium to intellectual and moral faculties, became a popular racial scientific field; craniometry, the measurement and dissection of human skulls, was its primary method. By the nineteenth century, race science had become a global enterprise,[88] and Agassiz was fully immersed when he arrived in the United States in the fall of 1846.

Among the first things Agassiz did in America was to view the prominent anatomist Samuel George Morton's skull collection in Philadelphia,[89] an early stop on his tour of the scientific community in the United States, which warmly embraced him.[90] Agassiz spent "four hours in contemplation" of the skulls of Native Americans and received a personal copy of Morton's *Crania Americana,* inscribed by the author. In a letter to his mother, Agassiz wrote that Morton's "collection alone merits a trip to the United States."[91] He also reflected on his first encounter with African Americans:[92] "It is impossible for me to repress the feeling that they are not the same blood as us."[93]

At this time, the United States was on the verge of establishing its own scientific institutions and schools of thought independent from those of Europe. Polygenism—which proposed not only a hierarchy of races but also separate creations of different races—was "an important agent in this transformation" because it was "of largely American origin" yet acquired authority from European scientists who had long pursued scientific theories of racial difference themselves.[94] Agassiz understood the importance of this moment in the nation's intellectual life and saw an opportunity. Some two years later, now a member of the Harvard faculty and building a celebrity status matched by few other scientists, he declared to the Boston Society of Natural History that American scientists "had been obliged to look up to Europe as our leader and guide in this pursuit," but "a short period of persevering labor . . . would place America in the position hitherto occupied by the Old World."[95]

Agassiz first formally articulated his embrace of polygenism at an 1850 meeting of the American Association for the Advancement of Science (AAAS) in Charleston, South Carolina.[96] In an essay published soon thereafter, he set out to disprove the "prevailing opinion, which ascribes to all living beings upon earth one common centre of origin, from which it is supposed they, in the course of time, spread over wider and wider areas, till they finally came into their present distribution."[97] His primary objective was "to show that there is no such statement in the book of Genesis: that this doctrine . . . is of very modern invention, and that it can be traced back for scarcely more than a century in the records of our science."[98] In another essay, he concluded that Blacks were at the bottom of a racial hierarchy ordained in nature and contended that "there has never been a regulated society of black men developed" in Africa, suggesting a "peculiar apathy . . . to the advantages afforded by civilized society."[99]

Such views were controversial even then. The first half of the nineteenth century represented a period of hardening of race as a scientific concept in the United States, at the height of debate over "monogenesis" versus "polygenesis," or the single versus separate origins of races.[100] Monogenists, who believed in a single human creation, immediately criticized Agassiz's arguments. Writing to her then fiancé, Elizabeth Cary noted the opposition building to his ideas: "Some of the Church people are out upon you in the papers, for your disrespect of Adam as the common father of mankind."[101] Congress was also, at this time, debating the Fugitive Slave Act, the passage of which would galvanize antislavery sentiment in New England.[102] Agassiz flatly denied that his research had bearing on the fraught political question of slavery,[103] although he asserted that it was "mock-philanthropy and mock-philosophy to assume that all races have the same abilities, enjoy the same powers, and show the same natural dispositions, and that in consequence of this equality they are entitled to the same position in human society."[104]

Agassiz was celebrated in the South, where he was invited to the homes of prominent slaveholders and gave iterations of his 1850 AAAS lecture.[105] Some of these visits were arranged by a local paleontologist and physician who welcomed Agassiz to plantations in Columbia, South Carolina to examine enslaved Africans as live research specimens. Following Agassiz's examination, Joseph T. Zealy made daguerreotype images of seven men and women for Agassiz's further study: Delia, Jack, Renty, Drana, Jem, Alfred, and Fassena.[106] In so doing, Zealy created what the *New York Times* described in 2020 as "some of history's cruelest, most contentious images—the first photographs, it is believed, of enslaved human beings."[107]

It was more than a century before historians retraced the identities and origins of the individuals represented in Agassiz's daguerreotypes. We now know that Delia, Renty's daughter, was an enslaved girl from Columbia, and that Jack was Drana's father. Fassena, noted in the daguerreotype as a carpenter, was Mandingo, originally from modern southern Mali and Northern Guinea. They are each pictured nude or nearly so.[108]

Agassiz returned to the South in 1851–1852 with his new wife, Elizabeth, who would become his frequent collaborator. The collection of research specimens—including human specimens—remained his focus.[109] In an 1852 letter, he begged pardon for his delayed arrival at his next destination, explaining that he "found . . . an excellent opportunity of examining the negros, of which I must avail myself."[110]

Agassiz's wide-ranging specimen collections were a celebrated part of life and learning at Harvard. In an 1850 report to the overseers, University President Jared Sparks highlighted Agassiz's, Wyman's, and the University's collections. Some of these were on display in Holden Chapel, used by the Medical School as a lecture hall and then assigned to the new Lawrence Scientific School, including a "curious collection of casts of skulls . . . which was purchased and presented to the University several years ago."[111]

Wyman, Agassiz, and Sturmann

In September of 1860, "an extraordinary importation from South Africa" arrived in Boston—five human beings described as "a Fuigo, a Zulu, a Kaffir, a Bushman, and a Hottentot, all sons of the forests and the desert who have hitherto lived the life of savages."[112] These living "specimens," had been acquired by the owners of the Boston Aquarial and Zoological Gardens for public exhibition. The announcement promised a one-of-a-kind experience, "seeing these specimens of human nature in a savage condition just as they appear in their native forests and wilds"—including "monkey tricks." Their names were given as Machiado, Macormo, Macuolo, Quaggu, and Sturmann.[113]

Advertisements described how the museum space was divided into two departments: the aquarial and the zoological.[114] The Africans were to be displayed alongside an assortment of "rare and beautiful animals and birds" including seals, kangaroos, and "Serpents."[115] "[R]efined and intellectual" ticketholders were promised performances of savagery on a regular schedule:

They will appear through the day, CLAD IN THEIR NATIVE DRESSES OF SKINS, ORNAMENTED WITH BEADS, FEATHERS AND PORCUPINE QUILLS, and every evening will go through the WAR, LOVE and FESTIVE DANCES,—(armed with their SPEARS, CLUBS, SHELLS, AND OTHER WEAPONS OF WAR AND OF THE CHASE,) and will also SING the NATIONAL SONGS of their SEVERAL TRIBES.[116]

The museum's owners created a scholarly veneer by commissioning a detailed pamphlet purporting to describe "the early life of each individual specimen of the nomadic tribes."[117] And Agassiz lent his scientific authority to the proceedings, addressing an inaugural gala on October 4, 1860.[118]

Three months later, when the popular showman P. T. Barnum exhibited the Africans in New York City, public outcry over the questionable nature of their "importation" prompted him to print a statement from Agassiz in local newspapers. Agassiz "testified" that they were not enslaved but "were shipped with the knowledge and consent of the local authorities," and that "nothing was done in securing them that would be objectionable either in a moral point of view or with reference to the laws of nations."[119] He did not identify these "local authorities," nor did he address the consent of Machiado, Macormo, Macuolo, Quaggu, and Sturmann themselves.

One of the five, Sturmann, took his own life on April 28, 1861, after more than six months on display.[120] The *Boston Evening Transcript* announced his death in a brief editorial:

> The young Hottentot at the Aquarial Gardens, yesterday terminated his life by hanging. He was seventeen years of age and used to drive a wagon at Port Natal. For several days he was noticed to act strangely, and, just before the commission of the fatal act, conveyed from the room, where he and his four companions domesticated, nearly every moveable article, in accordance with the practice of all suicides among his people. The other Africans at the Gardens are deeply affected by the death of their companion.[121]

Regardless of their distress, Machiado, Macormo, Macuolo, and Quaggu were "again on exhibition" on April 30.[122]

Sturmann's time as an object of study in the service of race science was only beginning: Wyman, who had met Sturmann while he was on display, dissected the teenager's body at Harvard, ultimately publishing his observations in an 1865 issue of the journal the *Anthropological Review*.[123] He took extensive measurements and compared them to those of a chimpanzee, a gorilla, and two Europeans. In a protracted discussion of Sturmann's pelvis, he noted that in some respects it came "nearer to that of the anthropoids [apes] than of the Caucasians"[124] but concluded it "belonged to the human family."[125]

Ultimately, Sturmann's remains were recorded in the catalog of the Warren Anatomical Museum:

> Item # 3237 cast of the head of a native Hottentot. The boy was seventeen years old, had been on exhibition for several months in this city; and finally hung himself. His skeleton is in the Museum of Comparative Zoology, at Cambridge, 1861."[126]

The casts of Sturmann's head remain in Harvard's collections.

Global Collecting and the Brazil Expedition

Over nearly three decades, Agassiz also engaged colleagues across the United States and around the world, especially in the Caribbean and Latin America, to collect and classify the natural world for what would become the Museum of Comparative Zoology.[127] He instructed his collectors—including patrons, friends, readers, and lecture audiences—to send him animals of all kinds from across New England, the United States, and the world.[128] His aim was to endow the United States with a museum that would rival the best collections in Europe. Agassiz initially acquired and stored most of the collection at his own cost, raising funds to support the effort from private donors, including Elizabeth Cary Agassiz's connections among the Boston elite.[129]

The search for specimens motivated Agassiz to organize his expedition to Brazil in 1865, in the midst of the Civil War. Polygenist ideas were losing favor following the publication of Charles Darwin's *On the Origin of Species* in 1859, and Agassiz identified Brazil as a prime location to continue his research and defend his claims.[130] In April 1865, with the support of a Boston financier,[131] Agassiz left for Brazil accompanied by Elizabeth and several Harvard students—including William James,[132] who would become an influential Harvard psychologist. Meanwhile, Alexander Agassiz, now a naturalist in his own right and directly involved in his father's work, assumed responsibility for the museum and handled Louis's correspondence, including discussions of the procurement of human remains from South America.[133]

Because of the country's racial diversity and its significant mixed-race population, Brazil had particular significance for Agassiz and other natural scientists of the nineteenth century.[134] In fact, race scientists had long identified Brazil as the embodiment of the dangers of race mixture, which they argued had produced a population that doomed the nation to backwardness.[135] Race mixture was Agassiz's focus when he commissioned a new set of photographs of Brazilian enslaved and free people. Agassiz personally oversaw the production of these images, which were taken by a local photographer and a Harvard student assistant.[136] The photographs likely were staged in the courtyard of the house in Brazil where Louis and Elizabeth had at one point resided with the research crew.[137]

Louis and Elizabeth cowrote *A Journey in Brazil,* published in 1868, which documented the expedition and presented their findings to a general audience in the travel narrative genre of the time. In the book's preface, Louis specifically acknowledged the important role his wife played in the endeavor:

> Partly for the entertainment of her friends, partly with the idea that I might make some use of it in knitting together the scientific reports of my journey by a thread of narrative, Mrs. Agassiz began this diary. I soon fell into the habit of giving her daily the more general results of my scientific observations, knowing that she would allow nothing to be lost which was worth preserving.[138]

Elizabeth's own correspondence confirms her deep involvement in writing and editing the manuscript.[139] Given this, it is interesting to note that the book remains silent about the Brazil photographs, even as it provides detailed depictions of other episodes, including Louis's sketch of their housemaid. Elizabeth is also thought to have expunged from other publications Louis's most flagrantly racist views.[140]

It is unclear whether the omission of the photographs reflects Elizabeth's discomfort with Louis's production of the images, all nude or seminude, her effort to safeguard Louis's reputation, or some other motivation. Whatever the reason, these omissions underscore Elizabeth's active participation in the expedition and publication. It is also evident from her work on *A Journey in Brazil* that she accepted prevailing racial hierarchies and stereotypes. For example, one passage in the book describes a gathering of enslaved people that Elizabeth and the crew witnessed while Louis was elsewhere:

> The dance and the song had, like the amusements of the negroes in all lands, an endless monotonous repetition. Looking at their half-naked figures and unintelligent faces, the question arose, so constantly suggested when we come in contact with this race, "What will they do with this great gift of freedom?" The only corrective for the half doubt is to consider the whites side by side with them: whatever one may think of the condition of slavery for the blacks, there can be no question as to its evil effects on their masters.[141]

Both Louis and Elizabeth were also interested in educational reform, so it is not surprising that they took time to observe the state of education across Brazil in the course of their travels. In one striking passage, they connect the deficits they perceive in Brazilians' education with the close contact between enslavers and the enslaved in private homes:

> Behind all defects in methods of instruction, there lies a fault of domestic education, to be lamented throughout Brazil. This is the constant association with black servants, and, worse still, with negro children. . . . Whether the low and vicious habits of the negroes are the result of slavery or not, they cannot be denied; and it is singular to see persons, otherwise careful and conscientious about their children, allowing them to live in the constant companionship of their blacks. . . . It shows how blind we may become, by custom, to the most palpable dangers.[142]

A complicated figure in her own right, some eleven years after the publication of *A Journey in Brazil*—and six years after her husband's death—Elizabeth played a critically important role in promoting educational access for women through the Harvard Annex, later Radcliffe College. Notably, and notwithstanding the racial prejudices she entertained while working alongside Louis in Brazil, Radcliffe College admitted and graduated Alberta Virginia Scott, its first black alumna, as part of its first graduating class in 1898, during Elizabeth's tenure as president (1882–1899).[143]

Charles William Eliot: A Paradoxical Racial Legacy

Charles William Eliot, Harvard's longest-serving president, in office for the four decades from 1869 to 1909, was an influential national figure. According to one historian, "by the turn of the century . . . his opinion and support were sought on every variety of public question."[144] He and his presidential administration represent a paradox: Harvard began admitting small numbers of Black students during his presidency; at the same time, Eliot himself and prominent Harvard faculty members promoted eugenics and endorsed racial segregation.

The first Black students to graduate from Harvard did so just two months after Eliot's election to the presidency.[145] The University saw its first Black graduate of the College, Richard T. Greener (AB 1870); first Black commencement orator, Robert H. Terrell (AB 1884); first Black class day speaker, Clement Morgan (AB 1890); and first Black recipient of a PhD, W. E. B. Du Bois (AB 1890; MA 1891; PhD 1895), during this period. Moreover, during Eliot's administration, William Monroe Trotter (AB 1895; AM 1896) became the first Black member of Phi Beta Kappa and Alain Locke the first Black Rhodes Scholar (1907).[146] Eliot's tenure also saw the hiring of Harvard's first Black faculty member, George F. Grant.[147]

Perhaps the most significant development occurred soon after Eliot became president, and it revealed the paradox at the heart of limited Black advancement at Harvard during his presidency. In 1896, Harvard awarded an honorary degree to a Black man for the very first time: Eliot bestowed the honor upon Booker T. Washington,[148] a man who had been born in slavery and who had made a mark as an author and as the principal of the Tuskegee Institute (later the Tuskegee College and today Tuskegee University).[149] By awarding Washington an honorary degree, Harvard expressed esteem for a Black man of great ability, and that was no small thing. But that was not all the award to Washington signified: it was a politically significant choice that gave Harvard's imprimatur to a man who achieved fame by urging Blacks to accommodate rather than fight racial exclusion, discrimination, and segregation.

Just months before Harvard honored him, Washington had gained national renown through his "Atlanta Compromise" address. In this 1895 speech, made to an audience of white Southerners during a time of rising white violence, political backlash, and legalized discrimination against descendants of slavery, Washington argued that Blacks should not agitate for racial equality or challenge segregation. "In all things that are purely social we can be as separate as the fingers, yet one as the hand in all things essential to mutual progress," he said.[150] Instead of pursuing the "extremest folly" of social equality, Blacks should pursue vocational education and work hard in the South, including manual labor in cotton mills.[151] Washington's proposal amounted to a "conservative social Darwinist proposition," according to one biographer, and it delighted whites who were eager to leave the race question behind and let Blacks fend for themselves. Washington's "compromise" enraged Black leaders bent on fighting racial inequality.[152] (In 1903, the Harvard graduate W. E. B. Du Bois would famously critique Washington's views in *The Souls of Black Folk.*[153])

It was in this context—Washington's endorsement of Black political quiescence—that Eliot personally awarded the honorary degree to him (and twelve others) during a June 24, 1896, ceremony in Sanders Theatre. Eliot praised Washington's remarks that evening at an alumni dinner, in which Washington—a self-described "humble representative" of the Black South—commended the "strong," "wealthy," and "learned" of Harvard and exhorted them to help the "ignorant" and "weak" masses rise to the "American standard."[154]

But Harvard did relatively little to help Blacks rise during Eliot's long presidency. Instead, Eliot himself, and Harvard's leadership more broadly, continued to advance ideas premised on biological racial difference—the same ideas deployed to support racial segregation. Eliot supported faculty who pursued eugenics, the selective breeding of human beings premised on racial hierarchy, and after his presidency would become a prominent public advocate for the field.[155] His views were "well within the intellectual mainstream" at Harvard and throughout the country at the time,[156] and coexisted with his enthusiasm for applied science as a means to identify new solutions for long-standing social ills. These interests were not merely academic; Eliot's views were also bound up with his politics—including his endorsement of segregation, opposition to interracial marriage, and support for eugenic sterilization—and shaped his administration of the University.

The Bussey Institution, founded in 1871 as an undergraduate department in agriculture with the proceeds of Boston merchant Benjamin Bussey's bequest to the University,[157] was reestablished under Eliot as a graduate school of applied biology.[158] Eliot supported the new school and its faculty, clearing the way for the geneticist William E. Castle's research into "what principles underlie the improvement of breeds" and his hereditary experiments on small mammals.[159] Castle and his ties to the global eugenicist movement are discussed in greater detail below.

Another beneficiary of Eliot's support was Dudley Allen Sargent, assistant professor of physical training (1879–1889) and director of Hemenway Gymnasium (1879–1919).[160] As head of Hemenway, Sargent established a system of rigorous physical exercises through which students might reform their bodies into the archetypal healthy, civilized man. He also, as described by Eliot, subjected "all students who desired to take part in athletic sports or severe physical exercises" to "thorough physical examination."[161] These intrusive physical examinations and his approach to physical education were motivated by his interest in "race improvement."[162]

Student athletes subject to Sargent's anthropometric evaluation began with a genealogical and family health form, which included parents' and grandparents' nationalities and parents' occupations, as well as a question about which parent the students believed they "most resemble[d]." After completing the form, the students' physical proportions were measured and plotted in a detailed chart that showed "relation, in size, strength, symmetry, and development, to the normal standard of your age and sex."[163] As part of these examinations, Sargent took nude photographs of many students, among them a young W. E. B. Du Bois.[164] He also measured and photographed students at Radcliffe and other colleges and universities, as well as men and women at gymnasiums and community organizations, such as YMCAs and YWCAs, and at major public events, including the 1893 World's Fair in Chicago.[165]

Sargent used his data to establish normative and idealized measurements for both sexes and commissioned drawings and sculptures to illustrate these findings.[166] Like other prominent eugenicists of the period, he was preoccupied with the notion that the white race was deteriorating under conditions of modernity and believed that as nations became more advanced, their citizens became unfit and lax.[167] He also openly endorsed racial hierarchy and held that "civilized" or "superior" races could be distinguished from "primitive" or "inferior" races based on body proportions.[168]

Eliot was also active in the public sphere, where he touted race science and the virtues of segregation. In the spring of 1909, before stepping down as president,[169] Eliot made a tour of the American South, where he was frequently asked to comment on questions of race. While in Memphis, Eliot attempted to address "race problems" in an interview with local reporters.[170] The resulting article spread like wildfire, with newspapers across the country, including in Boston, reprinting his statement that "there should be no admixture of racial stock":

> I believe for example, that the Irish should not intermarry with the Americans of English descent; that the Germans should not marry the Italians; that the Jews should not marry the French. Each race should maintain its own individuality. The experience of civilization shows that racial stocks are never mixed with profit, and that such unions do not bring forth the best and strongest children. . . . In the case of the negroes and the whites, the races should be kept apart in every respect. The South has a wise policy. I believe that Booker T. Washington has the right ideals and that Dubois is injuring the progress of his race with his views.[171]

Other newspapers quoted from the same interview Eliot's comparison of the South to other parts of the United States:

> In the South it is the negro problem. The same or similar problems exist in all parts of the country. In protestant Massachusetts, the land of Pilgrims and Puritans, the population today is mostly Catholic. There are Irish, Italian, and Portuguese that present the same race problem to that part of the country that the negroes do to the South. On the Pacific coast it is the same with the Japanese.[172]

Following public criticism of these comments, Eliot engaged in damage control; he acknowledged the value of immigrants and attempted to clarify his views on assimilation—namely that it should be gradual rather than sudden and achieved through education, industry, and policy rather than intermarriage. But he did not deny an aversion to racial mixing. While it was common in this era to oppose marriage between races of "widely different characteristics,"[173] Eliot had gone further, drawing lines between Europeans. One political cartoon depicted a stern Professor Eliot trying to instill his "no admixture" message in his only student—a laughing cupid.[174]

His statements did not go unnoticed by those few Black members of the Harvard community. A month after the interview, in April 1909, William Monroe Trotter wrote to Eliot "as an alumnus of Harvard, as a colored man, and as editor of a newspaper for colored Americans." Trotter, who cofounded the Niagara Movement, predecessor of the NAACP, with W. E. B. Du Bois, wanted to know if what he was reading in the press was true—whether the president of his alma mater really advocated "total segregation," approved of "the white South's method of dealing with colored Americans," and would concede to "admitting the colored people into the American brotherhood . . . only after 1000 years of 'civilization.'"[175]

Eliot's response two days later attempted some clarification of his opinions, which, he noted, were "not newly formed."[176] First, he explained, "The Whites and the Negroes had better live beside each other in entire amity, but separate, under equal laws." He expressed support for Black suffrage, albeit with a poll tax for all voters, and held that "political equality seems to me to have nothing whatever to do with what is called social equality" and will not lead to "social admixture."[177] He offered his own observations about the South, including his assessment that "it would take four or five generations more to teach the mass of the negro population that civilization is built on willingness to work hard six days in the week, and to be frugal all the time," partly because it would be "unreasonable to expect that people who had so recently been savages and slaves should all acquire in forty years the primary virtues of civilization." For good measure, Eliot concluded his letter with the assertion that "as to intermarriage between Whites and Blacks, all the best evidence seems to me to show that it is inexpedient."[178]

When Trotter responded the next day with additional questions about the application of Eliot's opinions to "actual conditions," noting that "I believe I am correct in saying the Colored people are quite anxious to know your views," he received no reply.[179] There is likewise no recorded response to Trotter's second prompt for a reply some five days later.

Eliot's stature and political savvy set him up to play an active supporting role in the rising eugenics movement in his post-presidency years. He warned that "the increase of liberty for all classes of the community seems to promote the rapid breeding of the defective, irresponsible and vicious" and advocated "preventing the feeble-minded from reproducing their like."[180] He stopped short of other Harvard affiliates—including his secretary, Frank W. Taussig, who went on to become a faculty member and argued that, although society "[had] not reached the stage where we can proceed to chloroform them once for all," the "feeble minded" could at least be "segregated, shut up in refuges and asylums, and prevented from propagating their kind."[181]

Charles B. Davenport, William E. Castle, and the International Eugenics Movement

As the eugenics movement took hold in the early twentieth century, another Harvard affiliate, Charles B. Davenport (AB 1889; AM 1890; PhD 1892), became one of its key leaders.[182] Davenport studied biology at Harvard and stayed on as an instructor until 1899, when he joined the faculty of the University of Chicago. In 1910, Davenport and his fellow eugenics leader Harry H. Laughlin established the Eugenics Record Office in Cold Spring Harbor, New York,[183] which became a center for the eugenics movement and produced a wide range of research and propaganda.[184] His 1911 book, *Heredity in Relation to Eugenics,* became the standard text for eugenics courses at colleges and universities across the country and was cited by more than a third of high-school biology textbooks of the era.[185] Like his fellow eugenicists, Davenport believed in biological differences among races and the distinctiveness and superiority of the white race, and he virulently opposed race mixing. He advocated for racial restrictions on immigration; "selective elimination" of undesirable people; and acceptance of "the principle of the inequality of generating strains" and "eugenical ideals . . . in mating," such that "strains with new and better combinations of traits may arise and our nation take front rank in culture among the nations of ancient and modern times."[186]

Davenport had a significant impact on his students during his decade as an instructor at the University. Among them was a young William Ernest Castle, who would himself go on to become a major figure in eugenics at Harvard and in the United States.[187] Castle enrolled at Harvard College in 1892, pursuing a second bachelor's degree—he had previously graduated from Denison University—in botany and zoology. Castle worked as a laboratory assistant for Davenport and completed a PhD under the direction of E. L. Mark, the professor of zoology who had also advised Davenport.[188] After teaching for two years at the University of Wisconsin and Knox College, Castle returned to Harvard in 1897 as an instructor and researcher in animal breeding, first at the Museum of Comparative Zoology, later at the Bussey Institution, and then at the University's center for agriculture and horticulture.[189]

Castle was a prominent member of the American Breeders' Association (today the American Genetic Association) and a founding member of the editorial board of the journal *Genetics.*[190] In 1912, he was chosen as a member of the American Consultative Committee at the First International Eugenics Congress in London, where Charles William Eliot was then serving as vice president.[191]

From 1910 to 1930, Castle taught Genetics and Eugenics, one of several courses on eugenics offered across Harvard at the time.[192] He published his lecture notes in 1916 in the textbook *Genetics and Eugenics: A Text-book for Students of Biology and a Reference Book for Animal and Plant Breeders*,[193] which deployed his research into the breeding of animals to advance eugenicist arguments about humans in a concluding chapter titled "The Possibility and Prospects of Breeding a Better Human Race."[194] On race mixing, Castle argued that "from the viewpoint of a superior race there is nothing to be gained by crossing with an inferior race. . . . From the viewpoint of the inferior race also the cross is undesirable if the two races live side by side, because each race will despise individuals of mixed race and this will lead to endless friction."[195] Moreover, to prevent the inheritance of undesirable traits, Castle concluded that "segregation" of the "feeble-minded" should be implemented in "schools and institutions under state control." When "segregation is impracticable," Castle argued, the "feeble-minded . . . should not be allowed to marry unless first sterilized."[196]

Such ideas, which led to compulsory sterilization practices in approximately thirty states and between 60,000 and 70,000 cases of eugenic sterilization in the United States,[197] were also a primary focus of Davenport's Eugenics Record Office (ERO).[198] The ERO quickly gained national and international prominence, and it sustained a dual mission to carry out research and advocate for eugenic research and eugenic policy among the public.[199] The organization received funding from the Gladys and Roland Harriman Foundation, the Rockefeller Foundation, and the Carnegie Corporation of New York—a total of $1.2 million between 1910 and 1940[200]—and established European connections, particularly with like-minded proponents of eugenics in interwar Germany.

Indeed, the ERO's *Eugenical News* introduced German eugenics to an American audience, praised a Nazi sterilization law that drew on ERO research, and became "the main propagandists for the German eugenical cause."[201] As president of the International Federation of Eugenic Organizations, Davenport himself helped restore German eugenicists to a place of prominence in the international movement after World War I.[202] At his alma mater, Davenport arranged for a delegation of German eugenicists to participate in Harvard's 1936 tercentenary celebration.[203]

W. E. B. Du Bois, a towering American intellectual and a tireless advocate for Black equality, was the first African American to earn a PhD at Harvard University. He went on to cofound the Niagara Movement—forerunner of the NAACP—and to teach at Atlanta University (the HBCU today known as Clark Atlanta University). HUD 290.04PF, olvwork408054 / Harvard University Archives

FIVE

Segregation, Marginalization, and Resistance at Harvard

Twentieth-Century Vestiges of Slavery

In the decades after the Civil War, in Massachusetts and in every corner of the nation, African Americans encountered roadblocks to achieving social mobility, including—perhaps especially—through education. White opposition to racially "mixed" schools, born of racist attitudes about Black ability and character promoted by slaveholders, blocked equal access to education.[1] Segregated, under-resourced, and inferior elementary and secondary schools became the norm for African Americans.

Harvard alumni played prominent roles on both sides of the struggle over school segregation. One critically important chapter in that struggle, which would have dire consequences nationwide for Blacks into the twentieth century, had occurred in Boston shortly before the Civil War. In *Roberts v. City of Boston,* an 1850 decision, the state helped normalize segregated schools. In that case—filed by the Harvard-educated lawyer and US senator Charles Sumner on behalf of a five-year-old Black girl—the Massachusetts Supreme Judicial Court held that racial segregation in the city's schools did not offend the law.[2] Chief Justice Lemuel Shaw—a Harvard alumnus (AB 1800), fellow, and overseer—authored the opinion for the court. But in 1855, after advocacy and a school boycott organized by Black abolitionists with important support from Sumner, Massachusetts passed legislation banning segregated schools—the first such law in the United States.[3] Nevertheless, decades later, in 1896, the US Supreme Court cited *Roberts* as authority when it held that racially "separate but equal" facilities did not violate the Fourteenth Amendment to the Constitution in *Plessy v. Ferguson*.[4]

In higher education, Blacks also found themselves in separate and unequal schools. It was left to historically Black colleges and universities—often founded by Black self-help organizations and religious societies, and which were offered some federal financial support beginning in 1865—to provide a measure of opportunity for Blacks.[5] But from the start, HBCUs were sorely under-resourced, and they remain so. Inadequate funding hobbled school leaders as they sought to fulfill the HBCUs' mission of racial uplift through postsecondary school access.[6]

Predominantly white universities did not fill the breach. In keeping with prevailing racial attitudes and the relegation of African Americans to HBCUs with limited funding, Harvard—like all but a few white universities—did relatively little to support the African American quest for advancement.[7]

To the contrary, Blacks still faced discrimination or plain indifference at Harvard and other white universities. Notwithstanding Harvard's rhetorical commitment in the Civil War's wake to recruit a nationally representative student body that would model political collegiality, the University's sights remained set on a white "upper crust." Harvard prized the admission of academically able Anglo-Saxon students from elite backgrounds—including wealthy white sons of the South—and it restricted the enrollment of so-called "outsiders."[8]

Abbott Lawrence Lowell and Discrimination in Admissions and Housing

Two major avenues for discrimination in the University setting, admissions and housing, figured prominently in the long Harvard presidency (1909–1933) of Abbott Lawrence Lowell. Lowell, who succeeded Charles William Eliot, guided Harvard through a period of significant growth—enrollment nearly doubled, and the endowment quintupled. His administration also gave rise to several highly publicized controversies related to discrimination on the basis of religion and race.[9]

Early in Lowell's presidency, the Faculty of Arts and Sciences voted to supplement the University's existing exam-based admissions system with an alternative "approved secondary school course" route.[10] In keeping with Harvard's long-standing vision of itself as a national institution, the express purpose of this change was to increase enrollments from outside New England as well as from public high schools, where students were less likely to receive preparation for college entrance exams.[11] The decision attracted notice well beyond the Harvard community: in a letter to Lowell, the businessman and philanthropist Andrew Carnegie lauded the University for creating a "clear path for the poor boy from bottom to top."[12] In practice, however, Lowell would work to limit the new process's effect upon the socioeconomic makeup of the student body,[13] and to instead promote discriminatory admissions practices.

As part of Harvard's evolving admissions policies, Lowell masterminded Harvard's well-documented efforts to exclude Jewish students in the early twentieth century. He did this in a variety of ways: first by privately tilting the admissions scale against Jewish transfer applicants[14] and adopting a national recruitment strategy focused on regions of the country with smaller Jewish populations,[15] and then by capping the number of Jewish students admitted and introducing new admissions criteria.[16] These criteria, including personal interviews and the requirement that all candidates submit photographs with their application materials, were approved by the faculty in January 1926.[17] And, at Lowell's behest, the Committee on Admission was granted discretion to execute, in his words, a "discrimination among individuals."[18]

Inside and outside of the Ivy League, universities deployed many of these same policies and practices, including photo requirements, interviews, admissions tests, and recruitment from private preparatory and other urban feeder schools in ways that discriminated against or disadvantaged Black students.[19]

But plain indifference or outright exclusion from white institutions of higher education were the more pressing problems for African Americans, as evinced by the small number of Blacks admitted to Harvard before, during, and well after the 64-year tenure of Presidents Eliot and Lowell.[20] Despite access to civic organizations in major cities that could

identify a pool of able Black students, the college enrolled meager numbers.[21] "The official view was that African Americans who had the grades
and money to come to Harvard were welcome," wrote two historians of
the institution, but no effort was made to find, recruit, or welcome
those students to campus.[22] Approximately 160 Black men matricu-
lated to Harvard College during the fifty-year period from 1890 to 1940,
an average of three per year, thirty per decade.[23] Such vanishingly
small numbers frequently left Black men isolated and marginalized on
campus.[24]

Those Blacks who did manage to enter Harvard's gates during the
nineteenth and early-to-mid-twentieth centuries excelled academically,
earning equal or better academic records than most white students, but
encountered slavery's legacies on campus.[25]

Lowell's perspective on questions of race—rooted in racial hierarchy
and eugenics—shaped campus life. He granted Charles B. Davenport
and the Eugenics Record Office (ERO) access to "the physical and intellectual records" of Harvard students for eugenics research.[26] And in
response to a request from a Harvard faculty member, Lowell lobbied a
US senator to support immigration quotas,[27] in keeping with his views
"that no democracy could be successful unless it was tolerably homogeneous; and that the presence of [different] races which did not inter-
mingle was unfortunate, as indeed it has been in the case of the negro."[28]

Lowell's views resulted in a notorious example of Black marginalization on campus. In the summer of 1922, when Harvard was already
under fire in the press over "the Jewish question"—the University's anti-
Jewish admissions policies—a new controversy developed: President
Lowell's signature innovation—a residential college experience for first
years that was meant to build community—excluded the handful of
Black Harvard students. The community Lowell sought to build included whites only.[29]

The seeds of this so-called "dormitory crisis" had been planted the
previous spring when William J. Knox Jr., a newly admitted Black
freshman from New Bedford, Massachusetts—and a great-nephew of
the Black abolitionist Harriet Jacobs[30]—was barred from living in the
freshman dormitories.[31] Knox had initially been granted a room but,

shortly after appearing in person for an entrance examination, he received a telegram asking that he return his registration card. One week later, Knox received a letter informing him that the freshman halls were full.[32]

Knox traveled to Cambridge with the fellow New Bedford native and recent Harvard College graduate Edwin B. Jourdain Jr. (AB 1921), then enrolled in Harvard Business School, to inquire after the change.[33] Jourdain had, after all, been permitted as a Black student to live in the freshman halls just a few years earlier. Dean Philip P. Chase informed Knox and Jourdain of Harvard's policy: while Black students were allowed in voluntary residence and dining halls, they were excluded from the freshman halls because residence in those dormitories was compulsory (for whites).[34] In Lowell's view, "Those students whose social prejudice against the negro is strong can hardly be compelled into an association that, rightly or wrongly, is repugnant to them."[35] Jourdain's admission into the halls was dismissed as a wartime inadvertence,[36] and Knox was offered a spot elsewhere.[37]

Jourdain pursued the matter further, seeking a conference with President Lowell.[38] According to Lowell, he told Jourdain "that negroes were well treated at Harvard and that it would be a mistake for them to urge admission to the Freshman Halls." Lowell also cautioned that, if "faced by the alternative of either admitting negroes to those halls . . . or of excluding negroes altogether, we might, or should, be compelled to adopt the latter, like some other colleges." News of this exchange spread, and Lowell's words were interpreted as a warning to those who might protest the policy, though he denied this was his intent. Lowell affirmed Harvard's duty to provide "the best possible opportunities for education," but doubled down on his position that Harvard did not owe Black students "inclusion in a compulsory social system with other people when it is not mutually agreeable."[39] Still focused on a national student body, it was, Lowell believed, "irrational to contend that on account of the two or three negroes in the freshman class, the College ought practically to drive away the large number of men from the South and West."[40]

The issue gained public attention in the summer of 1922, when word leaked to the *New York World* that a committee of seven white

Harvard alumni, including one Jewish graduate, was circulating a petition among fellow alumni to send to Lowell.[41] The petition, which gained more than 140 signatures,[42] "respectfully submit[ted]" that exclusion of Black students was a "Jim Crow policy" and argued that, while "the University owes the Southern man the best possible opportunity for education," it does "not owe him the surrender of our Northern ideas of democracy and our Harvard ideals of justice." If reversing the exclusionary policy meant a loss of Southerners "of intense race-consciousness," the petitioners wrote, "the College should accept that loss rather than surrender its standards."[43]

The administration showed no signs of budging until January, after added pressure from prominent Black alumni pushed the controversy onto the national stage and sparked another deluge of letters.[44] Roscoe Conkling Bruce (AB 1902), testing the policy, wrote to the registrar in December requesting a place in the freshman halls for his son.[45] Lowell's reply and the ensuing correspondence with Bruce were published in the *New York Times*. The paper also printed a statement from William Monroe Trotter, on behalf of the National Equal Rights League, decrying Harvard's "turn from democracy and freedom to race oppression, prejudice and hypocrisy."[46] Another published letter, from James Weldon Johnson on behalf of the NAACP, charged that "by capitulating to anti-negro prejudice in the freshman dormitories or anywhere else, Harvard University affirms that prejudice and strengthens it, and is but putting into effect the program proclaimed by the infamous Ku Klux Klan and its apologists."[47]

By the end of the month, Harvard's overseers called a special meeting to appoint a faculty committee to consider the issue.[48] In March and April, the governing bodies amended Lowell's policy on freshman housing; henceforth, "men of the white and colored races shall not be compelled to live and eat together, nor shall any man be excluded by reason of his color." It was not clear what the new policy meant in practice; but it was hardly a ringing endorsement of racial mixing in campus housing.[49]

The chilly racial climate on campus extended beyond this notorious incident. In other ways, African Americans encountered impediments to full acceptance.

During the early decades of the twentieth century, for instance, the talents of Black Harvard athletes earned them respect and recognition from University leaders and from other students on campus. But these athletes also encountered discrimination and exclusion, especially in intercollegiate play. Black football and baseball players sometimes faced harassment by other teams' fans. And universities in both the South and the North sometimes refused to play against Harvard teams that included Black players. Harvard administrators often bowed to these demands.[50] A controversy over a 1941 lacrosse match under Lowell's successor as president, James Bryant Conant, illustrated the problem and brought things to a head: William J. Bingham, Harvard's athletic director, benched Lucien Victor Alexis Jr. (AB 1942; MBA 1947), an African American lacrosse player, after the United States Naval Academy objected. "We were guests of the Naval Academy," Bingham said, "I had no choice."[51] After an outcry by Harvard students, the Harvard Corporation "suggested" that the athletic director make the University "principle" of non-discrimination known to other institutions.[52]

Even as white Harvard students appreciated the Black athletes who contributed to victories on the field, many were indifferent to the overall plight of African Americans. At a time of rising racist violence against African Americans and an NAACP campaign against lynching, for example, Harvard students made light of the resurgent Ku Klux Klan. The white terrorist organization was responsible for anti-Black harassment and murder and the dispossession of Black-owned property across the country.[53] Yet the students' general indifference was on full display at a Class Day ceremony in 1924: the "hit of the afternoon," according to one Boston newspaper, "was undoubtedly the class of '21"—the class to which Edwin B. Jourdain Jr. belonged[54]—"who came as a klavern of the Ku Klux Klan, white robes, pointed hoods with eyeholes and all."[55] The incident apparently did not spark public outcry or a response from the administration; the Class of 1921 continued to make light of the Klan in its newsletter years later.[56]

This was not the first time Harvard students had made light of the Klan. In 1923, the *Harvard Crimson* published stories about Klan activities around Halloween, and the *Harvard Lampoon* printed an entire issue on the Klan.[57] Such "pranks" are unlikely to have escaped the notice of the University's few Black students. In fact, the *Crimson* also reported on Harvard students' involvement in the Klan, coverage that prompted another response—a telegram to the president and Board of Overseers—from Johnson on behalf of the NAACP.[58]

Still, Black students generally could and did participate in campus clubs and activities. They wrote for undergraduate publications, debated, and won academic honors. Appreciative of the opportunities they gained at Harvard, many African Americans spoke fondly of the University. Others reacted with "ambivalence" to the reality of marginalization despite inclusion at the University.[59] The decidedly mixed experiences of Blacks at Harvard illustrated a "half-opened door," as one author aptly termed the Ivy League experience of African Americans during the early and middle decades of the twentieth century.[60]

Albert Bushnell Hart: A Complicated Mentor to W. E. B. Du Bois

Albert Bushnell Hart, who succeeded Lowell as Harvard's Eaton Professor of the Science of Government and was a contemporary of many of the University's prominent eugenicists, illustrates the ideological legacies of race science at Harvard in the late nineteenth and early twentieth centuries, even among some of the University's most progressive professors—of which he was one.

A faculty member in American history beginning in 1883, Hart held the Eaton Professorship from 1910 to 1926.[61] He was a prolific historian whose publications—including textbooks—shaped the teaching of American history at the high school and university level. He served as an early officer and president of the American Historical Association and was also president of the American Political Science Association, both during the time of the professionalization of academic disciplines in the United States.[62]

Hart's scholarship often focused on issues of race and class. Like many white scholars in this period, he depicted slavery as a generally benign institution that was more problematic in principle than in its execution. Presenting himself as "a son and grandson of abolitionists,"[63] he argued that "How far slavery, as a system, was inhuman and barbarous is difficult to decide."[64] He reasoned that "the evidence is overwhelming that many slaves were as well fed and housed as the poor whites of the neighborhood and were unconscious of serious injustice."[65]

Hart routinely elided or minimized racial violence in his work, in one case noting that "none but an extraordinarily stupid or cruel master would keep his slaves down to a point where they could not do full work."[66] In a history textbook written for use in American secondary schools he explained:

> It is not strange that slaves were sometimes cruelly treated. In those days prisoners and paupers were often ill treated. The object of a master was to make his slaves work and obey, whether they felt like it or not. If they refused, the master or overseer had to flog them or let them be idle. Sensible masters would not injure the value of a slave by too severe punishment.[67]

Hart cast such violence as understandable, if not wholly acceptable, given that "two negro slaves might do less work in a day than one hired white laborer in the North."[68] The slaves' "indolence was the despair of every slave-owner," he wrote; their "shiftlessness, waste of their master's property, neglect of his animals, were almost proverbial; and the looseness of the marriage-tie and immorality of even the best of the negroes were subjects of sorrow to those who felt the responsibility for them."[69]

Further, although vocally opposed to lynching—which he called "an opportunity for the most furious and brutal passion of which humanity is capable, under cover of moral duty, and without the slightest danger of a later accountability"[70]—Hart asserted that:

> One of the few advantages of slavery was that every slaveholder was police officer and judge and jury on his own plantation; petty offenses were punished by the overseer without further ceremony, serious crimes were easily dealt with, and the escape of the criminal was nearly impossible. Freedom . . . has combined with the influence of the press in popularizing crime, and perhaps with an innate African savagery, to make the black criminal a terrible scourge in the South.[71]

Despite such views, Hart strongly supported W. E. B. Du Bois during his time as a student at Harvard.[72] Citing his "distinct ability,"[73]

Hart recommended Du Bois for a scholarship that enabled him to continue his graduate studies. He also facilitated Du Bois's participation in the American Historical Association's 1891 meeting—making Du Bois the first Black scholar to present to that organization.[74] Du Bois's paper, "Enforcement of the Slave Trade Laws," was published the following year in the *Annual Report of the American Historical Association*.[75] But Hart's support of Black students was qualified: he believed that only a racially mixed few could succeed. The achievements of Du Bois or of Booker T. Washington, he wrote in an extended discussion of race in his 1910 book *The Southern South*, "prove nothing as to the genius of the races because they are mulattoes." He concluded that "few men of genius among the Negroes are pure blacks."[76]

While Hart was not an advocate for racial equality, neither was he a racist in the mold of the many eugenicists at Harvard. He certainly believed that whites were the superior race:

> There are a million or two exceptions, but they do not break the force of the eight or nine million of average Negroes. . . . Race measured by race, the Negro is inferior, and his past history in Africa and in America leads to the belief that he will remain inferior in race stamina and race achievement.[77]

Yet in a direct rebuke of his eugenicist colleagues, he declared "the Negro is entitled to be measured, not by brain calipers, not by two-meter rods, but by what he can do in the world."[78] Education was, for Hart, the consistent answer to "the vast and absorbing problem," namely "the presence of a non-European race, formerly servile, and permanently inferior to the white race."[79] He argued that educating all Blacks, regardless of aptitude, was worth the effort to reach those who— like Du Bois—were exceptional: "It is a favorite Southern delusion that education and Christian teaching have no effect on the animal propensities of Negroes; there are thousands of examples to the contrary."[80] Hart, also a Howard University trustee, concluded that the "most hopeful thing" is the "work of institutions like Fisk, Atlanta, and Talladega."[81] "Education does not necessarily make virtue, but it is a safeguard."[82]

Black Students at Harvard: A Legacy of Resistance

Just as legacies of slavery continued to shape campus life long after the Civil War and well into the twentieth century, so too did Black resistance. Throughout the postbellum era and into the twentieth century, Black students confronted and resisted marginalization, earning their Harvard educations and, ultimately, reshaping the nation.

W. E. B. Du Bois

W. E. B. Du Bois once recalled: "I was in Harvard, but not of it, and realized all the irony of my singing 'Fair Harvard.'"[83] Reflecting decades later on his experience as a black student at Harvard, Du Bois declared that the University had "a galaxy of great men and fine teachers," Albert Bushnell Hart among them. Yet, he wrote, "I went to Harvard as a Negro . . . recognizing myself as a member of a segregated caste whose situation I accepted."[84] Of his social relationships, he wrote: "Following the attitudes which I had adopted in the South, I sought no friendships among my white fellow students, nor even acquaintanceships. Of course I wanted friends, but I could not seek them."[85] A lover of music and singing, he was rejected from the Glee Club: "I ought to have known that Harvard could not afford to have a Negro on its Glee Club traveling about the country."[86] Even moments of triumph were tinged: When Du Bois and his fellow Black student Clement G. Morgan were selected as Commencement speakers, Francis Greenwood Peabody—Plummer Professor of Christian Morals at Harvard Divinity School and preacher to the University—moved to consult the Harvard Corporation as to whether it was appropriate to select two Black students for this honor.[87] Their answer was no; Du Bois spoke, but Morgan did not.[88] In the end, Du Bois was lauded for his address "Jefferson Davis: Representative of Civilization."[89] Yet even a Harvard professor who recounted a "trustee's" view that the paper was "masterly in every way" felt compelled to add that "Du Bois is from Great Barrington, Massachusetts, and doubtless has some white blood in his veins."[90]

Du Bois arrived at Harvard having already completed his undergraduate studies at the historically black Fisk University in Nashville,

Tennessee. Harvard, unwilling to accept his Fisk credential, required Du Bois to complete a second bachelor's degree.[91] Fisk, like other Black institutions, was not accredited; the Southern Association of Colleges did not grant accreditation to Fisk or any other Black college in this era.[92] Du Bois enrolled in the College as a junior and graduated *cum laude* in history in 1890.[93] He completed a master's degree in 1891 and earned his PhD in 1895.

During his time at Harvard, Du Bois's financial struggles set him even further apart from many of his white classmates. As an undergraduate, he had to rely on outside funding and charitable loans to cover tuition and living expenses.[94] Unable to afford student housing, he did not live on campus; and his landlady, Mary Taylor, a Black woman from Nova Scotia, let him "owe the rent."[95] As a graduate student, Du Bois was better financially equipped: he had inherited money from his grandfather, and, with the help of recommendations from Hart and another Harvard professor, James Bradley Thayer, Du Bois was awarded the Henry Bromfield Rogers Memorial Fellowship from 1890 to 1892.[96]

Du Bois's experience as a Harvard alumnus mirrored, in some ways, the marginalization he faced on campus. In his autobiography, he wrote of his discomfort at visiting the Harvard Club of New York around 1950 as the guest of a white classmate and club member.[97] Some eight years earlier, in 1942, Du Bois had received what appears to be a form letter recruiting new members, prompted by the club's loss of income with so many members leaving for the warfront.[98] Du Bois responded:

> My dear Sir: Your letter . . . rather astonished me. I have been graduated from Harvard College over fifty years and this is the first time during that period that I have been asked to join a Harvard Club. I have assumed that the reason for this reticence was that I am of Negro descent. Possibly, however, Harvard is learning something from this war for democracy and has changed her attitudes. If this is true, I shall be very glad to hear from you and to become a member.[99]

There are no records of a reply from the club or a membership in Du Bois's name.[100]

As much as Du Bois's experience with the Harvard community—as both student and alumnus—illustrates the racism and disenfranchisement of that era on campus, it is also a powerful story of resistance. He directly and publicly challenged ideas and ideologies advanced by Harvard professors and administrators, including Dean Nathaniel Southgate Shaler and President Charles William Eliot.[101] His dissertation, titled "The Suppression of the African Slave Trade to the United States of America, 1638–1870," pushed against the common understanding of slavery at the time, casting it as a moral failure with lasting consequences.[102]

Another piece from Du Bois's graduate student years, "Harvard and the South," not only illustrates his willingness to enter the fraught discourse on the post–Civil War South but also offers glimpses into his experience, having been privy to intellectual discussions in which he was uniquely implicated because of his race. The paper argues that the Civil War was "at core the result of a vast economic mistake" and that the solution to the South's problems of the day "lies in the trained leadership toward correct economic ideas" and "the intellectual impetus of the broadly trained university man."[103] In one particularly telling passage, Du Bois notes his distance from the "Northern student of Southern affairs," who, he writes, "wavers between calling the whites rascals, or the Negroes idiots." The Northern student, he writes, "cannot decide whether to make out my Southern fellow student as a case of total depravity; or me as a specimen of the anthropoid ape." Then, directly challenging his classmates' stereotypes, he adds: "With as little personal bias as could be expected under the circumstances, I respectfully submit that he need do neither."[104] Du Bois subtly acknowledges the prejudice—whether scientific, social, or religious in nature—of his Harvard audience:

> If the Southern people can once be brought to see that it is to their highest economic advantage to have their working classes as intelligent and ambitious and with as great political privileges as possible, I care not what they or you think as to the origen and destiny of the Negro people.[105]

Long after earning his PhD, Du Bois remained active within the Harvard community, including attending reunions, and he continued to push Hart, with whom he stayed in regular contact, on matters of representation. For example, Du Bois responded to a letter from Hart wishing him well on his 50th birthday with the following note:

> My dear Prof. Hart: I want to thank you very much for the kind letter which you sent on my birthday. I have been noticing that "The American Year Book" with which you are connected, always says surprisingly little about the Negro of America and elsewhere. Cannot something be done about this?[106]

Du Bois also worked to hold the University accountable.[107] In 1922 and 1923, leading up to the petition against President Abbott Lawrence Lowell's exclusion of Black students from freshman dormitories, Du Bois consulted with the organizing alumni, sharing suggestions and contacts.[108] He was "shocked" and enraged by the exclusion of the high-achieving Blacks admitted to Harvard. And he brought national attention to the issue by unleashing what biographer David Levering Lewis called a "double-barreled" critique of anti-Black discrimination and the use of anti-Jewish quotas by "Fair (!) Harvard" in the August 1922 issue of *Crisis,* the magazine of the NAACP.[109] The dormitory exclusion distressed Du Bois because it showed that "mainstream America recognized no amount of merit, conceded not even the most minimal authority . . . however rarely talented, insofar as Negro citizens were concerned."[110]

Du Bois's role in cofounding the NAACP—the nation's oldest civil rights organization—was his most profound act of resistance to the marginalization of African Americans in American society. Under the aegis of that organization and its lawyers, Black Americans struggled against discrimination in the political process, housing, public accommodations, the criminal legal system, and education.[111] The organization's legal strategy against segregation prevailed in *Brown v. Board of Education* (1954), one of the most celebrated cases in the canon of American constitutional law.[112] Thurgood Marshall and a team that included the Harvard-educated Black lawyers Charles Hamilton Houston

(LLB 1922, SJD 1923), William H. Hastie (LLB 1930; SJD 1933), and William T. Coleman Jr. (LLB 1946) played leading roles in the lawsuit that "reconsecrated American ideals."[113]

Ewart G. Guinier

Ewart G. Guinier, who would go on to serve as chair of Harvard's Department of Afro-American Studies at its founding in 1969,[114] was a student well after Du Bois had left campus. He enrolled at Harvard in 1929, during Abbott Lawrence Lowell's presidency, and was subject to the admissions practices Lowell had put in place. After graduating with honors from Boston's English High School, Guinier applied and was accepted to both Dartmouth College and Harvard.[115] While Dartmouth offered a full scholarship including room and board, Harvard offered nothing. But Guinier was determined to attend the University. He turned down the full scholarship at Dartmouth and worked summers and throughout the school year to pay his way at Harvard.[116]

Despite Harvard's new, ostensibly nondiscriminatory housing policy, Guinier was notified that he "had been granted permission to live at home"—permission he had not requested. As a freshman, Guinier would commute to campus from Roxbury, and during his sophomore year, he stayed in Brookline. Both locations are several miles from campus.[117]

Guinier's first week at Harvard was jarring.[118] When he attended the freshman assembly to hear Lowell speak, he recalled:

> There seemed to be a thousand people in the hall. I was the only Black. As we left the meeting I could hear conversations being started all around me,—but no one looked me in the eye, no one spoke to me. As I walked toward a group, they would move away.[119]

Later, Guinier was excited to encounter a familiar face—a former schoolmate—working the desk of the freshman library, but again, he was ignored. It was not until shopping for textbooks at the Harvard Coop that Guinier met another Black student, Ralph Bunche (MA 1928; PhD 1934), who welcomed him to Harvard. Bunche, who became an acclaimed diplomat, would go on to receive the Nobel Peace Prize in 1950 and play an important role in the Civil Rights Movement.[120] "He was the first person who spoke to me voluntarily," said Guinier, "and gave me some sense of community and connection with Harvard."[121] Bunche also told Guinier to look for a job at one of the private student eating clubs that catered to wealthy white students, where he could work alongside other Black students.[122]

Classes were not much better, and Guinier's professors rarely called on him.[123] He was "invisible to everyone around me," treated as a "nonperson," he recalled.[124] Things improved when he joined Alpha Phi Alpha and Omega Psi Phi, two Black fraternities with local chapters, but he suffered from health problems, and his family faced financial difficulties.[125] Guinier was forced to transfer to City College in New York in 1931.[126]

Undeterred by these challenges, Guinier completed his undergraduate studies and went on to earn a master's degree from Columbia University and a law degree from New York University. He became a prominent trade unionist, served as international secretary for the United Public Workers of America, and was the first Black candidate to be nominated by a political party—the American Labor Party—for the Manhattan borough presidency.[127]

In a turn of events that illustrates both Black intellectual resistance to inequality and institutional change over time, the history of the Guinier family and of Harvard remain deeply entwined. Both Guinier's daughter, Lani Guinier (Radcliffe AB 1971), and his grandson, Nikolas Bowie (AM 2011, JD 2014, PhD 2018), followed him to Harvard first as students and later as members of the faculty. In 1998, Lani Guinier made history as the first Black woman to hold a tenured professorship at Harvard Law School.[128]

African American Women at Radcliffe College

The story of African Americans and Harvard during the twentieth century includes the experiences of Black women at Radcliffe College. The history of Radcliffe is, itself, a tale of resistance. It was founded in 1879 as the Society for the Collegiate Instruction of Women, or the "Harvard Annex," to create opportunities for women then excluded from the University. Elizabeth Cary Agassiz, the author and naturalist described above and a "bold" reformer "devoted to the cause of women's higher education," served as its first president.[129] Coeducation developed at Harvard in fits and starts; although Harvard professors taught the women of Radcliffe according to the University's standards, women did not receive Harvard degrees until 1963.[130]

Radcliffe stood out among its peers on the matter of access for African American women: it consistently enrolled more Black women than other Seven Sisters colleges. It was "by far the leader" among these peers.[131] Nevertheless, the women educated at Radcliffe College (and the Annex) overwhelmingly were white, and they initially hailed predominantly from the Anglo-Saxon upper classes.[132] Radcliffe admitted its first Jewish students in 1893, and Alberta Virginia Scott (AB 1894), the first Black woman to graduate from the College, was admitted in 1894.[133] Thereafter, Radcliffe admitted a steady trickle of Black women, who invariably were "highly motivated and high achievers" according to one historian of the College.[134] Another historian characterized these women as "an African American female elite."[135]

While the relatively few Black women educated at Radcliffe welcomed the opportunity to be a part of a community of women scholars, they also encountered discrimination. They were denied campus housing and scholarships—significant barriers to educational access and academic success.[136] Yet, many of these same women went on to play important roles in building a better and more equitable nation.

Two such women, Eva Beatrice Dykes (AB 1917; AM 1918; PhD 1921) and Caroline Bond Day (AB 1919; AM 1930), arrived at Radcliffe in the 1910s with degrees in hand from historically Black colleges—Howard and Atlanta Universities, respectively. Like W. E. B. Du Bois, the women were forced to repeat their undergraduate degrees at Radcliffe before proceeding on to graduate studies.[137] They were among fewer than fifteen Black students who attended Radcliffe before 1920,[138] and neither was allowed to live on campus. Radcliffe would not permit a Black woman to live in the dormitories until 1925—two years *after* Harvard officially ended its discriminatory housing policy.[139] Neither Dykes nor Day wrote much about their experiences at Radcliffe, but both seem to have viewed the College positively—at least in comparison to their baseline, the Black experience in the American South, where both women had grown up.[140] Yet, both women also explored slavery and its legacies in their work, and they devoted considerable time in their careers to striving to right the wrongs African Americans confronted in American society.

Eva Beatrice Dykes

Eva Beatrice Dykes earned a bachelor's degree, summa cum laude, from Howard University in 1914;[141] a second bachelor's degree, magna cum laude, from Radcliffe in 1917; and, in 1921, she became the first African American woman to complete the requirements for a PhD in the United States, one of three Black women in the country to earn a PhD that year. A distinguished scholar of English literature, in her work Dykes foregrounded white authors' little-discussed views on race and slavery and elevated the prose, poetry, and song of Black writers.[142]

Dykes went on to teach at several Black institutions, including Walden University in Nashville, Tennessee; Dunbar High School, her alma mater, in Washington, DC; Howard University, where she taught English from 1929 to 1944; and finally Oakwood College—today Oakwood University—in Huntsville, Alabama.[143] At Oakwood, where she taught from 1944 until 1968, Dykes served as chair of the English department and the Division of Humanities and played a key role in securing accreditation for the institution in 1958.[144] An accomplished musician, Dykes also founded the Aeolians of Oakwood University, now a world-renowned choir recognized as "an authoritative exponent of Negro spirituals and Work songs which express the yearnings of their forefathers to be free."[145]

Much of Dykes's scholarship analyzes attitudes toward Blacks and toward slavery among canonical Western writers of the eighteenth and nineteenth centuries. In her 1942 book *The Negro in English Romantic Thought, or a Study of Sympathy for the Oppressed,* she explores the explicit attitudes of a long list of English Romantic writers toward Blacks and slavery, examining "not only poems and essays but also letters, memoirs, journals, lives, records of conversations, speeches, and anecdotes, which indicate very intimately the trend of English thought."[146]

The Ku Klux Klan, founded in the South in 1865,[1] gained considerable membership in the West and Midwest in the early twentieth century.[2] At its peak in 1925, the Klan claimed tens of thousands of members in every state of New England, including Massachusetts.[3]

Between February 1922 and October 1923, the student-run newspaper the *Harvard Crimson* reported an underground Ku Klux Klan presence on campus. Articles described isolated incidents of intimidation or recruitment, alleged student participation in area Klan chapters, and suggested the presence of an organized chapter of the Klan on campus. Such reports were published alongside Klan-related satire.

These issues received passing attention from Harvard administrators and alumni and from the national media. In 1922, for example, administrators responded to a white student's reports that the local Klan had threatened him by dismissing the threats as "undoubtedly part of a joke."[2] While the *Crimson*'s report of Klan activity on campus in early 1922 drew little comment, similar reports in the fall of 1923 made national news in the wake of controversies over Harvard's discriminatory housing and admissions policies.[4] The Klan's own newspaper eagerly recirculated and expanded on the reports;[5] the *New York Times* cited Harvard Regent Matthew Luce's assessment of their veracity;[6] and James Weldon Johnson, secretary of the NAACP, an organization then in the midst of an anti-lynching campaign,[7] wrote, "it would be better to close the university than to permit it to become a vehicle for disseminating the poison of race and religious hatred upon which the infamous Klan depends in recruiting its membership." He further warned that "nation wide experience with the Klan has demonstrated that where it has not been dealt with sternly and promptly [it] has become futile to attempt to do so later."[8]

Most, however, continued to dismiss the reports. Student reactions ranged from flippant to annoyed.[9] And the Harvard Alumni Bulletin lectured the *Crimson*, suggesting "an abatement in the firecracker brand of undergraduate journalism."[10] The *Crimson*, however, stood by its reporting "that there was a comparatively large number of Klansmen within the walls of the University."[11]

Regardless of whether the student newspaper's reports of Klan activity on campus were reliable or exaggerated, or fabricated as an ill-advised scheme to make light of the Klan, they would almost certainly have caused distress, particularly for Black students keenly aware of a national context of anti-Black harassment, murder, and theft of property.[12]

She used this methodology to recover not only long-ignored arguments against slavery by celebrated white writers but also to recover the work of Black creators. Through her coedited textbook, *Readings from Negro Authors, for Schools and Colleges, with a Bibliography of Negro Literature,* Dykes introduced Black writers to American students.[147] Elsewhere, she wrote that the examination of the lives and work of Black authors and artists powerfully illustrated "the variety of ways in which that cancer of American life, race prejudice, is eating the spiritual bowels of American morale and undermining the progress of the United States as a nation,—prejudice in labor, in education, in journalism, in the artistic world, in the courts of justice, in the church and in society in general."[148] To study Black American achievements was, for Dykes, to highlight the damages of racism and to demonstrate the need for "that racial unity which is the objective of every well-thinking person of the twentieth century."[149]

Caroline Bond Day

Caroline Bond Day, born in Montgomery, Alabama, studied under Du Bois at Atlanta University, graduating with a bachelor's degree in 1912. She entered Radcliffe College in 1916 and began work on a second undergraduate degree, which she earned in 1919.[150] She studied anthropology under Earnest A. Hooton, an instructor and the curator of somatology—the study of human variation and classification—at Harvard's Peabody Museum, who was sympathetic to at least some of the eugenicist views of his era.[151] Under Hooton's guidance, she began research into mixed-race families that would form the core of her pathbreaking master's work.[152]

After completing her second bachelor's degree, Day served as a social worker, including with the YWCA and at a settlement house in Washington, DC, and taught at several HBCUs, including Atlanta University; Howard University; North Carolina College for Negroes, now North Carolina Central University; Paul Quinn College, then in Waco, Texas, where she was the dean of women; and Prairie View State College, now Prairie View A&M, also in Texas. She also continued to pursue her research in her spare time.[153]

Day took leave from teaching in the late 1920s to return to Radcliffe for graduate studies, supported by a grant from the Bureau of International Research (BIR) of Harvard University to her mentor Earnest Hooton.[154] While working in Hooton's lab, she leveraged her own social networks to recruit 2,537 individuals from 346 mixed-race families[155]— an "inaccessible class" for white anthropologists[156]—to participate in her research. These individuals entrusted her with sociological and genealogical information, physical measurements, family photographs, and even locks of hair.[157] Day's thesis, *A Study of Some Negro-White Families in the United States,* was published in 1932, with a foreword by Hooton, by the Peabody Museum of Harvard University as part of a Harvard African Studies series.[158]

Day's highly technical work pushed back against the race scientists and eugenicists at Harvard and elsewhere, arguing that race is not a fixed category and that by no measure are people of color as a group inferior to whites. This work is still hailed today as a groundbreaking demonstration, using the same tools deployed by race scientists from Louis Agassiz to Charles B. Davenport, that Black and mixed-race Americans are not systematically inferior to whites.[159]

These and numerous other acts illustrate the counter-history of resistance embedded in Harvard's history.

Harvard, Radcliffe, and Racial Change

The presence of Black students at Harvard and Radcliffe increased significantly during the late 1960s: the racial transformation resulted partly from law—in particular, the antidiscrimination mandate of the Civil Rights Act of 1964—and partly from pressure brought to bear on the University by its own students. Among them was a young Lani Guinier:

> My posse wanted to express our concern that there were very few black women being admitted to Radcliffe. We sat in in the corridor leading up to the dean's office. We were told to be very "ladylike"; I remember well. This was our ladylike approach, but I think we got their attention. They certainly started admitting more students of color.[160]

University leadership played an important role as well. During the late 1950s and early 1960s, under the leadership of Wilbur J. Bender (AB 1927; dean of Harvard College, 1947–2952; dean of admissions, 1952–1960) and Fred Glimp (dean of admissions, 1960–1967; dean of Harvard College, 1967–1969) as deans of admissions and financial aid at Harvard, the number of Blacks and other people of color began to increase. These changes flowed from active recruitment, expanded financial aid, and explicit advocacy for student body diversity.[161]

Efforts to recruit greater numbers of students from modest backgrounds had begun a decade earlier during the administration of President James Bryant Conant (1933–1953), but African Americans did not then benefit from them. A "dominant figure in American higher education,"[162] Conant in the 1930s created national scholarships that broadened the University's geographic reach and provided aid according to financial need.[163] After World War II, Harvard under Conant enrolled large numbers of veterans subsidized under the GI Bill, with such students constituting nearly three quarters of students enrolled at the University in 1946–1947.[164] But Conant repeatedly declined to undertake efforts to improve race relations or aid Black students, although he claimed to be "interested in the racial problem."[165] Nevertheless, the changes he put in place to aid veterans and students in need of financial aid helped open the University's doors to larger numbers of Black students during the mid-to-late 1960s.

It was after the postwar boom that Bender—a former veterans' counselor and dean of Harvard College as well as a child of a working-class Mennonite family—was appointed dean of admissions and financial aid. His mandate was to find and recruit "the diverse groups needed to make a healthy student body." Harvard College would endeavor to increase recruitment of academically able students from all corners of the nation and from relatively modest backgrounds, while continuing to admit able children of alumni and of the upper classes.[166] With Bender and later Glimp at the helm, admissions began to evolve into a larger office, and one guided by formal admissions policy with an interest in composing a diverse student body, at least by some measures; in other words, an operation that would be more recognizable to those familiar with University admissions today was taking shape.[167] In 1959, according to one account, some eighteen Black men numbered among the freshman matriculants to Harvard College.[168] That figure represented an improvement over the average enrolled per year in prior decades, but the number of Black men on campus remained small.[169]

Harvard and Radcliffe student protests during the late 1960s, organized in the context of the civil rights, women's liberation, and antiwar movements, accelerated the trend toward the recruitment and admission of students of color, including Native American and Hispanic students, as well as students in need of financial assistance.[170] The Black presence at the two colleges tripled as a percentage of the student body between the beginning and end of the 1960s (from 2 percent in the early 1960s to 7 percent in 1969).[171] By the end of the decade, amid increasing student protests on a wide range of pressing issues, the Association of African and Afro-American Students (referred to as AFRO) and like-minded student activists sought to reform the curriculum. They would see their demand for the creation of an Afro-American studies department begin to bear fruit in 1968–1969, when a faculty committee recommended the establishment of an Afro-American studies program but not a department.[172] Ultimately, in April 1969, not long after Harvard President Nathan M. Pusey (1953–1971) controversially called in the police to disperse (predominantly white) student protesters, the faculty approved the creation of the Department of Afro-American Studies[173] (now the Department of African and African American Studies).

Meanwhile, the upward trend in admissions of students of color continued during the 1970s. More than 400 Black students applied to join the Harvard College class of 1975, of whom 109 were admitted and 90 enrolled.[174] The University's long-serving dean of admissions and financial aid, William R. Fitzsimmons (AB 1967, EdM 1969, EdD 1971), first joined the admissions office in 1972. He, along with David L. Evans—a son of Arkansas sharecroppers who earned a degree from Princeton University and served for five decades in Harvard's admissions office—became nationally known for leading the University's efforts to recruit a diverse student body.[175]

Harvard's Role as a Champion of Racial Diversity in Higher Education

The 1970s also marked the point at which the University became a proponent of the consideration of race in admissions and a leader in defending such practices.[176]

Under the leadership of then-President Derek Bok, Harvard University, along with several other leading educational institutions,[177] expressed unequivocal support for race-conscious admissions when the US Supreme Court first considered a challenge to these efforts. *Regents of the University of California v. Bakke,* a 1978 case in which a rejected white applicant sued a state-supported medical school, set the terms of the legal debate over race-conscious admissions in higher education. In an amicus brief, Harvard argued that "the inclusion of qualified minority group members in a student body" was necessary for "important educational objectives."[178] The brief built on the scholarship of Harvard Law School Dean Erwin N. Griswold[179] and began by, in essence, repudiating the long period during which Harvard and other predominantly white universities did little to recruit African Americans to campus. The lack of racial diversity on campuses through the 1960s, the University acknowledged, had created a "sort of white myopia," which narrowed the perspectives of both students and professors and deprived universities of scores of future leaders.[180]

Harvard's admissions policy, as well as the University's argument that the educational benefits of diverse learning environments constitute a compelling state interest, were both cited in the controlling opinion written by Justice Lewis F. Powell Jr.[181] Powell "even appended a summary of Harvard's policy to his opinion to provide a kind of template."[182] For this reason, Harvard's admissions program has often been cited as a model for race-conscious admissions.

In every major subsequent case challenging race-conscious admissions, Harvard presidents—including Derek Bok, Neil L. Rudenstine, Lawrence H. Summers, Drew Gilpin Faust, and Lawrence S. Bacow—have remained steadfast proponents of diversity in education. In 1996, the University joined amicus briefs filed by the Association of American Law Schools[183] and the Association of American Medical Colleges,[184] in support of the University of Texas's admissions program.

Harvard, along with other universities, also supported the University of Michigan through amicus filings in the *Grutter v. Bollinger* and *Gratz v. Bollinger* cases. The briefs argued that Michigan's efforts to achieve the "educational benefits of diversity"—the accepted rationale from *Bakke*—were essential in higher education.[185]

In the *Grutter* opinion, Justice Sandra Day O'Connor, like Justice Powell before her, cited Harvard's practices as a model of constitutionally acceptable race-conscious admissions.[186] She wrote that Michigan Law's "claim of a compelling interest is furthered bolstered by its *amici,* who point to the educational benefits that flow from student body diversity." Moreover, she cited *The Shape of the River: Long-Term Consequences of Considering Race in College and University Admissions*—a landmark study of race-conscious admissions policies and their positive long-term consequences—published by former Harvard President Derek Bok five years prior, in 1998.[187] Bok and his coauthor, former Princeton President William G. Bowen, had also served as expert witnesses for the University of Michigan.[188]

Harvard University, in conjunction with other schools, also filed an amicus brief when the US Supreme Court again considered the admissions policies of the University of Texas.[189] The brief asked the court to reaffirm *Grutter,* arguing—just as the University had in prior briefs—that diversity is an important interest for educational institutions and that race-neutral alternative practices are inadequate. The brief emphasized that the schools did not employ "race or ethnicity as a *classification* in [their] admissions policies" but rather considered "myriad factors including race and ethnicity . . . [as] influenced by the Harvard Plan approved by Justice Powell in *Bakke* and [the] Court in *Grutter.*"[190] Separately, then–Harvard Law School Dean Martha Minow filed an amicus brief with the dean of Yale Law School, contending that "considering race as a part of an individualized, holistic [admissions] process is entirety consistent with the Fourteenth Amendment" and that overturning *Grutter* would have "significant adverse consequences."[191]

The University continues to support race-conscious admissions, most recently in a pending case that challenges its own practices, which both the United States District Court and the United States Court of Appeals for the First Circuit have upheld as constitutional.[192] Following the United States District Court ruling, President Lawrence S. Bacow sent an e-mail to Harvard affiliates reaffirming that the College's use of race in admission "enriches the education of every student."[193] "Everyone admitted to Harvard College has something unique to offer our community," he continued, "and today we reaffirm the importance of diversity—and everything it represents to the world."[194]

Recognizing that financial barriers also limit universities' ability to recruit diverse cohorts of students, Harvard has also been a national leader in expanding financial assistance to ensure that all admitted students can afford a Harvard education. President Lawrence Summers in 2004 announced a major increase in aid for students from families of modest means; the University would no longer require parents with incomes below $40,000 to financially contribute to the cost of their children's Harvard College education.[195] The College's financial aid program has continued to expand, including through generous donor support.[196] Today, 55 percent of Harvard students receive scholarship aid, and 20 percent pay nothing at all.[197]

These steps do not erase the University's exclusion of Black students nor its anemic efforts to recruit and welcome Black students to campus into the twentieth century. But they do illustrate profound and positive racial change on Harvard's campus over time.

The Challenge of Belonging

While it is important to acknowledge progress in student body diversity and the University's commitment to it, the challenges that accompanied the demographic transformation on campus, described above, must also be acknowledged. Even after their numerical presence on campus substantially increased, some African American students reported marginalization on and off campus.

A Presidential Task Force on Inclusion and Belonging, established in 2016 by President Drew Gilpin Faust (2007–2018), documented many of these challenges in its 2018 report. The Committee on Harvard & the Legacy of Slavery affirms and incorporates by reference the task force's findings.

The task force also urged new actions to promote inclusion and ensure that all members of the Harvard community, across lines of race and ethnicity, feel welcome.[198] In response, the University installed its first chief diversity and inclusion officer in August 2020, and that office, along with offices or individuals tasked with advancing diversity and inclusion in every Harvard school, is taking concrete steps to promote inclusion and equity across campus.[199]

In these and in other ways, the University seeks continued momentum toward the achievement of a multiracial, multiethnic community where all students can thrive.

SIX

Conclusion and Recommendations to the President and Fellows of Harvard College

INSTITUTIONS CAN AND DO CHANGE, as the attitudes of the people inside them evolve. Over the nearly four hundred years since its founding, in 1636, Harvard University has changed in many ways. It evolved from a seminary founded in a cow pasture into a university known for its excellence in numerous disciplines. It evolved from a college defined by its enrollment of white men from elite backgrounds to a university that educates students from all backgrounds, regardless of gender, race, nationality, or economic status. By the early 1970s, Harvard and Radcliffe no longer were preserves of upper crust, Anglo-Saxon white men and women.

Under the weight of sweeping changes in law and society that some of its own graduates helped to bring about, Harvard—an institution entangled with American slavery and its legacies in the many ways documented in this report—is now reckoning with this past and seeking to make amends for these wrongs.

Much remains to be done as we seek to live up to our highest ideals. But by undertaking these endeavors in good faith and with a commitment to meaningful action, the University imbues *Veritas* with new meaning and renews its commitment to excellence.

The damage caused by Harvard's entanglements with slavery and its legacies warrant action—efforts to remedy the persistent educational and social harms that human bondage caused to descendants, to the campus community, and to surrounding cities, the Commonwealth, and the nation. Such action cannot possibly address the many complex and damaging legacies of slavery in and beyond the United States, but nonetheless, action is vital. Harvard should take responsibility for its past, and it should leverage its strengths in the pursuit of meaningful repair.

If undertaken, the actions that the committee recommends would be voluntary, rather than the result of legal obligation.[1] But the absence of a legal requirement does not negate the importance of undertaking these efforts, nor does it diminish the moral case for action. Institutions often take steps that uphold their values absent any formal requirement to do so. Harvard, for example, routinely donates services and provides other benefits to communities and organizations in Greater Boston in pursuit of "a vibrant and shared future."[2] And in recent years, dozens of other universities, along with corporations, churches, and municipalities, have instituted remedies for complicity with slavery, all on a voluntary basis.[3]

It is particularly appropriate for universities to take such steps: American society depends on universities to reflect and promote its highest ideals. The gap between the missions and values of universities—the pursuit of knowledge, truth seeking, integrity, and opportunity—and the reality of involvement with slavery is stark. And while a university's participation in human bondage through direct ownership or buying and selling of people might be deemed the highest level of culpability, financial entanglements and intellectual leadership that lent universities' prestige to theories of racial hierarchy have also resulted in lasting harm.[4] That universities continued to exclude or discriminate against descendants of enslaved people into the middle of the twentieth century deepens their complicity with this history of oppression.

Each of these forms of culpability—direct participation, financial ties, intellectual leadership, and discrimination—applies to Harvard, where the routine admission of descendants of slavery is a relatively recent phenomenon in a 385-year history. And the responsibility for involvement with slavery is shared across the institution—by presidents, fellows of the Corporation, overseers, faculty, staff, donors, students, and namesakes memorialized all over campus.

Several principles underpin the committee's recommendations:

To be meaningful, remedies must be visible, lasting, grounded in a sustained process of engagement, and linked to the nature of the damage done. Harvard's efforts should also be commensurate with this University's place in the American educational landscape. We must lead in this realm, no less than in others.

Harvard must set a powerful example as it reckons with its own past. We must pursue not only truth, vital though that is, but also reconciliation. Doing so requires a range of actions—visible and continuing— that address the harms of slavery and its legacies, many of which still reverberate today, affecting descendants of slavery in the community and indeed the nation.

These actions must include monetary and nonmonetary efforts.[5] Slavery was a system that, through violence, deprived the enslaved of the value of their own labor, creating a persistent multigenerational racial wealth gap that continues to disadvantage descendants of the enslaved. And the legacies of slavery—exclusion, segregation, marginalization, criminalization, disenfranchisement, and more—compounded its damage. The economic and social costs of categorical exclusion from and discrimination in education—not only but perhaps especially at Harvard—are profound.

Harvard is not alone in this work, nor is it first. The actions and experiences of other universities establish informative precedent. Brown University, the first among the Ivy League to formally acknowledge its ties to slavery, under the leadership of President Ruth J. Simmons, led the way. Years ago, Brown made significant investments in support of local educational institutions, including a $10 million endowment to promote academic excellence for K–12 students in Providence, of which approximately $2 million was raised from donors, with the remaining $8 million authorized by the Brown Corporation. Brown's actions also included loan forgiveness for graduate students who serve urban schools and students in the local area, fellowships in support of slavery studies, faculty fellowships for youth outreach, and more. More recently, the Princeton Theological Seminary pledged to create a $27.6 million reparative endowment, established scholarship funds, and hired new staff.

The University of Glasgow pledged £20 million to research slavery and its legacies around the world. The University of Virginia erected a $7 million memorial, built a new dormitory named for enslaved people who labored on campus, and established scholarships and fellowships for descendants of slavery. And in 2019, Georgetown University announced a fund that would raise $400,000 annually to benefit the descendants of enslaved people that the college sold in 1838, following a nonbinding referendum passed by Georgetown students.[6] In keeping with its position in higher education, Harvard should make a significant monetary commitment, and it should invest in remedies of equal or greater breadth than other universities.

We believe that Harvard's intellectual, reputational, and financial resources should be marshaled in its efforts to remedy the harms of the University's ties to slavery, just as past representatives of Harvard deployed these same resources and caused harm. Some of the committee's recommendations, below, are for wholly new endeavors; many others seek to build upon important existing programs and partnerships at Harvard, which we suggest should be strengthened and expanded. All must be sustained over time, and metrics should be established to ensure accountability. Through lasting efforts institutionalized as integral parts of Harvard's culture and curriculum, the University can create new legacies of service, innovation, equity, and leadership. We can renew our commitment to *Veritas*, and imbue it with deeper meaning.

We present seven broad recommendations that seek to remedy harms to descendants, to our community and the nation, and to campus life and learning.

Recommendation 1:
Engage and Support Descendant Communities by Leveraging Harvard's Excellence in Education

We recommend that the University leverage its scholarly excellence and expertise in education to confront systemic and enduring inequities that impact descendant communities in the United States—including in the American South, locus of the system of plantation slavery that produced cotton and fed the lucrative textile manufacturing companies of the Northeast—as well as descendant communities in the Caribbean.[7] The University should address these inequities in close and genuine partnership with institutions such as schools, community colleges, tribal colleges, universities, and nonprofit organizations already engaged in this work.[8]

We recommend a particular focus on the creation, expansion, and dissemination of world-class learning opportunities—including curricular and pedagogical innovations, expanded access to existing resources, and outstanding teacher training—especially to support historically marginalized children and youth from birth through high school and college. Harvard's pathbreaking work in early childhood development; in K–12 civic, moral, and social-emotional learning; in arts and STEM education; in higher education access and success; and in other fields could be leveraged to support children, educators, and parents in descendant communities locally nationally, and internationally. This could include offerings modeled on the Cambridge-Harvard Summer Academy of the Harvard Graduate School of Education or Harvard's Crimson Summer Academy.

This pursuit might be facilitated or enhanced by taking advantage of the University's new digital education nonprofit, established to "advance inclusion by driving innovations in learning that enrich and support people at all stages of education" through "partnerships with organizations that are doing outstanding work to identify, address, and close learning gaps."[9]

In creating and implementing such programs, we urge collaboration with experts outside of Harvard. We particularly suggest partnerships with local colleges and nonprofits engaged in work with demonstrated efficacy. These institutions disproportionately serve students from disadvantaged backgrounds, many of whom likely are descendants of enslaved people.

Finally, we suggest that the University broadly share what it learns through these partnerships. Harvard should, with its partner institutions, seek to establish and model best practices to support other historically white institutions that wish to address systemic and enduring educational inequities rooted in slavery and its legacies.

Recommendation 2:
Honor Enslaved People through Memorialization, Research, Curricula, and Knowledge Dissemination

In pursuit of truth and reconciliation, we recommend that the University create opportunities for all members of the Harvard community, especially students, to acknowledge and engage with the history of slavery and its legacies at Harvard. Toward this end, we recommend that the University recognize and honor the enslaved people whose labor facilitated the founding, growth, and evolution of Harvard through a permanent and imposing physical memorial, convening space, or both.

Moreover, in an effort to invest in current and future generations of scholars within and outside of the University, we recommend that Harvard—already home to many scholars and programmatic endeavors related to slavery and its legacies in and beyond education—provide ongoing financial support for scholarship and curricula that seek to understand, analyze, and promote solutions to persistent racial inequities that plague descendant communities.

We further recommend that the University provide ongoing financial support for the production of knowledge and curricula about Harvard's ties to slavery and for the dissemination of such knowledge to alumni and members of the public as well as to students, staff, and faculty across the University.

Recommendation 3:
Develop Enduring Partnerships with Black Colleges and Universities

Historically Black Colleges and Universities have educated a significant share of African American professionals who have helped lead the country in creating a more equitable society, one that acknowledges that the intelligence, talents, and contributions of all groups must be recognized, nurtured, and drawn upon for the benefit of the nation. Thurgood Marshall, former associate justice of the Supreme Court; Martin Luther King Jr., minister and civil rights activist; and the Nobel Prize laureate Toni Morrison were all educated at HBCUs. The quality and importance of these institutions cannot be denied.

Yet, as a result of the nation's history of separate and unequal systems of education, HBCUs have often been underfunded and excluded from the benefits that many other universities enjoy. In spite of this long-standing disparity in treatment, Harvard, like other major universities, has greatly benefitted from the enrollment of HBCU alumni in its graduate and professional programs. These students have added immeasurably to the quality of education afforded all students at Harvard and have expanded knowledge and understanding in many disciplines.

In light of the invaluable role of HBCUs in the educational landscape and the persistent underfunding of these colleges, we believe the University should develop enduring partnerships with HBCUs. We suggest that it do so through the expansion of existing collaborations between Harvard's schools and research-focused HBCUs.[10]

To promote enriching and long-lasting bonds between the universities, we recommend that Harvard encourage and fund summer, semester, or yearlong visiting appointments to Harvard by interested faculty from HBCU partner institutions and similar visiting appointments by Harvard faculty to HBCU partners. We also recommend that the University encourage and subsidize summer, semester, or yearlong visits to Harvard by interested students who are juniors at HBCU partner institutions and by interested Harvard students in their junior years to HBCU partners, through a new "Du Bois Scholars Program." These faculty and student visits would promote intellectual exchange and research collaborations between Harvard and HBCUs, particularly in STEM fields, and would also financially support HBCU partner institutions in two ways: first, by providing to Du Bois scholars who visit Harvard as juniors the generous financial aid routinely available to Harvard students, thus in many cases reducing overall college costs, and, second, by providing to faculty of HBCUs the financial support for sabbaticals routinely available to Harvard faculty.

Similarly, we recommend the University promote and fund visiting fellowships for affiliates of Harvard libraries and affiliates of HBCU partner libraries, efforts that would promote archival preservation, digitization, and other collaborations to document and safeguard African American history.

Finally, we suggest that the University broadly share what it learns through these partnerships. Harvard should, with its HBCU partners, seek to establish and model best practices to other historically white institutions that wish to address systemic and enduring educational inequities rooted in slavery and its legacies.

Recommendation 4:
Identify, Engage, and Support Direct Descendants

We recommend that the University endeavor to identify the direct descendants of enslaved individuals who labored on Harvard's campus and of those who were enslaved by Harvard leadership, faculty, or staff. The University's acknowledgement of direct descendants' lineage, through a Harvard & the Legacy of Slavery Remembrance Program, is a vital step in its quest for truth, reconciliation, and repair.

We further recommend that, in recognition of this lineage, the University engage with these descendants through dialogue, programming, information sharing, relationship building, and educational support. Through such efforts, these descendants can recover their histories, tell their stories, and pursue empowering knowledge.

Recommendation 5:
Honor, Engage, and Support Native Communities

Indigenous history has special significance to Harvard's founding and evolution. Slavery in New England began with the enslavement of Native Americans, and Harvard leaders and staff members enslaved and sold Indigenous people as well as people of African descent. Moreover, Harvard's Indian College, which reflected both political and financial expediency and the broader colonial effort to Christianize, enrolled just five Native students, only one of whom received a degree in his lifetime. Legacies of Indigenous slavery and colonialism, while not discussed at length in this report, persist in Massachusetts and across the United States.

Recognizing this special significance, we recommend that the University provide financial support for research, dissemination of knowledge, recruitment of students from tribal communities, and other reparative efforts benefiting members of New England's Native communities.

We further recommend that the University organize a landmark conference, under the auspices of the Harvard University Native American Program, to advance a national dialogue on the history and legacies of Indigenous slavery and colonialism in the United States, catalyze deep research, and establish new partnerships with Indigenous communities.

Recommendation 6:
Establish an Endowed Legacy of Slavery Fund to Support the University's Reparative Efforts

The profound harm caused by the University's entanglements with slavery and its legacies cannot be valued in monetary terms alone. Nevertheless, the commitment of significant resources can and does signify Harvard's acknowledgement of wrongdoing and a responsibility to undertake a sustained process of repair: financial expenditures are a necessary predicate to and foundation for redress.

Therefore, we recommend the creation of a Legacy of Slavery Fund—generously funded, preserved in an endowment, and strategically invested—to support implementation of these recommendations.

Recommendation 7:
Ensure Institutional Accountability

Finally, we recommend that the University establish an accountable institutional apparatus fully empowered to lead—during an implementation phase of this Presidential Initiative—the operationalization of the committee's recommendations and coordination of all Harvard Schools' participation in these efforts, in the spirit of One Harvard. This includes a commitment to ongoing engagement, dialogue, information sharing, and relationship building with community members and stakeholders in Cambridge and the greater Boston area in order to foster discussion and solicit input on the long path forward.

We further suggest annual reporting on and evaluation of the implementation process and, if necessary, the revision of these recommendations in ways consistent with their goals.

Harvard's past entanglements with slavery and its legacies cannot be undone, but the present and future are ours—as a University community—to shape. The history revealed here and the committee's recommendations for action can inspire renewed commitment to truth, institutional reform, and community engagement. Through these endeavors we can advance both the University's commitment to the transformative power of education and our mission to develop ethical leaders who respect the "rights, differences, and dignity" of all people.[11]

List of Human Beings Enslaved by Prominent Harvard Affiliates

Notes about Organization and Criteria for Inclusion

This list of individuals enslaved by Harvard leadership, faculty, staff, and donors is almost certainly an undercount. Records of enslavement in the colonial era are irregular, and the list omits some individuals who are likely to have been enslaved but for whom sufficient documentation could not be located. This is an important area for future research in the spirit of the committee's fourth recommendation to the President and Fellows of Harvard College.

The enslaved individuals listed below were identified through research in city vital records, church records, published memoirs, and personal papers, including correspondence, journals, wills, and probate records. Many were previously identified in published scholarship, although their connections to Harvard were often not highlighted. Dates appended to the names of enslaved people reflect the first and, where applicable, last date of documentation for each individual, not the duration of their enslavement.

The list includes individuals who are referred to in extant records as a Harvard affiliate's "servant," "man," or "woman" and who are also identified as being of African or Indigenous descent. This reflects the fact, noted by leading historians of the era, that the term "slave" was not commonly used in colonial New England in reference to enslaved people. For example, in her authoritative work *New England Bound: Slavery and Colonization in Early America,* Wendy Warren explains:

> English people in the early seventeenth century only sporadically used the word "slave" to describe people of African or Indian descent in perpetual servitude, in New England or elsewhere. More often, the words "negro" and "negro servant" and, in some cases, "Indian servant" demarcated chattel status for Africans and Indians in the English Atlantic colonies. Counterintuitively, where "slave" was used in New England records during the seventeenth century, it generally referred to English captives held in North African slavery, or even as a figure of speech to connote some sort of debased state. This slowly changed over the century; more than sixty years later, an observer on Barbados would note, "These two words, *Negro* and *Slave* being by custom grown Homogeneous and Convertible; even as *Negro* and *Christian, Englishman* and *Heathen,* are . . . made *Opposites.*"[1]

The list is organized by enslaver, rather than by enslaved individual, in order to support further research to identify those people who were enslaved by Harvard affiliates; source materials are, in general, similarly organized. As this work continues, however, it is critical that researchers center enslaved people in order to appropriately honor their memories and, as the committee recommends, to enable descendants to "recover their histories, tell their stories, and pursue empowering knowledge."[2]

Finally, unless otherwise noted, Harvard affiliations are drawn from the *Quinquennial Catalogue of the Officers and Graduates of Harvard University, 1636–1915.*[3] The relationships of named Harvard affiliates to buildings and physical spaces on campus are drawn from the Harvard Property Information Resource Center's online database.[4]

Table A.1. Enslaved by Presidents of Harvard

Enslaver	Harvard Affiliation(s)	Enslaved Persons	Documentation Dates	Memorialization(s)
Presidents				
Nathaniel Eaton (1609–1674)	Schoolmaster (1637–1639)[1]	"The Moor"	1639[2]	A plaque on Wadsworth Gate and brass markers nearby on Massachusetts Avenue mark the site of Eaton's home, the first building occupied by Harvard College.[3]
Increase Mather (1639–1723)	President (1692–1701) Rector (1686–1692) Acting President (1685–1686)	"The Spaniard"	ca. 1681[4]–1719[5]	Mather House[6]
Benjamin Wadsworth (1670–1737)	President (1725–1737) Fellow (1697–1707; 1712–1725)	Titus Venus	1728–1740[7] 1726–1740[9]	Wadsworth House Wadsworth Gate (also known as the Class of 1857 Gate) A plaque installed in 2016 on the east side of Wadsworth House acknowledges Titus and Venus as enslaved persons who lived and worked there.[8]
Edward Holyoke (1689–1769)	President (1737–1769) Librarian (1709–1712) Tutor (1712–1716) Fellow (1713–1716)	Juba Bilhah Bilhah's newborn son Dinah	1744–1748[10] 1755–1765[13] 1762[14] 1757–1819[15]	A plaque installed in 2016 on the east side of Wadsworth House acknowledges Juba and Bilhah as enslaved persons who lived and worked there.[11] Holyoke Street in Cambridge, south of Harvard Yard[12]
Joseph Willard (1738–1804)	President (1781–1804) Tutor (1766–1772) Fellow (1768–1772)	Cesar	1789[16]	Willard Street in Cambridge, west of Harvard Square[17]

Table A.2. Enslaved by Harvard Fellows and Overseers

Enslaver	Harvard Affiliation(s)	Enslaved Persons	Documentation Dates	Memorialization(s)
Fellows and Overseers[1]				
Governor John Winthrop (1588–1649)	Overseer (1637–1649)[2]	The wife of Pequot sachem Mononotto	1637[3]	Winthrop House is named for Governor John Winthrop and his direct descendant Professor John Winthrop (see below).[4]
		Two unnamed sons of Mononotto	1637[7]	A sculpture of Governor Winthrop is displayed in Annenberg Hall, the freshman dining hall in Memorial Hall.[5]
		At least four additional unnamed Indigenous people: two men and two women	1637–1639[8]	A portrait of Governor Winthrop is in the Harvard University Portrait Collection.[6]
Israel Stoughton (1603–1644)	Overseer (1637–1644)[9]	Unnamed Pequot woman Dorcas	1637[11] 1641–1653[13]	Stoughton Hall is named for Israel's son, colonial lieutenant governor and Harvard overseer and benefactor William Stoughton (AB 1650).[12]
	Donor of 300 acres of land at his death in 1644[10]			
John Endecott / Endicott (1600–1665)	Overseer (1642–1665)[14]	Unnamed Pequot boy	1637[15]	
Hugh Peter(s) (1598–1660)	Overseer (1637–1641)[16]	Hope	1637–1640[17]	
Governor John Leverett (1616–1679)	Overseer (1673–1679)[18]	As governor of the Massachusetts Bay Colony, Leverett authorized	1675–1678[19]	Leverett House is named for Governor Leverett's grandson and namesake, Harvard President John Leverett (served 1708–1724).[20]

		the capture, enslavement, and distribution of hundreds of Native men, women, and children taken captive in King Philip's War		
Governor Joseph Dudley (1647–1720)	Overseer (1702–1715)[21]	An unnamed "Indian" girl Peter Brill	1679 1687[23] 1713–1722[24]	The Dudley Community and three associated Harvard residences are named for Joseph Dudley's father, the Massachusetts governor and Harvard overseer Thomas Dudley.[22]
Cotton Mather (1663–1728)	Fellow (1690–1703) Overseer (1707–1724)[25]	An unnamed "Spanish Indian," believed to be the same individual as "The Spaniard," above Onesimus "a little boy" Obadiah	ca. 1681[26] 1706–1716[28] 1716[29] 1717[30]	Mather House is named for Cotton Mather's father, Harvard President Increase Mather (president, 1692–1701; rector, 1686–1692; acting president, 1685–1686).[27]
William Brattle (1662–1717)	Tutor (1685–1697) Fellow (1703–1717) Treasurer (1713–1715) Minister of First Church, Cambridge (1696–1717)[31]	Scipio Cicely	1697–1705[32] 1714[35]	Brattle Street and Brattle Square are all named for William Brattle's family, and the William Brattle House is named for his son.[33] Cicely's tombstone stands in the Old Burying Ground in Harvard Square.[34]
Paul Dudley (1675–1751)	Fellow (1697–1700) Donated £133 in 1750 to fund an annual lecture[36]	Unnamed "negro boy" Guinea	1705[37] 1745[39]	The Dudley Community and three associated Harvard residences are named for Paul Dudley's grandfather, the Massachusetts governor and Harvard overseer Thomas Dudley.[38]

(Continued)

Table A.2. (continued)

Enslaver	Harvard Affiliation(s)	Enslaved Persons	Documentation Dates	Memorialization(s)
Nathaniel Appleton (1693–1784)	Fellow (1717–1779) Minister of First Church, Cambridge (1717–1783)[40]	Pompey	1729[41]	
William Brattle (1706–1776)[42]	Overseer (n.d.) Trustee of the Hopkins Foundation (n.d.)[43]	Philicia Zillah	1731[44] 1738[47]	A portrait of William Brattle is in the Harvard University Portrait Collection.[45] The William Brattle House in Harvard Square is named for this William Brattle, who built it. Brattle Street and Brattle Square are named for his family.[46]
Francis Foxcroft (1695–1768)	Overseer (1732–1757?)[48]	Flora Leos	1737–1742[49] 1749[50]	Foxcroft House (1822–1926) once occupied the corner of Kirkland and Oxford Streets; it was demolished to make way for the Lowell Lecture Hall.
Lieutenant Governor Spencer Phip(p)s (1685–1757)	Overseer (1720–1757)[51] Trustee of the Hopkins Foundation (1720–?)[52]	Tobe Cuffy Zillah Rose James	1714[53] 1739–1741[54] 1739[55] 1745[56] 1755[57]	
Ebenezer Storer (1730–1807)	Treasurer (1777–1807)	Unnamed "Negro servant" London	1757[58] 1771[59]	

John Hancock (1736/7–1793)	Treasurer (1773–1777)	Cato 1764–1777[60] Frank 1768–1771[61] Agnes 1777[62] Violet 1777[63] Hannibal 1777[64]	
Thomas Hubbard (1702–1773)	Treasurer (1752–1773) Donor of £300 and books at his death in 1773	Unnamed people referred to as "Negores"[65] 1774[66]	
Lieutenant Governor Thomas Oliver (1734–1815)	Overseer (1774–1776)[67]	Buff 1783 Cato 1783 Jerry 1783 Jeoffry 1783 Samuel 1783 Mira 1783 Jude 1783 Sarah 1783 Jenny 1783 Violet 1783 "Young Jerry" 1783[68] Unknown number of enslaved people in Antigua ca. 1760–ca. 1815[69]	Oliver built Elmwood, also known as the Oliver–Gerry–Lowell House, which has been the residence of University presidents since the 1970s.

Table A.3. Enslaved by Harvard Faculty Members

Enslaver	Harvard Affiliation(s)	Enslaved Persons	Documentation Dates	Memorialization(s)
Edward Wigglesworth (1693–1765)	Hollis Professor of Divinity (1721–1765) Fellow (1724–1765)	Hannibal[1]	1736–1755[2]	Wigglesworth Hall is built on the site of Edward Wigglesworth's home and named for his father.
Henry Flynt (1675–1760)	Tutor (1699–1754) Fellow (1700–1760) Secretary of the Board of Fellows (1712–1758) Acting President (1736–1737)	Toney	1738[3]	A portrait of Flynt is in the Harvard University Portrait Collection.[4]
Judah Monis (1683–1764)	Instructor in Hebrew (1722–1760)	Cuffy Cicely	1741[5] 1747[6]	
John Winthrop (1714–1779)	Hollis Professor of Mathematics and Natural Philosophy (1738–1779) Fellow (1765–1779) Acting President of Harvard (1773–1774)	George Scipio	1759[7] 1761[12]	Winthrop House is named for Professor John Winthrop and his ancestor Governor John Winthrop.[8] A portrait of Professor Winthrop is in the Harvard University Portrait Collection.[9] Winthrop Street and the adjacent Winthrop Square, southwest of Harvard Yard, is named for Professor Winthrop.[10] There is a City of Cambridge historic marker at the site of Professor Winthrop's home in Winthrop Square.[11]

Table A.4. Enslaved by Harvard Staff Members

Enslaver	Harvard Affiliation(s)	Enslaved Persons	Documentation Dates	Memorialization(s)
Thomas Danforth (1623–1699)	Treasurer (1650–1668) Steward (1668–1682) Overseer (1679–1686; 1689–1692)	Philip Ffeild	1700[1]	
Andrew Bordman (II) (1671–1747)	Steward and Cook (1703–1747)[2]	Cuffe Rose Jane " of Rose" Flora "of Rose" Jeffrey " of Rose" Cesar "of Rose" Lucy Peter	1716/17[3] 1718–1730[6] 1718–1740[7] 1723[8] 1731–1739[9] 1733[10] 1740[11] 1758[12]	The Bordman home, where enslaved people lived and worked, was purchased by Harvard in 1794 and used as the College House. The land where that building stood, at the corner of Massachusetts Avenue and Dunster Street, is now part of the site of the Smith Student Center.[4] Jane's tombstone stands in the Old Burying Ground in Harvard Square.[5]
Jonathan Hastings (1709–1783)	Steward (1750–1779)	Cato Anne Rose "of Anne" Cato "of Anne"	1761[13] 1771[15] 1771[16] 1774[17]	A stone tablet next to the Littauer Center marks the site of Hastings's home, north of Harvard Yard.[14]

Table A.5. Enslaved by Major Donors to Harvard

Enslaver	Harvard Affiliation(s)	Enslaved Persons	Documentation Dates	Memorialization(s)
Edward Hopkins (1600–1657)	Funded the Hopkins Foundation, established in 1710s with Harvard as a primary beneficiary[1]	Unnamed person referred to as "the Negar"	1658[2]	Hopkins is the namesake of the town of Hopkinton, Massachusetts, which was created in the 1715 and administered to generate revenue for the University through 1832.[3]
John Hull (1624–1683)	Donated £100 in 1683[4]	As treasurer of the Massachusetts Bay Colony, Hull managed the sale of dozens of Native men, women, and children taken captive in King Philip's War	1675–1676[5]	Hull's name is included on a list of "Notable Alumni" published online by the Boston Latin School—the oldest public school in the United States—that highlights "centuries of former Latin School students who have gone on to be leaders in a variety of fields."[6]
Edmund Trowbridge (1709–1793)	Endowed the Alford Professorship of Natural Religion, Moral Philosophy, and Civil Polity (1798)[7] Tutored Harvard students in law and boarded them in his home[8]	York Violet Violet's unnamed mother	1742[9] 1767[12] 1767[13]	Trowbridge Street east of Harvard Yard in Cambridge[10] Harvard Law School owns a portrait of Trowbridge[11]
John Cuming/ Cummings (1728–1788)	Benefactor of Harvard Medical School[14]	Brister Freeman Jem	1753–1822[15] 1755–1788[16]	

Person	Connection to institution	Dates	Enslaved people	Legacy
Thomas Hancock (1703–1764)	Funded a professorship	1763[17] 1763[18]	Unnamed people referred to as "Negroes" Cato	Hancock Professorship of Hebrew and Other Oriental Languages
Isaac Royall Jr. (1719–1781)	Funded the first professorship in law at Harvard, forerunner of the Harvard Law School	1732–1783[19]	With his father, owned more than 60 enslaved individuals in Massachusetts	Royall Professorship of Law; Harvard Law School owns a portrait of Isaac Royall Jr. and his family[20]; Royall House and Slave Quarters, in Medford, Massachusetts[21]
James Perkins[23] (1761–1822)	Funded a professorship; Donor to and officer of the Massachusetts General Hospital, the first HMS teaching hospital,[24] at its founding[25]; Director of the effort to create the Theological School of Cambridge, now Harvard Divinity School	1732–1783[22] 1790s–1831[26] 1789–1793[27]	Unknown number of enslaved people in Antigua; Mousse / Deyaha; An unknown number of enslaved people traded in St. Domingue (Haiti)	Perkins Professorship of Astronomy and Mathematics
Thomas Handasyd Perkins (1764–1854)	Donor to and officer of Massachusetts General Hospital at its founding[28]	1789–1793[29]	An unknown number of enslaved people traded in St. Domingue (Haiti)	Perkins School for the Blind, in Watertown, Massachusetts[30]
Samuel Gardner Perkins (1767–1847)	Donor to Massachusetts General Hospital at its founding[31]; Donor to the Massachusetts Professorship of Natural History at Harvard[32]	1789–1793[33]	An unknown number of enslaved traded in St. Domingue (Haiti)	The Perkins Room in Massachusetts Hall is named for a descendant of Samuel Gardner Perkins.[34]

(Continued)

Table A.5. (continued)

Enslaver	Harvard Affiliation(s)	Enslaved Persons	Documentation Dates	Memorialization(s)
Israel Thorndike (1755–1832)	Donated the Ebeling Map Collection to the Harvard Library[35] Vice president of "A Society for the Promotion of Theological Education in Harvard University," member of the Committee for Procuring Subscriptions, and donor at the founding of Harvard Divinity School[36] Donor to Massachusetts General Hospital[37]	An unknown number of enslaved people traded in the Caribbean	1791–1793[38]	A professorship in orthopedic surgery at Harvard Medical School is named for a descendant of Israel Thorndike.[39]
Moses Brown (1748–1820)	Donor to Harvard Divinity School[40]	An unknown number of enslaved people traded in the West Indies	1791–1793[41]	
Edwin F. Atkins (1850–1926)	Donated property in Cuba and over $100,000[42]	95 Cuban *patrocinados*, formerly enslaved people who were required by law to pay in order to leave the plantation properties to which they were legally bound	1884[43]	The Atkins Institution in Cuba (botanical gardens was operated by Harvard until the Cuban Revolution in 1961)[44]

A Note on Process

The release of this report is at once the beginning of Harvard's commitment to a meaningful and sustained process of repair and the culmination of an initiative that involved deep research and the active participation of a wide range of stakeholders. Process matters greatly in work of this kind, and the initiative's efforts to engage a wide range of experts and share its work with a broad audience are described below. The committee is grateful to all those who supported this undertaking.

As noted in Section One of this report, Harvard's twenty-ninth president, Lawrence S. Bacow, established the Presidential Initiative on Harvard & the Legacy of Slavery in 2019. He appointed a committee representative of all the University's schools and charged this group with diving deep into our history and its relationship to the present. President Bacow asked the committee to "give additional dimension to our understanding of the impact of slavery" at Harvard. This work, he said, should "have a strong grounding in rigorous research and critical perspectives" that "will inform . . . our understanding of facts" and "how we might address the ramifications of what we learn." President Bacow also asked the committee to "concentrate on connections, impact, and contributions that are specific to our Harvard community" and "provide opportunities to convene academic events, activities, and conversations that will encourage our broader University community to think seriously and rigorously about the continuing impact and legacy of slavery in 2019 and beyond."[1]

This charge built on earlier work. In 2016, Drew Gilpin Faust, the University's twenty-eighth president, publicly acknowledged that "Harvard was directly complicit in America's system of racial bondage from the College's earliest days in the 17th century until slavery in Massachusetts ended in 1783, and Harvard continued to be indirectly involved through extensive financial and other ties to the slave South up to the time of emancipation."[2] She established a committee on the University and slavery[3] that, with the aid of the researcher Caitlin Galante DeAngelis (PhD 2014), conducted a preliminary investigation upon which this report builds. These initial efforts included, in 2016, a public ceremony in which then-President Faust and the late civil rights leader US Congressman John Lewis unveiled a plaque affixed to Wadsworth House in Harvard Yard that acknowledges the unfree labor of four enslaved people—Titus, Venus, Juba, and Bilhah—who lived there and worked for two Harvard presidents and their families.[4] A 2017 conference at the Radcliffe Institute for Advanced Study, organized at Faust's suggestion with the support of then–Radcliffe Dean Lizabeth Cohen, brought together prominent thinkers about universities and slavery from around the country.[5]

The work of excavating and confronting the truths that this committee now discloses has been, and continues to be, a community-wide endeavor. Whereas prior histories of Harvard scarcely mentioned the University's ties to slavery,[6] Harvard scholars and students have worked assiduously in recent years to reveal painful truths. Beginning in 2007, Laird Bell Professor of History Sven Beckert and his undergraduate students began investigating Harvard's ties to slavery in a multiyear series of research seminars, releasing a report on their findings in 2011.[7] At Harvard Law School in 2008, Royall Professor of Law Janet Halley explored the history of the slave-owning colonial benefactor Isaac Royall Jr.,[8] sharing knowledge that helped spur student protests decrying the Law School's shield, which featured the Royall family crest.[9] Martha Minow, 300th Anniversary University Professor and then-dean of Harvard Law School, established a committee that recommended the retiring of the shield.[10] In 2017, Harvard Law School dedicated a memorial on the School's campus to the enslaved people whose labor generated Royall's wealth.[11] In 2020, Harvard Medical School students petitioned against the "Oliver Wendell Holmes" academic society because of namesake Oliver Wendell Holmes Sr.'s role in the expulsion of Black students in 1850 and his promotion of so-called race science.[12] Upon the recommendation of a faculty subcommittee and with the approval of Dean George Q. Daley, the society was renamed for William Augustus Hinton (SB 1905; MD 1912), a clinical professor of bacteriology and immunology at HMS and the first Black full professor at Harvard.[13]

Moreover, as this committee conducted its work, many Harvard alumni engaged with it, including some with family connections to slavery and others who were present on campus during the era of segregation, bearing witness to parts of the history documented in this report. It welcomed broad audiences through more than a dozen events, all of which were free and open to the public. And, with support from the presidential initiative, Harvard students from multiple schools and departments also aided and augmented our efforts through research and the production of poetry and dramatic art.[14]

Consultative Process

In preparing this report and recommendations, the committee consulted a wide range of experts and organizations that provided invaluable input. In particular, committee members met with King Boston and Höweler + Yoon to explore approaches to memorialization; with leaders of the Royall House and Slave Quarters and the Museum of African American History in Boston and Nantucket on questions of public history and partnership; with major library and HBCU leaders on archival collaborations; with University of California system leaders on innovations in education access; and with leaders of the Boston Foundation, the University of Massachusetts Boston, Bunker Hill Community College, Roxbury Community College, and other educational and service organizations that support descendant communities in Massachusetts. Committee members and staff also participated in the City of Cambridge Committee on City Art, Monuments, and Markers and engaged with the Cambridge Historical Commission, History Cambridge (formerly Cambridge Historical Society) and the new Slave Legacy History Coalition, led by Dennis Lloyd, a descendant of Darby Vassall, whose story is discussed in Sections One and Three of this report.

Harvard is one of many institutions reckoning with historical ties to slavery, and the committee also benefited from partnership with the Universities Studying Slavery consortium as well as generous advice from faculty members, administrators, and advocates involved with similar efforts at other universities. The committee chair is particularly grateful to Prairie

View A&M President Ruth Simmons, who convened the Brown University Steering Committee on Slavery and Justice as president of that university in 2003, and to James Campbell, the Edgar E. Robinson Professor in United States History at Stanford University (formerly of Brown University); David Blight, Sterling Professor of History, of African American Studies, and of American Studies at Yale; David Collins, associate professor and Haub Director of Catholic Studies at Georgetown University; Kirt von Daacke, assistant dean and associate professor of history at the University of Virginia; and Martha A. Sandweiss, professor of history at Princeton.

Within Harvard, the committee consulted with the Steering Committee on Human Remains in Harvard Museum Collections, chaired by the historian of science and medicine Evelynn M. Hammonds, who also served on the legacy of slavery committee; with the Committee to Articulate Principles on Renaming, chaired by Harvard President Emerita Drew Gilpin Faust; and with the Faculty of Arts and Sciences Task Force on Visual Culture and Signage, chaired by Robin Kelsey, dean of arts and humanities. Leaders and staff of the Harvard Museum of Comparative Zoology, the Harvard Peabody Museum of Archaeology and Ethnology, and the Warren Anatomical Museum also provided support. The committee also benefited from consultation and partnership with the University's Office of Equity, Diversity, Inclusion, and Belonging; the Hutchins Center for African and African American Research and its director, Henry Louis Gates Jr.; the Charles Warren Center for Studies in American History; the Harvard Office for the Arts; the Department of Music; the American Repertory Theater; and several students involved with the Harvard Generational African American Students Association.

We received particular support from the Harvard University Archives, Houghton Library, and the Schlesinger Library on the History of Women in America at Harvard Radcliffe Institute, all of which granted our researchers safe physical access during the COVID-19 pandemic and digitized parts of their collections for us. Many other Harvard libraries and departments digitized materials and provided additional support, including:

Arnold Arboretum Horticultural Library and Archives

Baker Library, Harvard Business School

Countway Library, Harvard Medical School, Harvard School of Dental Medicine, and Harvard T. H. Chan School of Public Health

Department of African and African American Studies, Harvard Faculty of Arts and Sciences

Ernst Mayr Library of the Museum of Comparative Zoology

Frances Loeb Library, Harvard Graduate School of Design

Harvard Fine Arts Library

Harvard Law School Library

We also engaged with numerous libraries and special collections in eastern Massachusetts and across the United States. In particular, the leadership and staff at the Massachusetts Historical Society and the Boston Athenaeum provided us with invaluable guidance and access to their collections. Colleagues at the William L. Clements Library at the University of Michigan and the Moorland-Spingarn Research Center at Howard University digitized items in their collections for our use, and staff at the Schomburg Center for Research in Black Culture at the New York Public Library and the Robert S. Cox Special Collections and University Archives Research Center at the University of Massachusetts Amherst assisted us in accessing important materials. We also consulted the collections of the American Philosophical Society Library, the Boston Public Library, the Milton (Massachusetts) Historical Society, and the Williams Research Center at the Historic New Orleans Collections.

Research and Creative Projects

Harvard faculty and students engaged in a wide range of research and creative projects with support from the Presidential Initiative on Harvard & the Legacy of Slavery. You can learn more about their work online.

Student Research and Creative Project Grant Recipients

Aabid Allibhai (GSAS; HLS)

Clara Amenyo (GSD)

Busola Banjoh (Harvard College)

Daniel Barcia (HBS; HLS; Harvard College)

Phoebe Braithwaite (GSAS)

Gianna Cacciatore (HDS; GSE; Harvard College)

Darien Carr (GSD; Harvard College)

Alexandre Chaumette (Harvard College)

Bettie Closs (Harvard College)

Isabel Cole (Harvard College)

Bennett Comerford (GSAS)

Jarrett Drake (GSAS)

Stacey Fabo (Harvard College)

Winona Guo (Harvard College)

Catherine Huang (GSE)

Shandra Jones (GSE)

Heidi Lai (Harvard College)

Sarah Mallory (GSAS)

Kyra March (Harvard College)

Orlee Marini-Rapoport (Harvard College)

Mary McNeil (GSAS)

Garry Mitchell (GSE)

Elifmina Mizrahi (GSD)

Thandi Nyambose (GSD)

Eve O'Connor (GSAS)

Ogechukwu Ogbogu (Harvard College)

Suzannah Omonuk (HDS)

Nicole Piepenbrink (GSD)

Cresa Pugh (GSAS)

Kiana Rawji (Harvard College)

Avi Robinson (GSD)

Malachi Robinson (Harvard College)

Divya Saraf (GSD)

Jack "Alex" White III (Harvard College)

Cecilia Zhou (Harvard College)

Abbreviations:

- *GSAS: Harvard Graduate School of Arts and Sciences*
- *GSD: Harvard Graduate School of Design*
- *GSE: Harvard Graduate School of Education*
- *HBS: Harvard Business School*
- *HDS: Harvard Divinity School*
- *HLS: Harvard Law School*

Faculty-led Research Projects

When Campus Is Closed: Privilege, Poverty, and Pandemic Life at Harvard University

Researcher: Anthony Abraham Jack, assistant professor of education, Harvard Graduate School of Education, and Shutzer Assistant Professor, Harvard Radcliffe Institute

This study examines the impact of the convergence of a reckoning over long-standing racial inequalities, a global pandemic, and—for many—an economic crisis. Jack and his research team have interviewed 120 Black, white, Latinx, Asian, and Native undergraduates, with particular emphasis on understanding the experiences of generational African American students at Harvard. This research informed the recommendations presented in Section Six of this report.

Mapping Post-Mortem Segregation: A Survey of the Old Burying Ground in Cambridge

Researchers: Aja Lans, 2021–2023 postdoctoral fellow, Inequality in America Initiative; Jason Ur, Stephen Phillips Professor of Archaeology and Ethnology; and Andrew Bair, PhD candidate, Harvard Department of Archaeology

Compared to the white colonial settler population, Black residents of colonial Cambridge are currently nearly invisible in death, with only two headstones known to mark gravesites of "negro servants" in the Old Burying Ground in Harvard Square. Yet the documentary record shows that there were many more enslaved persons living and working in Cambridge and at Harvard. What became of them in death? Can we find them and give them the same visibility afforded to white colonists? To answer these questions, this project brings the tools of historical archaeology, spatial analysis, and archeological remote sensing to the Old Burying Ground in an effort to locate the graves of marginalized members of the colonial Cambridge community.

Student Researchers and Creative Partners

Many undergraduate and graduate students, as well as recent graduates and postdoctoral fellows, played critical roles in the work of the initiative, including as researchers working on the report and on supported projects, as participants in a film accompanying the report, and as voice actors for a virtual walking tour that provides an introduction to the landscape of enslavement—and of resistance—in and around Harvard Yard.

Busola Banjoh (Harvard College)

Becca Spindel Bassett (HRI; GSE)

D'Wayne Bell (GSE)

Lucian Bessmer (GSE)

Vincent Bish (HKS; GSE)

Robert Clinton (HLS)

Mycah Conner (GSAS)

Galadriel A. Coury (Harvard College)

Theodore Delwiche (Harvard College)

Emily Farnsworth (HDS)

Noah Gold (Harvard College)

Ethan Goodnight (GSAS)

Laura Greenberg (GSD)

Lindsey Hightower (Harvard College)

Hiram Jackson (HDS)

Chelsea Jno Baptiste (GSD)

Orelia Jonathan (GSE)

Shandra Jones (GSE)

Aja Lans (GSAS)

Sydney Lewis (Harvard College)

Kyra March (Harvard College)

Suzannah Omonuk (HDS)

Samantha O'Sullivan (Harvard College)

Phyllis Pawa (HDS)

Franco Paz (GSAS)

James Ramsey (HDS; HLS; Harvard College)

Claire Rostov (HDS)

Mini Saxena (HLS)

Ajay Singh (Harvard College)

Nicholas Spragg (HDS)

Isabel Strauss (GSD; Harvard College)

Ellie Taylor (Harvard College)

Caroline Tucker (GSE)

Kemeyawi Wahpepah (GSAS; Harvard College)

Suleyman Wellings-Longmore (HLS)

Nicole Yapp (HLS)

Jacqueline Zoeller (Harvard College)

Abbreviations:

- *GSAS: Harvard Graduate School of Arts and Sciences*
- *GSD: Harvard Graduate School of Design*
- *GSE: Harvard Graduate School of Education*
- *HBS: Harvard Business School*
- *HDS: Harvard Divinity School*
- *HLS: Harvard Law School*
- *HRI: Harvard Radcliffe Institute*

Public Programming

The Presidential Initiative on Harvard & the Legacy of Slavery (H&LS) is a University-wide effort anchored at Harvard Radcliffe Institute (HRI). The following public lectures and discussions were organized by HRI in partnership with, and with funding from, the presidential initiative. Recordings of these events are available online.

2019–2020

Naming Racism, June 2020

As part of a series on health inequity in the age of COVID-19, Camara Phyllis Jones and the H&LS committee member David R. Williams explored how we might overcome "the somnolence of racism denial," dismantle the system of racism, and put in its place a system in which all people can thrive.

American Policing and Protest, June 2020

Monica C. Bell and Laurence Ralph, with Brandon Terry as moderator, discussed contemporary police violence against people of color along with ethical issues that we must consider as we attempt to envision how our nation might be transformed.

2020–2021

Perfecters of This Democracy: A Conversation with Nikole Hannah-Jones, September 2020

Nikole Hannah-Jones and the H&LS committee chair, Tomiko Brown-Nagin, engaged in conversation about pressing issues of race, civil rights, injustice, desegregation, and resegregation.

The Enduring Legacy of Slavery and Racism in the North, October 2020

Kyera Singleton, Manisha Sinha, and John Stauffer, with the moderator and H&LS committee member Tiya Miles, examined the role and impact of slavery in the North, the influence of scientific racism, and the response of Black abolitionists.

This event was presented in collaboration with the Peabody Museum of Archaeology and Ethnology and the Harvard Museums of Science and Culture.

Obesity, COVID-19, and Systemic Racism, October 2020

Sara Bleich and Sabrina Strings explored how uneven distribution of social support drives obesity; how framing affects policy; and how lack of research fuels speculation and reinforces racist stereotypes.

The Impact of 2020 on Higher Education: Colleges, COVID-19, and a Time of Racial Reckoning, November 2020

Eddie R. Cole, the H&LS-funded researcher Anthony Abraham Jack, and Jennifer Morton, with the moderator Kemeyawi Wahpepah, discussed how higher education can and should rise to the challenges of 2020 and beyond.

Harvard & the Legacy of Slavery: Reckoning with the Past to Understand the Present, March 2021

The H&LS committee chair, Tomiko Brown-Nagin, and the committee members Tiya Miles and Martha Minow explored the charge of the initiative and the work then underway to explore Harvard's historical entanglements with slavery and its legacies, along with the initiative's efforts to support student and community engagement.

The Intentional Museum, March 2021

Christy Coleman, Makeda Best, and the H&LS committee member Sven Beckert, with the moderator and H&LS committee chair Tomiko Brown-Nagin, discussed the power that museums have to genuinely engage with communities around what matters most to them.

This event was presented in collaboration with the Harvard Museums of Science & Culture and the Harvard Art Museums.

Racial Inequity and Housing Instability in Boston: Past, Present, and Future, April 2021

Tatiana Cruz and Lydia Edwards, with Chris Herbert as moderator, discussed how millions of Americans have long struggled to pay for housing, with communities of color additionally burdened by housing discrimination and historical race-based policies, such as legalized segregation, redlining, and mortgage discrimination, with a specific focus on Greater Boston.

This event was presented in collaboration with the Royall House and Slave Quarters, in Medford, Massachusetts.

Medical Racism from 1619 to the Present: History Matters, May 2021

Jim Downs and Susan M. Reverby, with the moderator and H&LS committee member Evelynn M. Hammonds, examined the roots in slavery of contemporary African American mistrust of the healthcare system, the lack of trust in medical providers fostered by experiences of everyday racism, and the African American community's long dependence, born of necessity, on care from within the community.

This event was presented in collaboration with the Project on Race & Gender in Science & Medicine at the Hutchins Center for African & African American Research at Harvard University.

2021–2022

Book Talk with Clint Smith, July 2021

First in a two-part series, featuring Clint Smith, author of *How the Word Is Passed: A Reckoning with the History of Slavery Across America* (Little, Brown and Company, 2021).

This event was presented in collaboration with the Royall House and Slave Quarters, in Medford, Massachusetts.

Book Talk with Tiya Miles, July 2021

Second in a two-part series, featuring the H&LS committee member Tiya Miles, author of *All That She Carried: The Journey of Ashley's Sack, a Black Family Keepsake* (Random House, 2021), the 2021 National Book Award Winner for Nonfiction.

Opening Discussion for *Brown II*, September 2021

Tomashi Jackson and the H&LS committee chair, Tomiko Brown-Nagin, engaged in a wide-ranging conversation to mark the opening of Jackson's Harvard Radcliffe Institute exhibition, *Brown II,* in the Johnson-Kulukundis Family Gallery.

This event was presented in collaboration with the Royall House and Slave Quarters, in Medford, Massachusetts.

Feeding the Nation: Michael W. Twitty on American Foodways and the History of Enslavement, March 2022

Michael W. Twitty shared insights about the role of enslaved people in shaping American foodways, as well as the critical importance of including stories of the enslaved prominently in public history and historical interpretation, followed by a conversation with the H&LS committee chair, Tomiko Brown-Nagin.

This event was presented in collaboration with the Royall House and Slave Quarters, in Medford, Massachusetts.

Lift Ev'ry Voice: Celebrating the Music of Black Americans, April 2022

A discussion and concert by the Aeolians of Oakwood University, Kuumba Singers of Harvard College, and Harvard Choruses. The Aeolians was founded in 1946 by Eva Beatrice Dykes, a professor of English at Oakwood who in 1921 had become the first Black woman to earn a doctoral degree from Radcliffe College (the women's college affiliated with Harvard).

This event was part of the Eileen Southern Initiative, housed in the Harvard University Department of Music.

Inclusions: Envisioning Justice on Harvard's Campus, April 2022

Inclusions—a participatory, student-generated art installation—served as the inspiration for this conversation about the intersection of art, visual culture, and representation at Harvard. Tracy Smith joined the student creators Kiana Rawji '23 and Cecilia Zhou '23 in a discussion focusing on how we can use art to envision justice, moderated by the H&LS committee member Stephen Gray.

This event was presented in partnership with Harvard College student artists, the Office for the Arts at Harvard (OFA), the Harvard John A. Paulson School of Engineering and Applied Sciences, the OFA Ceramics Program, and The Monument Project.

Who Is Policing the Police? April 2022

An exploration of what real police accountability looks like, including perspectives of current and former law enforcement officers, activists, and academics.

This event was presented in partnership with the Harvard Generational African American Students Association.

"Telling the Truth about All This": Reckoning with Slavery and Its Legacies at Harvard and Beyond, April 2022

> "Nations reel and stagger on their way; they make hideous mistakes; they commit frightful wrongs; they do great and beautiful things. And shall we not best guide humanity by telling the truth about all this, so far as the truth is ascertainable?"
>
> —W.E.B. Du Bois, *Black Reconstruction in America, 1860–1880* (1935)

Over the past two decades, universities around the world have begun to engage with their legacies related to slavery. Many have issued reports detailing some of their historical ties to slavery, the substantial financial benefits the institutions and their affiliates extracted from slave economies, and universities' intellectual contributions to racist ideologies and practices. At the same time, this research has uncovered a long history of African American resistance, and we are just beginning to address the impact of legacies of slavery on Black students at these institutions into the twenty-first century.

With this history uncovered, we must now ask: What must institutions of higher education do? What types of repair work can and should we undertake? We will explore these questions in our conference through discussions about a range of topics, including engagement with descendant communities, legacies of slavery in libraries and museums, and novel public engagement and educational opportunities.

NOTES

1: Introduction

1. "Harvard Shields," Harvard University, accessed October 9, 2021, https://www.harvard.edu/about-harvard/harvard-history/harvard-shields/; for an explanation of Harvard's motto and its history, see Corydon Ireland, "Seal of Approval," *Harvard Gazette*, May 14, 2015, https://news.harvard.edu/gazette /story/2015/05/seal-of-approval/.

2. See Section Two of this report; Appendix A lists individuals enslaved by Harvard leadership, faculty, staff, and donors. This list is not comprehensive, as records of enslavement in the colonial era are irregular and the list omits individuals who are likely to have been enslaved but for whom sufficient documentation could not be located. This is an important area for future research.

3. See Sections Three and Four of this report; Emory Junior West, "Harvard and the Black Man, 1636–1850," in *Blacks at Harvard: A Documentary History of African-American Experience At Harvard and Radcliffe*, ed. Werner Sollors et al. (New York, NY: NYU Press, 1993), 435–437; Sven Beckert, Katherine Stevens, and the students of the Harvard and Slavery Research Seminar, *Harvard and Slavery: Seeking a Forgotten History* (Cambridge, MA: Harvard University, 2011), 7–8, 10–12, 19–20, http://www.harvardandslavery.com/wp-content/uploads /2011/11/Harvard-Slavery-Book-111110.pdf; John S. Rosenberg, "Harvard's Slave Connections," News, *Harvard Magazine*, April 6, 2016, https://www .harvardmagazine.com/2016/04/harvard-acknowledges-slave-connections; Stephen Smith and Kate Ellis, "Shackled Legacy: History Shows Slavery Helped Build Many U.S. Colleges and Universities," *APM Reports*, September 4,

2017, https://www.apmreports.org/episode/2017/09/04/shackled-legacy. See also Craig Wilder, *Ebony & Ivy: Race, Slavery, and the Troubled History of American Universities* (New York, NY: Bloomsbury Press, 2013); Leslie M. Harris, James T. Campbell, and Alfred L. Brophy, eds., *Slavery and the University: Histories and Legacies* (Athens, GA: University of Georgia Press, 2019).

4. Brown University, under the leadership of Ruth Simmons, began the effort to uncover ties between the university's founders and slavery. See Brown University, *Slavery and Justice: Report of the Brown University Steering Committee on Slavery and Justice*, 2016, https://slaveryandjustice.brown.edu/sites/g/files/dprerj1501/files/reports/SlaveryAndJustice2006.pdf. See also, for example, Georgetown University, *Report of the Working Group on Slavery, Memory, and Reconciliation to the President of Georgetown University*, June 3, 2016, accessed February 17, 2022, https://www.americamagazine.org/sites/default/files/attachments/working_group_on_slavery_memory_and_reconciliation_final_report.pdf, and University of Virginia, *President's Commission on Slavery and the University*, 2018, https://slavery.virginia.edu/wp-content/uploads/2021/03/PCSU-Report-FINAL_July-2018.pdf.

5. See "Universities Studying Slavery," President's Commission on Slavery and the University, University of Virginia, accessed February 7, 2022, https://slavery.virginia.edu/universities-studying-slavery/. See also Wilder, *Ebony & Ivy* and Harris et al., eds., *Slavery and the University*.

6. See "The History of Harvard," Harvard University, accessed October 15, 2021, https://www.harvard.edu/about-harvard/harvard-history/. For a well-known history of Harvard, written by the University's official historian for the university's Tercentenary, see Samuel Eliot Morison, *Three Centuries of Harvard 1636–1936* (Cambridge, MA: Harvard University, 1936); see also Beckert et al., 7–8, 10–12, 19–20.

7. The admitted class of 2025 at Harvard College was historically diverse. According to the College Admissions website, the class was 15.9% African American, 25.9% Asian American, 12.5% Hispanic / Latino, 1.1% Native American, and 0.5% Native Hawaiian. "Admissions Statistics," Harvard College Admissions & Financial Aid, accessed October 12, 2021, https://college.harvard.edu/admissions/admissions-statistics.

Note that in reporting such statistics and quoting historical sources throughout this report, for the sake of clarity we generally use the terminology of the source document.

8. See Section Five of this report. As early as 1977, under the leadership of President Derek Bok, the University advocated for the use of race-conscious admissions policies to increase diversity at colleges and universities across the

country. The University filed an amicus brief in Regents of the University of California v. Bakke, arguing before the Supreme Court that maintaining a racially diverse student body achieves important educational goals. Brief for Columbia University et al. as Amici Curiae Supporting Petitioner, Regents of the University of California v. Bakke, 438 U.S. 265 (1978) (No. 76-811). The University continues to defend race conscious admissions: As President Lawrence S. Bacow noted in a recent statement, "Considering race as one factor among many in admissions decisions produces a more diverse student body which strengthens the learning environment for all." "SCOTUS Statement from President Bacow," Harvard Admissions Lawsuit, Harvard University, accessed February 7, 2022, https://www.harvard.edu/admissionscase/2022/01 /24/scotus-statement/.

9. See "Presidential Task Force on Inclusion and Belonging," Harvard University, accessed February 7, 2022, https://inclusionandbelongingtaskforce .harvard.edu/. Established by Harvard President Emerita Drew Gilpin Faust, the members of the Task Force were Danielle Allen (co-chair); Archon Fung (co-chair); Meredith Weenick (co-chair); Katrina Armstrong; Ali Asani; Anita Berrizbeitia; Iris Bohnet; Mohan Boodram; Pat Byrne; Elson Callejas; Tez "Bank" Chantaruchirakorn; Eric Chavez; Daniel Cnossen; Andrew Manuel Crespo; Chuck Curti; Tania deLuzuriaga; Alberto de Salvatierra; Erin Driver-Linn; Erika Eitland; Frances Frei; Eden Girma; Marc Goodheart; Annette Gordon-Reed; Kent Haeffner; Natasha Hicks; Elizabeth Hinton; Andrew Ho; Chris Hopson; Kiera Hudson; Bob Iuliano; Vincent James; Jack Jennings; Lisa Kamisher; Jordan Kennedy; Cameron Khansarinia; Stephanie Khurana; Avi Loeb; Diane Lopez; Sophia Lozano; Michael Lynton; Vinny Manoharan; Dave Miller; Anshi Moreno-Jimenez; Tim Murphy; William Oh; Shaiba Rather; Joan Reede; Meredith Rosenthal; Liam Schwartz; Marcia Sells; Edirin Sido; Judy Singer; Jonathan Walton; Sarah Wu; Kenji Yoshino.

10. See "Black Studies at the Crossroads: A Discussion with Henry Louis Gates Jr.," *The Journal of Blacks in Higher Education*, last modified April 20, 2011, https://www.jbhe.com/features/55_gatesinterview.html; Manisha Aggarwal-Schifellite, "African and African American Studies at 50," *Harvard Gazette*, February 26, 2020, https://news.harvard.edu/gazette/story/2020/02/african -and-african-american-studies-at-five-decades/. See also the Department of African and African American Studies at Harvard, accessed February 17, 2022, https://aaas.fas.harvard.edu/home.

11. Audrey M. Apollon and Leah J. Teichholtz, "Harvard University Native American Program Celebrates 50th Anniversary, Plans for the Future," *Harvard Crimson*, March 15, 2021, https://www.thecrimson.com/article/2021/3/15

/hunap-celebrates-50th-anniversary/. See also "Mission," Harvard University Native American Program, accessed February 17, 2022, https://hunap.harvard .edu/mission.

12. See "Initiative on Harvard and the Legacy of Slavery," Office of the President, Harvard University, accessed October 12, 2021, https://www.harvard.edu /president/news/2019/initiative-on-harvard-and-the-legacy-of-slavery/.

13. See Drew G. Faust, "Recognizing Slavery at Harvard," *Harvard Crimson*, March 20, 2016, https://www.thecrimson.com/article/2016/3/30/faust-harvard -slavery/.

14. The members of the committee were: Sven Beckert (co-chair); Evelyn Brooks Higginbotham (co-chair); Alejandro de la Fuente; Annette Gordon-Reed; Evelynn M. Hammonds; and John Stauffer.

15. Titus and Venus were enslaved by Benjamin Wadsworth, President of Harvard University from 1725 to 1737. Juba and Bilhah were enslaved by Edward Holyoke, President of Harvard from 1737 to 1769. See Christina Pazzanese, "To Titus, Venus, Bilhah, and Juba," *Harvard Gazette*, April 6, 2016, https://news.harvard.edu/gazette/story/2016/04/to-titus-venus-bilhah-and -juba/. Titus, Venus, Juba, and Bilhah, along with many of the individuals discussed here, were brought to light in Beckert et al., *Harvard and Slavery*, and by Caitlin Galante DeAngelis, Harvard and Slavery Research Associate, 2017–2019.

Note that all pre-1752 dates have been updated to the New Style system following the Gregorian calendar, in which the calendar year runs from January 1 to December 31. See "The 1752 Calendar Change," Colonial Records & Topics, Connecticut State Library, accessed February 17, 2022, https:// libguides.ctstatelibrary.org/hg/colonialresearch/calendar.

16. See Lydia Lyle Gibson, "A Vast Slave Society," Research, *Harvard Magazine*, March 6, 2017, https://www.harvardmagazine.com/2017/03/a-vast-slave -society; Claire E. Parker, "Conference Encourages Reparations for Harvard's Ties to Slavery," *Harvard Crimson*, March 5, 2017, https://www.thecrimson .com/article/2017/3/5/conference-encourages-slavery-reparations/.

17. See Samuel Eliot Morison, *The Founding of Harvard College* (Cambridge, MA: Harvard University, 1935), 232–233, 425; "The History of Harvard," Harvard University; Conrad Edick Wright, *Revolutionary Generation: Harvard Men and the Consequences of Independence* (Amherst, MA: University of Massachusetts Press in association with Massachusetts Historical Society, 2005), and Bernard Bailyn et al., *Glimpses of the Harvard Past* (Cambridge, MA: Harvard University Press, 1986).

18. Beckert et al., *Harvard and Slavery.*

19. Janet Halley, "My Isaac Royall Legacy," *Harvard BlackLetter Law Journal* 24 (2008), http://www.law.harvard.edu/faculty/jhalley/cv/24.Harvard.Black letter.117.pdf. On the Royalls, see also Alexandra A. Chan, *Slavery in the Age of Reason: Archeology at a New England Farm* (Knoxville, TN: University of Tennessee Press, 2007); C. S. Manegold, "The Master," part 3 in *Ten Hills Farm: The Forgotten History of Slavery in the North* (Princeton, NJ: Princeton University Press, 2010); and Daniel R. Coquillette and Bruce A. Kimball, *On the Battlefield of Merit: Harvard Law School, the First Century* (Cambridge, MA: Harvard University Press, 2015), 75, 81–88.

20. See "Royall Must Fall: The Shield is Retired," Exhibit Addenda, Harvard Law School, accessed February 9, 2022, https://exhibits.law.harvard.edu/royall -must-fall-shield-retired. Isaac Royall, Jr. (1719–1781) lived just over three miles from Harvard Yard. The Royall House and Slave Quarters, where the Royalls enslaved more than sixty people and lived off of the wealth generated by yet more enslaved people who labored on the family's sugar plantation in Antigua, has been a historic site for over a century. Since 2005, the Royall House and Slave Quarters has reoriented its programming to focus on educating the public about the lives of the people enslaved there and, more broadly, the history of slavery in New England. See The Royall House & Slave Quarters, accessed October 12, 2021, https://royallhouse.org/.

21. The members of Harvard Law School's 2016 shield committee were: Bruce H. Mann (chair); Mawuse Oliver Barker-Vormawor; James E. Bowers; Tomiko Brown-Nagin; Annette Gordon-Reed; Janet Halley; Rena Karefa-Johnson; Robert J. Katz; Samuel Moyn; S. Darrick Northington; Annie Rittgers; and Yih-hsien Shen. See Harvard Law School, *Recommendation to the President and Fellows of Harvard College on the Shield Approved for the Law School*, March 2016, https://today.law.harvard.edu/wp-content/uploads/2016 /03/Shield-Committee-Report.pdf, and Annette Gordon-Reed, *A Different View*, March 2016, https://today.law.harvard.edu/wp-content/uploads/2016/03 /Shield_Committee-Different_View.pdf. The law school recently unveiled a new shield, which makes clear that "Harvard Law School stands for truth, law, and justice," see "The Harvard Law School Shield," Harvard Law School, accessed February 17, 2022, https://hls.harvard.edu/about/the-harvard-law -school-shield/.

22. Brigit Katz, "Harvard Law School Marks Ties to Slavery in New Plaque," Smart News, *Smithsonian Magazine*, September 6, 2017, https://www .smithsonianmag.com/smart-news/harvard-law-school-marks-ties-slavery -new-plaque-180964784/.

23. See Section Four of this report.

24. The members of the sub-committee were: Nawal Nour (co-chair); Fidencio Saldaña (co-chair); M. William Lensch (organizer and member); Jalen Benson; Terésa Carter; Anthony D'Amico; Marcela del Carmen; Emily Gustainis; Dominic Hall; Beth MacGillivray; Stephen Maiorisi; Alisha Nanji; Jane Neill; LaShyra Nolen; Scott Podolsky; Joan Reede; Tania Rodriguez; Raquel Sofia Sandoval; Joanna Swift; and Alana Van Dervort. See M.R.F. Buckley, "Winds of Change: Holmes Academic Society Renamed in Honor of Physician-Scientist William Augustus Hinton," *Harvard Gazette*, September 23, 2020, https://news.harvard.edu/gazette/story/2020/09/harvard -medical-schools-holmes-academic-society-renamed/. See also "Guiding Principles for Artwork and Cultural Representations," Harvard Medical School, accessed February 17, 2022, https://hms.harvard.edu/about-hms /campus-culture/diversity-inclusion/guiding-principles-artwork-cultural -representations.

25. See, for example, Colleen Walsh, "Initiative on Legacy of Slavery at Harvard Picks Up Steam," *Harvard Gazette*, October 15, 2020, https://news.harvard .edu/gazette/story/2020/10/radcliffe-based-program-rolls-out-research -efforts/; Colleen Walsh, "A Poem for Venus," *Harvard Gazette*, April 15, 2021, https://news.harvard.edu/gazette/story/2021/04/student-poem-gives-voice -to-enslaved-woman-on-campus-in-18th-century/. See also Appendix A.

26. See, for example, Margaret Ellen Newell, *Brethren by Nature: New England Indians, Colonists, and the Origins of American Slavery* (Ithaca, NY: Cornell University Press, 2015), 4: "historians have produced almost as many books about New England as there were English colonial residents, as Edmund Morgan famously joked. They have reconstructed the compelling narrative of the Puritan migration, the complexity of the English immigrants' rich religious and intellectual life, and the intricacies of the society and innovative economy they helped create. Many of these works stressed the uniqueness of New England culture and sought there the origins of American exceptionalism. With a few notable exceptions, though, the history of slavery in general and of Indian slavery in particular remains stubbornly absent from these narratives."

27. On the region's history, see Mark Peterson, *The City-State of Boston: The Rise and Fall of An Atlantic Power, 163–1865* (Princeton, NJ: Princeton University Press, 2019).

28. Newell, *Brethren by Nature*; Peterson, *City-State of Boston*, 49–52; Jill Lepore, *In the Name of War: King Philip's War and the Origins of American Identity* (New York, NY: Vintage, 1998), xii–xiii, 174–177.

29. Peterson, *City-State of Boston*, 19.

30. Wendy Warren, "The Key of the Indies," chap. 2 in *New England Bound: Slavery and Colonization in Early America* (New York, NY: Liveright, 2016).

31. Peterson, *City-State of Boston*, 19.

32. Warren, *New England Bound*, 45–46. Warren notes that there are many more documented direct voyages between New England and the Caribbean, although their cargoes are not well documented. Any slave-trading activities on the part of New Englanders amounted to smuggling, because the Royal African Company had been granted a monopoly on the English slave trade, and so authorities in New England had a vested interest in hiding such activities—and their profits—from the English government. See Warren, "Unplanting and Replanting," chap. 3 in *New England Bound*.

33. Warren, *New England Bound*, 35; see also Thomas G. Barnes, *The book of the general lawes and libertyes concerning the inhabitants of the Massachusets: Reproduced in facsimile from the unique 1648 edition in the Huntington Library* (San Marino, CA: Huntington Library, 1975).

Newell argues that the regulation of slavery in the Body of Liberties was meant largely to define the legal status of Native people captured during the Pequot War in the late 1630s. She further notes that, when Native peoples were granted certain rights of citizenship after their defeat in King Philip's war, colonial courts used laws such as the Body of Liberties to enslave them through "the sentencing of Indians to terms of servitude and even slavery as punishment for crime and debt." See *Brethren by Nature*, 6, 11, 53–58, and "To be sold 'in any part of ye kings Dominyons': Judicial Enslavement of New England Indians," chap. 9.

34. See Section Two of this report and Appendix A. See also Beckert et al., *Harvard and Slavery*, 8–9.

Newell acknowledges that "[n]umerous historians have argued that slavery was more of an ornamental or status institution in the North rather than an economic investment, but others have marshaled persuasive evidence to the contrary," *Brethren by Nature*, see 171–172, quote on 287 n. 37, citing Robert E. Desrochers Jr., "Slave-for-Sale Advertisements and Slavery in Massachusetts, *The William and Mary Quarterly* 59, no. 3 (July 2002); Lorenzo Johnston Greene, *The Negro in Colonial New England, 1620–1776* (New York, NY: Columbia University Press; P. S. King & Staples, ltd., 1942), 123; Joanne Pope Melish, *Disowning Slavery: Gradual Emancipation and "Race" in New England, 1780–1860* (Ithaca, NY: Cornell University Press, 1998), 1618–1620; and Rachel Chernos-Lin, "The Rhode Island Slave-Traders: Butchers, Bakers and Candlestick Makers," *Slavery and Abolition* 23, no. 3 (September 2002): 21–38. See also Warren, "Visible Slaves," chap. 4 in *New England Bound*.

35. See Section Three of this report.

36. The quote is from Eric Kimball, "'What have we to do with slavery?' New Englanders and the Slave Economies of the West Indies," chap. 8 in *Slavery's Capitalism: A New History of American Economic Development*, ed. Sven Beckert and Seth Rockman (Philadelphia, PA: University of Pennsylvania Press, 2016). For more, see Sven Beckert, *Empire of Cotton: A Global History* (New York, NY: Alfred A. Knopf, 2014).

37. For sources discussing Harvard's accumulation of wealth vis-a-vis slavery, see Beckert et al., *Harvard and Slavery*, 11–12.

38. For scholarship discussing the many laws, policies, practices, norms, and attitudes that remained as relics of slavery despite its legal prohibition, see generally Leon F. Litwack, *Been in the Storm So Long: The Aftermath of Slavery* (New York, NY: Knopf, 1979); Tera W. Hunter, *To 'Joy My Freedom: Southern Black Women's Lives and Labors after the Civil War* (Cambridge, MA: Harvard University Press, 1997); Kate Masur, *An Example for All the Land: Emancipation and the Struggle over Equality in Washington, DC* (Chapel Hill, NC: University of North Carolina Press, 2010), 214–256; Eric Foner, *Forever Free: The Story of Emancipation and Reconstruction* (New York, NY: Knopf, 2005), 189–213; John Hope Franklin, *Reconstruction: after the Civil War* (Chicago, IL: University of Chicago Press, 1961); Ariela J. Gross, *What Blood Won't Tell: A History of Race on Trial in America* (Cambridge, MA: Harvard University Press, 2008), 4–5, 9–11, 70–110.

39. See generally Donald M. Jacobs, ed., *Courage and Conscience: Black and White Abolitionists in Boston* (Bloomington, IN: Indiana University Press, 1993); Manisha Sinha, *The Slave's Cause: A History of Abolitionism* (New Haven: Yale University Press, 2016), 41–42, 67–72, 454. These anti-slavery activists, however, encountered significant resistance. See Josh S. Cutler, *The Boston Gentleman's Mob: Maria Chapman and the Antislavery Riot of 1835* (Charleston, SC: The History Press, 2021). This history is sometimes forgotten. On the complex association between historical memory in discussions of slavery and antislavery see Margot Minardi, *Making Slavery History: Abolitionism and the Politics of Memory in Massachusetts* (New York, NY: Oxford University Press, 2012), and Ana Lucia Araujo, *Slavery in the Age of Memory: Engaging the Past* (New York, NY: Bloomsbury Publishing, 2020).

40. Joseph Marr Cronin, *Reforming Boston's Schools, 1930 to the Present: Overcoming Corruption and Racial Segregation* (New York, NY: Palgrave Macmillan, 2008), 5, 25–26; Eric Foner, *Reconstruction: America's Unfinished Revolution,*

1863–1877 (New York, NY: Harper & Row, 1988), 26; Kazuteru Omori, "Race-Neutral Individualism and Resurgence of the Color Line: Massachusetts Civil Rights Legislation, 1855–1895," *Journal of American Ethnic History* 22, no. 1 (2002): 32–58; Janette Thomas Greenwood, "A Community within a Community," in *First Fruits of Freedom: The Migration of Former Slaves and Their Search for Equality in Worcester, Massachusetts, 1862–1900* (Chapel Hill, NC: University of North Carolina Press, 2010), 131–173; Tony Hill, "Ethnicity and Education," Boston Review, July 23, 2014, https://bostonreview.net/us/tony-hill-ethnicity-and-education.

41. Sollors et al., eds., *Blacks at Harvard*, xix, 3, 22; Ronald Takaki, "Aesculapius Was a White Man: Antebellum Racism and Male Chauvinism at Harvard Medical School," *Phylon* 32, no. 2 (1978): 128–134; Doris Y. Wilkinson, "The 1850 Harvard Medical School dispute and the admission of African American students," *Harvard Library Bulletin* 3, no. 3 (Fall 1992): 13–27; see also Nora N. Nercessian, *Against All Odds: The Legacy of Students of African Descent at Harvard Medical School before Affirmative Action, 1850–1968* (Hollis, NH: Puritan Press, 2004).

42. Wilkinson, "1850 Harvard Medical School," 14, 16.

43. See Carla Bosco, "Harvard University and the Fugitive Slave Act," *New England Quarterly: A Historical Review of New England Life and Letters* 79, no. 2 (2006): 227–247.

44. Bosco, "Fugitive Slave Act," 229–230, 239. See Section Four of this report.

45. Bosco, "Fugitive Slave Act," 242–243.

46. The names of Harvard men who died in service to the Union are displayed in Memorial Hall. See Morison, *Three Centuries of Harvard*, 302–303.

47. See Section Four of this report.

48. Adam S. Cohen, "Harvard's Eugenics Era," Features, *Harvard Magazine*, March–April 2016, https://www.harvardmagazine.com/2016/03/harvards-eugenics-era.

49. Charles Patton Blacker, *Eugenics: Galton and After* (Cambridge, MA: Harvard University Press, 1952). On eugenics and Nazi Germany's extermination campaigns, see Morton A. Aldrich et al., *Eugenics: Twelve University Lectures* (New York, NY: Dodd, Mead and Company, 1914).

50. See Section Five of this report.

51. Because of universities' unique role as sites of research and education, the idea of intellectual leadership as a category of entanglement and a form of

culpability with slavery is particularly important. Yet it is also a complicated matter: Many universities rightly prize intellectual freedom, and therefore strive not to proscribe or circumscribe the intellectual output of their faculty. Harvard is no exception in this regard, and the discussion of past wrongs is not a departure from this core institutional value. It affirms academic freedom: As this report documents, rather than upholding the principle of academic freedom and the pursuit of *Veritas*, the University, on several occasions, sought to moderate or suppress anti-slavery views within the community.

Moreover, the committee does not propose a retrospective evaluation of all the ideas that have emerged from Harvard and may have caused harm. Rather, this report describes specific actions and ideas advanced by Harvard faculty and leaders with the University's institutional backing—actions and ideas that caused enduring harm, and which we, as a University community, must no longer honor.

52. See U.S. Const. amends. XIII, XIV, XV; see also Eric Foner, "What is Freedom? The Thirteenth Amendment," chap. 1, "Toward Equality: The Fourteenth Amendment," chap. 2, and "The Right to Vote: The Fifteenth Amendment," chap. 3 in *The Second Founding: How the Civil War and Reconstruction Remade the Constitution* (New York, NY: W.W. Norton & Company, 2019).

53. On the white vigilante violence that followed formerly enslaved Blacks when they tried to exercise their newly found freedom, see Foner, *Reconstruction* 119–123, 425–430. W. E. B. Du Bois, *Black Reconstruction in America: An Essay Toward a History of the Part Which Black Folk Played in the Attempt to Reconstruct Democracy in America, 1860–1880* (New York, NY: Russell & Russell, 1935), 221–230, describes, for example, the insufficient resources given to the Freedmen's Bureau, a federal agency design to aid the formerly enslaved in the South, as the result of political pushback from Southern whites.

54. Morison, *Three Centuries of Harvard*, 323.

55. This language is drawn from an address by Charles William Eliot, president of Harvard from 1869–1909, quoted in Morison, *Three Centuries of Harvard*, 322.

56. Morison, *Three Centuries of Harvard*, 322. On the Overseers' aspirations for Harvard during this period, see also ibid., 324–331.

57. Bobby L. Lovett, *America's Historically Black Colleges and Universities: A Narrative History, 1837–2009* (Macon, GA: Mercer University Press, 2011), 5.

58. Wayne J. Urban and Jennings L. Wagoner, Jr., *American Education: A History* (New York, NY: Routledge, 2009), 116–127. On higher education in the

Commonwealth, see George Gary Bush, *History of Higher Education in Massachusetts* (Washington, DC: G.P.O., 1891).

59. See Lovett, *Black Colleges and Universities*, 4–5; Urban and Wagoner, Jr., *American Education*, 167–168.

60. Roberts v. City of Boston, 59 Mass. 198, 5 Cush. 198 (1849). See David Herbert Donald, *Charles Sumner and the Coming of the Civil War* (Naperville, IL: Sourcebooks, Inc., 2009), 151. Sumner asserted: "The separation of the schools, so far from being for the benefit of both races, is an injury to both." See also *Roberts*, 59 Mass. at 204.

61. "Lemuel Shaw," Commonwealth of Massachusetts, accessed February 17, 2022, https://www.mass.gov/person/lemuel-shaw-0; *Roberts*, 59 Mass. at 209 (1850).

62. See Carleton Mabee, "A Negro Boycott to Integrate Boston Schools," *New England Quarterly* 41, no. 3 (September 1968): 341–361.

63. Plessy v. Ferguson, 163 U.S. 544 (1896) (Harlan, J., dissenting) coined the oft-quoted phrase "separate but equal"; see also *Plessy,* 544–545 (discussing *Roberts*); Douglas J. Ficker, "From *Roberts* to *Plessy*: Education Segregation and the 'Separate But Equal' Doctrine," *The Journal of African American History* 84, no. 4 (1999): 301–314. Even philanthropists who aided schools supported the practice of racial segregation and systematically provided less funding to southern Black schools. See Urban and Wagoner Jr., *American Education*, 166–171.

64. For a discussion on racial segregation in elementary and secondary education, see Urban and Wagoner, Jr., *American Education*, 165–168; for HBCUs, see generally Lovett, *Black Colleges and Universities*.

65. See Lovett, *Black Colleges and Universities*, xii–xiii; James D. Anderson, *Education of Blacks in the South, 1860–1935* (Chapel Hill, NC: University of North Carolina Press, 1988), 239, 248–249; Walter R. Allen et al., "Historically Black Colleges and Universities: Honoring the Past, Engaging the Present, Touching the Future," *The Journal of Negro Education* 76, no. 3 (2007): 263, 267.

66. There was little support for mixed schools anywhere in the North. See Urban and Wagoner, Jr., *American Education*, 165; Sollors et al., eds., *Blacks at Harvard*, 1–4; West, "Harvard and the Black Man."

67. Marcia Graham Synnott, *The Half-Opened Door: Discrimination and Admissions at Harvard, Yale, and Princeton, 1900–1970* (New York, NY: Routledge, 2010), 38; Jerome Karabel, *The Chosen: The Hidden History of Admission and Exclusion at Harvard, Yale and Princeton* (New York, NY: Houghton

Mifflin Harcourt, 2005), 39–41 and chap. 3, "Harvard and the Battle over Restriction."

68. Synnott, *The Half-Opened Door*, 38, 40, 47, 207–208, 220; Sollors et al., eds., *Blacks at Harvard*, 2–3.

69. Synnott, *The Half-Opened Door*, 47.

70. See Muriel Spence, "Minority Women at Radcliffe: Talent, Character, and Endurance," *Radcliffe Quarterly* 72, no. 3 (September 1986): 20–22, https://nrs.harvard.edu/urn-3:RAD.ARCH:4609952?n=130.

71. Morison, *Three Centuries of Harvard*, 391–392.

72. Linda M. Perkins, "The African American Female Elite: The Early History of African American Women in the Seven Sister Colleges, 1880–1960," *Harvard Educational Review* 67, no. 4 (December 1997): 726–729. Like the history of women at Harvard generally, the history of women of color at Harvard and Radcliffe has seldom been a subject of description or analysis. See Laurel Thatcher Ulrich, ed., *Yards and Gates: Gender in Harvard and Radcliffe History* (New York, NY: Palgrave, 2004), and Laurel Thatcher Ulrich, "Harvard's Womanless History: Completing the University's Self-Portrait," Features, *Harvard Magazine*, December 18, 2018, https://www.harvardmagazine.com/2018/12/harvards-womanless-history.

73. See Perkins, "African American Female Elite," 729; Morison, *Three Centuries of Harvard*, 392. The pattern of limited Black enrollment at Harvard and Radcliffe persisted into the mid-1960s. See Section Five of this report.

74. Synnott, *The Half-Opened Door*, 47.

75. Sollors et al., eds., *Blacks at Harvard*, xxi–xxiii; Perkins, "African American Female Elite," 728–729.

76. See Nell I. Painter, "Jim Crow at Harvard: 1923," *The New England Quarterly* 44, no. 4 (1971): 627–634; Sollors et al., eds., *Blacks at Harvard*, xxi–xxiii; Synnott, *The Half-Opened Door*, 49–50. For more on this controversy during the Lowell presidency, see Section Five of this report.

77. Raymond Wolters, "The New Negro on Campus," in *Blacks at Harvard*, 195–202. See also "Attacks Harvard On Negro Question: J. Weldon Johnson Denounces the Exclusion of Negroes From Its Dormitories," *New York Times*, January 13, 1923, https://nyti.ms/3nJaq96.

78. Synnott, *The Half-Opened Door*, 48–49.

79. Synnott, *The Half-Opened Door*, 47; on his exclusion from the glee club and social marginalization, see W. E. B. Du Bois, "A Negro Student at Har-

vard at the End of the 19th Century," *Massachusetts Review* 1, no. 5 (May 1960): 439–458.

80. See Section Four of this report.

81. Richard Norton Smith, *The Harvard Century: The Making of a University to a Nation* (New York, NY: Simon & Schuster, 1986), 13.

82. See Beckert et al., *Harvard and Slavery*, 9–10.

83. See, for example, W. E. B. Du Bois, *The Souls of Black Folk* (New Haven, CT: Yale University Press, 2015); W. E. B. Du Bois, *The Problem of the Color Line at the Turn of the Twentieth Century: The Essential Early Essays* (New York, NY: Fordham Scholarship Online, 2015); W. E. B. Du Bois, *The Negro* (Philadelphia, PA: University of Pennsylvania Press, 2014); see generally David Levering Lewis, *W. E. B. Du Bois, 1868–1919: Biography of a Race* (New York, NY: H. Holt, 1993) and *W. E. B. Du Bois: The Fight for Equality and the American Century, 1919–1963* (New York, NY: Holt and Company, 2000).

84. See Patricia Sullivan, *Lift Every Voice: The NAACP and the Making of the Civil Rights Movement* (New York, NY: The New Press, 2010); see also Kerri K. Greenidge, *Black Radical: The Life and Times of William Monroe Trotter* (New York, NY: Liveright Publishing Corporation, 2020).

85. Although formally vice-dean, Houston "had the responsibilities of a dean" and was Howard Law School's "dean in all but title," according to a Howard University profile. See Steven D. Jamar, "Charles Hamilton Houston (1895–1950)," Brown@50, Howard University School of Law, accessed February 17, 2022, http://law.howard.edu/brownat50/BrownBios/BioCharlesHHouston .html.

86. See Genna Rae McNeil, *Groundwork: Charles Hamilton Houston and the Struggle for Civil Rights* (Philadelphia, PA: University of Pennsylvania Press, 1984).

87. Sollors et al., eds., *Blacks at Harvard*, 3

88. On the history of Radcliffe College, see "History," Harvard Radcliffe Institute, accessed November 5, 2021, https://www.radcliffe.harvard.edu/about -the-institute/history; see also Sally Schwager, "Taking up the challenge: the origins of Radcliffe," in Ulrich, *Yards and Gates,* 87–116.

89. For a detailed biography see "Eva Dykes, Transcript," Harvard Radcliffe Institute, i–iii. Dykes was also profiled in Sollors et al., *Blacks at Harvard*, 160–167.

90. For example, Harvard Law Professor Felix Frankfurter, a Jewish immigrant to the United States from Austria, who went on to become Associate

Justice of the U.S. Supreme Court, mentored Houston. See McNeil, *Groundwork*, 53, 63–64. Du Bois counted William James and Albert Bushnell Hart as mentors. See Sollors et al., eds., *Blacks at Harvard*, xx, 5.

91.   Richard Kluger, *Simple Justice: The History of Brown v. Board of Education and Black America's Struggle for Equality* (New York, NY: Vintage, 2004), 713.

92.   William T. Martin Riches, *The Civil Rights Movement: Struggle and Resistance* (New York, NY: Red Globe Press, 2017).

93.   Drew Gilpin Faust, Harvard President Emerita, chaired the Committee to Articulate Principles on Renaming that produced principles and guidelines on renaming, see "Report of the Committee to Articulate Principles on Renaming," accessed March 4, 2022, https://www.harvard.edu/president/wp -content/uploads/sites/2/2021/12/Committee-to-Articulate-Principles-on -Renaming-Final-Report1.pdf. In recent years, Harvard community members have raised objections to certain individuals honored on campus. See Andrew M. Duehren and Daphne C. Thompson, "In Debate Over Names, History and Race Relations Collide," *Harvard Crimson*, January 19, 2016, https://www.thecrimson.com/article/2016/1/19/faust-name-title-changes-/; Sydnie M. Cobb, "Harvard Affiliates Petition to Rename Mather House Due to Slaveholding Namesake," *Harvard Crimson*, June 16, 2020, https://www .thecrimson.com/article/2020/6/16/mather-name-change-petition/; John S. Rosenberg, "Lowell, Not Coming to Dinner," News, *Harvard Magazine*, March 27, 2019, https://www.harvardmagazine.com/2019/03/harvard-lowell -house-changes-portraits-display. The question extends beyond Harvard. Many of the names cited in this report also are memorialized at locations in Boston, Cambridge, and beyond because of these individuals' generous support of educational, civic, and cultural organizations.

94.   "Steering Committee on Human Remains in Harvard Museum Collections," Office of the President, Harvard University, accessed October 13, 2021, https://www.harvard.edu/president/news/2021/steering-committee-on -human-remains-in-harvard-museum-collections/. The charge states: "Our University is home to some of the most extraordinary scholarly resources in the world, including museum collections comprising some 30 million artifacts, objects, and specimens. Among these are the remains of more than 22,000 individuals, most of them held by either the Peabody Museum of Archaeology and Ethnology or the Warren Anatomical Museum. It is a staggering figure—made even more so because of its imprecision. We know much about some of these individuals because they were accompanied by detailed records of their unique experiences, but others were afforded no biographical

information. . . . Earlier this year, the Peabody undertook a review of its collections as part of an assessment of its ethical stewardship practices and in the spirit of continuing efforts to understand the legacy of slavery at Harvard. As a result, I was informed of the remains of fifteen individuals of African descent who were or were likely to have been alive during the period of American enslavement."

2: Slavery in New England and at Harvard

1.   Some Black scholars were making this argument already in the 1930s and 1940s. See Greene, *Negro in Colonial New England,* 68–69.

2.   Peterson, *City-State of Boston,* 19.

3.   Warren, "The Key of the Indies," chap. 2, and "Unplanting and Replanting," chap. 3 in *New England Bound.*

4.   Peterson, *City-State of Boston,* 19.

5.   Warren, *New England Bound,* 45–46. Warren notes that there are many more direct voyages between New England and the Caribbean, although their cargoes are not well documented. Any slave-trading activities on the part of New Englanders amounted to smuggling, because the Royal African Company had been granted a monopoly on the English slave trade, and so authorities in New England had a vested interest in hiding such activities—and their profits—from the English government. For a full discussion, see "Unplanting and Replanting," chap. 3 in *New England Bound.*

6.   Warren, *New England Bound,* 35; see also Barnes, *Book of the general lawes and libertyes.*

7.   "Throughout New England before 1700, and in subregions thereafter, Native Americans represented the dominant form of nonwhite labor," Newell, *Brethren by Nature,* 5. See also Warren, *New England Bound* and Jared Ross Hardesty, *Black Lives, Native Lands, White Worlds: A History of Slavery in New England* (Amherst and Boston: Bright Leaf, An Imprint of University of Massachusetts Press, 2019).

8.   The enslavement of the Pequots was the first large-scale, institutionalized distribution of people as property in the British North American colonies. See Newell, "'David's warre': The Pequot War and the Origins of Slavery," chap. 1 in *Brethren by Nature.*

Due to a navigational error the Pequot prisoners of war were in fact sold in the Puritan colony of Providence Island. They did not arrive in Bermuda until 1640. See Newell, *Brethren by Nature,* 50–51; Ethel Boissevain, "Whatever Became of the New England Indians Shipped to Bermuda to be Sold as

Slaves?" *Man in the Northeast* 21 (1981): 103–114; F. Van Wyck Mason, "Bermuda's Pequots," *Harvard Alumni Bulletin* 39 (February 26, 1937): 616–620; Karen Ordahl Kupperman, *Providence Island, 1630–1641: The Other Puritan Colony* (Cambridge, UK: Cambridge University Press, 1993).

9.   John Langdon Sibley, *Biographical sketches of graduates of Harvard University in Cambridge, Massachusetts, Volume I, 1642–1658* (Cambridge, MA: Charles William Sever, University Bookstore, 1873), 1–7, https://books.google.com/books?id=SRZSAQAAMAAJ.

10.   Newell, *Brethren by Nature*, 40–41, 79; Manegold, *Ten Hills Farm*, 42; Francis J. Bremer, *John Winthrop: America's Forgotten Founding Father* (New York: Oxford University Press, 2003), 273. See also John Winthrop to William Bradford, Winthrop Family Papers, Massachusetts Historical Society, accessed August 27, 2021, https://www.masshist.org/publications/winthrop/index.php/view/PWF03d358.

11.   George Francis Dow, *Slave Ships and Slaving* (Reprint, New York, NY: Dover Publications 2002), 267; George Henry Preble, "Notes on Early Ship-Building in Massachusetts," *The New-England Historical and Genealogical Register and Antiquarian Journal* 25, no. 1 (1871): 17; James Kendall Hosmer, ed., *Winthrop's Journal: History of New England, 1630–1649*, vol. 1, (New York, NY: Charles Scribner's Sons, 1908), 260, https://books.google.com/books?id=Iwo6FnGALocC.

12.   On Eaton's tenure as schoolmaster, see Morison, *Three Centuries of Harvard*, 7–10. See also Susan E. Maycock and Charles M. Sullivan, *Building Old Cambridge: Architecture and Development* (Cambridge, MA: MIT Press, 2016), 8; Margery Somers Foster, *Out of Smalle Beginnings: An Economic History of Harvard College in the Puritan Period (1636 to 1712)* (Boston, MA: Belknap Press of Harvard University Press, 1962), 5–6. On "the Moor," see John Winthrop, *The History of New England from 1630 to 1649*, vol. 1, ed. James Savage (Boston, MA: Little, Brown, 1853), 372–375, https://books.google.com/books?id=KIarrcIX7QAC. Winthrop's description of the Moor was reprinted in Sibley, *Biographical sketches of graduates*, 5.

13.   Patrick Copeland to John Winthrop, December 4, 1639, Papers of the Winthrop Family, vol. 4, Massachusetts Historical Society.

14.   John Irwin Cooper, "The West Indies, Bermuda and American Mainland Colleges," *Jamaican Historical Review* 2, no. 1 (December 1, 1949): 2.

15.   Records of the Governor and Company of the Massachusetts Bay in New England, vol. 4, pt. 1, *Records, 1650–1660* (Boston, MA: William White, 1854), 136, accessed February 4, 2022, https://books.google.com/books?id=XG9OAQAAMAAJ.

16. Robin Stephen McMahon, "Contested Boundaries: The Harvard Land Grants as an Archetype for Intercolonial Competition for Land," *Connecticut History Review* 56, no. 2 (Fall 2017): 203–209.

17. *Charter of 1650,* Harvard University Archives, https://iiif.lib.harvard.edu /manifests/view/ids:6597921$1i. For a transcription, see "Harvard Charter of 1650," Harvard Library, Harvard University, accessed February 4, 2022, https:// guides.library.harvard.edu/c.php?g=880222&p=6323072; Foster, *Smalle Beginnings,* 2.

18. Lisa Brooks, *Our Beloved Kin: A New History of King Philip's War* (New Haven, CT: Yale University Press, 2018), 81–82, 97–99; Foster, *Smalle Beginnings,* 107–109, 117–118.

19. *Charter of 1650,* Harvard University Archives.

20. Brooks, *Our Beloved Kin,* 102–106. See also "Digging Veritas—The Indian College," Peabody Museum of Archaeology & Ethnology, Harvard University, accessed January 25, 2022, https://peabody.harvard.edu/galleries /digging-veritas-indian-college.

21. "A Degree Delivered: Harvard honors Native American who completed course work in 1665," *Harvard Gazette,* May 26, 2011, https://news.harvard .edu/gazette/story/2011/05/a-degree-delivered/.

22. Maycock and Sullivan, *Building Old Cambridge,* 755.

23. Du Bois, *Black Reconstruction,* 7.

24. United States Bureau of the Census, *A century of population growth from the first census of the United States to the twelfth, 1790–1900* (Baltimore, MD: Genealogical Publishing Company, 1969), 5, https://www2.census.gov/library /publications/decennial/1900/century-of-growth/1790-1900-century-of -growth-part-1.pdf.

25. White indentured servants in the New England colonies faced harsher conditions than those in England, but in general could count on masters to honor the agreed upon duration of their indenture and release them at the end of their terms. For Native people, however, masters routinely ignored terms of indenture and held servants for life—sometimes forcing their children into servitude as well—effectively rendering them enslaved in practice regardless of whether the law allowed it or not. See Newell, 12–15, "'As good if not better then the Moorish Slaves': Law, Slavery, and the Second Native Diaspora," chap. 7, and "To be sold 'in any part of ye kings Dominyons': Judicial Enslavement of New England Indians," chap. 9 in *Brethren by Nature.*

26. *Edward Randolph: including his letters and official papers from the New England, middle, and southern colonies in America, with other documents relating*

chiefly to the vacating of the royal charter of the colony of Massachusetts Bay, 1676–1703, with historical illustrations and a memoir by Robert Noxon Toppan, 5 vols. (Boston, MA: The Prince Society, 1898), 2:236, https://books.google.com /books?id=iaAUAAAAYAAJ.

27. *Collections of the Massachusetts Historical Society,* 3rd ser., vol. 8 (Boston, MA: Charles C. Little and James Brown, 1843), 337, https://archive.org/details /s3collections07massuoft/page/304/mode/2up?view=theater, quoted in George Henry Moore, *Notes on the history of slavery in Massachusetts* (New York, NY: D. Appleton & Co., 1866), 49, https://books.google.com/books?id=ohsEAA AAYAAJ. Brackets in original.

28. The monopoly's revocation allowed the colonists to legally enter the African slave trade. Prior to this change they had relied on New England traders who enslaved people off the eastern coast of Africa and smuggled them into the colonies—a much longer though altogether less perilous journey. See "An Act to Settle the Trade to Africa," July 5, 1698, in *Documents Illustrative of the History of the Slave Trade to America,* 4 vols., ed. Elizabeth Donnan (Washington, DC: Carnegie Institution of Washington, 1930), 1:421–429.

29. W. E. B. Du Bois, *The Suppression of the African Slave Trade to the United States of America, 1638–1870* (New York, NY: Longmans, Green, and Co., 1896), 31, https://books.google.com/books?id=fUgXAAAAYAAJ.

30. Warren, "The Selling of Adam," chap. 7 in *New England Bound.*

31. The import duties were part of a clause attached to a law prohibiting interracial sexual relations. See "An Act for the Better Preventing of a Spurious and Mixt Issue, 1705" in ed. Donnan, *Slave Trade to America,* 3:20.

32. "An Act to Encourage the Importation of White Servants, 1709," in *The acts and resolves, public and private, of the province of the Massachusetts bay: to which are prefixed the charters of the province. With historical and explanatory notes, and an appendix. Published under chapter 87 of the Resolves of the General court of the commonwealth for the year 1867,* vol. 1 (Boston, MA: Wright & Potter, printers to the state, 1869–1922), 634, https://books.google.com/books ?id=fQZHAQAAIAAJ.

33. For 1708 figures, see Moore, *History of Slavery,* 49. For 1720 figures, see "An Answer to the First Query Propos'd by the Right Honorable the Lords of Trade &c Referring to the Province of the Massachusetts Bay," in James Phinney Baxter, ed., *History of the State of Maine Containing the Baxter Manuscripts,* 24 vols. (Portland, ME: Lefavor-Tower Company, 1907), 10:106–107, https://archive.org/details/baxtermanuscript02lcbaxt/page/n7/mode/2up.

    "Though enslaved people never made up more than 5 or 10 percent of the population in New England's largest towns, and far less than that in rural areas, they nonetheless played a significant role in keeping the region's pre-modern economy functioning and growing," Warren, *New England Bound*, 133.

34. Lawrence William Towner, *A Good Master Well Served: Masters and Servants in Colonial Massachusetts, 1620–1750* (New York, NY: Garland Publishing, 1998), 88.

35. See Appendix A for a list of individuals enslaved by Harvard leadership, faculty, staff, and donors. This list is not comprehensive, as records of enslavement in the colonial era are irregular and the list omits individuals who are likely to have been enslaved but for whom sufficient documentation could not be located. This is an important area for future research.

36. "Wadsworth House Plaque Dedication," Office of the President, Harvard University, accessed February 4, 2022, https://www.harvard.edu/president /speeches-faust/2016/wadsworth-house-plaque-dedication/.

37. See Appendix A.

38. One sign of relative social standing is family ties: Ruth Bordman, sister to Steward Aaron Bordman who held the position from 1687 to 1703, was married to Harvard President Benjamin Wadsworth (President, 1725–1737). Clifford K. Shipton, *Sibley's Harvard Graduates,* vol. 4, *Biographical Sketches of Those Who Attended Harvard University, 1690–1700* (Cambridge, MA: Harvard University Press, 1933), 84. Wadsworth sometimes referred to "my brother Bordman" in correspondence. See, for example, Benjamin Wadsworth, Diary, 1725–1736, box 1, seq. 126, Papers of Benjamin Wadsworth, UAI 15.868, Harvard University Archives, https://nrs.harvard.edu/urn-3:HUL.ARCH:3333813 ?n=126.

39. For a complete list of stewards up to 1890, see Harvard University, *Quinquennial Catalogue of the Officers and Graduates of Harvard University, 1636–1890* (Cambridge, MA: John Wilson and Son, 1890), 56, https://books.google .com/books?id=zh9OAAAAMAAJ. During the period 1636–1779, the stewards were:

?–1649, Matthew Day
1649–1660, Thomas Chesholme
1660–?, John Shearman
?–1668, William Bordman
1668–1682, Thomas Danforth
1682–1687, Andrew Bordman
1687–1703, Aaron Bordman (brother of the prior Steward)
1703–1747, Andrew Bordman II (nephew of Aaron Bordman)
1747–1750, Andrew Bordman III (son of Andrew Bordman II)
1750–1779, Jonathan Hastings

Family relationships are described in Shipton, *Sibley's Harvard Graduates,* vol. 4, 19, n. 1. For more detail, see Appendix A.

40. See Appendix A.

Thomas Danforth, Treasurer (1650–1668) and later Steward (1668–1682), enslaved a man named Phillip Ffeild. In his will, Danforth declared "that the negro man Philip ffeild should serve Mr. Foxcroft four years, and then be a free man." See *An Historic Guide to Cambridge,* compiled by members of the Hannah Winthrop Chapter of the National Society of the Daughters of the American Revolution (Cambridge, MA: self pub., 1907), 161, https:// books.google.com/books?id=ckIVAAAAYAAJ, cited in Warren, *New England Bound,* 154.

Jonathan Hastings, Steward from 1750 to 1779, is documented to have enslaved four people: Cato, Anne, and Anne's children Rose and Cato. See Shepard Congregational Society, *The Manual of the First Church in Cambridge (Congregational), Corner of Garden and Mason Streets, Cambridge, Massachusetts* (Boston, MA: Press of Samuel Usher, 1900), 30, https://books.google .com/books?id=mQAFEN3KfGsC, and *Records of the Church of Christ at Cambridge in New England, 1632–1830: Comprising the Ministerial Records of Baptisms, Marriages, Deaths, Admission to Covenant and Communion, Dismissals and Church Proceedings,* copied and ed. Stephen Paschall Sharples, (Boston, MA: Eben Putnam, 1906), 172, 224, 226, 233, 234, https://books.google.com /books?vid=HARVARD:32044017338153. See also Samuel Phillips 5th to father Samuel Phillips the 4th, December 4, 1767, box 1, folder 21, Phillips family collection, Phillips Academy Archives and Special Collections, Andover, Massachusetts, https://phillipsacademyarchives.net/collections/phillips-family -papers/samuel-phillips-5th-to-father-samuel-phillips-the-4th/.

Andrew Bordman (II), Steward from 1703 to 1747, is described in the following paragraphs.

41. Deed of sale, January 1, 1716/7, box 2, folder 3, Papers of the Bordman family, 1686–1837, HUGS 1228, Harvard University Archives, https://iiif.lib .harvard.edu/manifests/view/drs:52823945$1i.

42. Notebook, 1686–1741, box 3, Papers of the Bordman family, 1686–1837, HUG 1228, Harvard University Archives, https://iiif.lib.harvard.edu/manifests /view/drs:52760842$61i.

43. According to leading historians of this era, the term "slave" was not commonly used in New England in the colonial era in reference to enslaved people. For example, in her authoritative work *New England Bound: Slavery and Colonization in Early America,* Warren notes:

English people in the early seventeenth century only sporadically used the word "slave" to describe people of African or Indian descent in perpetual servitude, in New England or elsewhere. More often, the words "negro" and "negro servant" and, in some cases, "Indian servant" demarcated chattel status for Africans and Indians in the English Atlantic colonies. Counterintuitively, where "slave" was used in New England records during the seventeenth century, it generally referred to English captives held in North African slavery, or even as a figure of speech to connote some sort of debased state. This slowly changed over the century; more than sixty years later, an observer on Barbados would note, "These two words, *Negro* and *Slave* being by custom grown Homogeneous and Convertible; even as *Negro* and *Christian, Englishman* and *Heathen,* are . . . made *Opposites.*" (32)

Warren cites, in this passage, C. N. Degler, "Slavery and the Genesis of American Race Prejudice," *Comparative Studies in Society and History* 2, no. 1 (October 1959): 54–55; Margaret Ellen Newell, "Indian Slavery in Colonial New England," chap. 2 in *Indian Slavery in Colonial America,* edited and with an introduction by Alan Gallay (Lincoln, NE: University of Nebraska Press, 2009), 34; Edmund S. Morgan, *The Puritan Family: Religion and Domestic Relations in Seventeenth-Century New England* (New York, NY: Harper and Row, 1966), 109; and suggests that readers see also Linda M. Heywood and John K. Thornton, "'Canniball Negroes,' Atlantic Creoles, and the Identity of New England's Charter Generation," *African Diaspora* 4, no. 1 (2011): 79–80. See also Greene, *Negro in Colonial New England,* 168; Richard S. Dunn, *Sugar and Slaves: The Rise of the Planter Class in the English West Indies, 1624–1713* (Chapel Hill, NC: UNC Press, 1972), 228; Allegra di Bonaventura, *For Adam's Sake: A Family Saga in Colonial New England* (New York, NY: Liveright Publishing Corporation, 2013), 17; Newell, *Brethren by Nature,* 12–13.

Accordingly, this report includes people who are referred to in extant records as someone's "servant," "man," or "woman," and who are also explicitly identified as "negro," "mulatto," or "Indian." See Appendix A for a more complete list.

44. Harvard University, *Quinquennial Catalogue of the Officers and Graduates of Harvard University, 1636–1915* (Cambridge, MA: Harvard University Press, 1915), 120, https://books.google.com/books?id=JiNOAAAAMAAJ; Harris, *Epitaphs,* 48, 90. Online at https://books.google.com/books?id=wrXW6T1MeKUC&source=gbs_navlinks_s.

First Church (Congregational) in Cambridge, where William Brattle served as minister and where Harvard faculty and students were required to attend services from the College's founding until the early nineteenth century, since

2011 has been examining its historical involvement with slavery through written research, visual art, and community engagement efforts. See "Owning Our History," First Church in Cambridge, accessed January 14, 2022, https://www .firstchurchcambridge.org/owning-our-history/.

45.   Rose is also identified as "negro of Mr. Bordman" in church records. See *Church of Christ at Cambridge,* 145. On children inheriting the status of their mother, see Newell, *Brethren by Nature,* 167; Warren, *New England Bound,* 156.

46.   *Church of Christ at Cambridge,* 109.

47.   *Vital Records of Cambridge Massachusetts to the Year 1850,* vol. 2, *Marriages and Deaths,* compiled by Thomas W. Baldwin, (Boston, MA: Wright & Potter Print. Company, 1910), 442, https://books.google.com/books?id=lc8UAAA AYAAJ. On Elizabeth Bordman as the wife of Andrew Bordman, see *Vitals Records of Cambridge,* 2:41.

48.   This tax assessment from 1749 lists only one Bordman, not one of the Stewards of Harvard. The largest slaveholder listed in the First Parish—what is now Cambridge—listed four slaves between the ages of 12 and 50, while all other enslavers list only one. Town of Cambridge Tax Valuation Sheet, 1749, Cambridge Historical Commission Archival Collections, cited in Maycock and Sullivan, *Building Old Cambridge,* 20, table 1.1.

49.   Harvard University, *Quinquennial Catalogue, 1636–1915,* 8, 131; Clifford K. Shipton, *Sibley's Harvard Graduates, Volume IX, 1731–1735: Biographical Sketches of Those Who Attended Harvard College in the Classes 1731–1735 with Bibliographic and Other Notes* (Boston, MA: Massachusetts Historical Society, 1956), 241–264.

50.   "About," Winthrop House, Harvard College, accessed January 25, 2022, https://winthrop.harvard.edu/about.

51.   John Winthrop, Annotated almanac, 1759, box 5, vol. 4, seq. 5, Papers of John and Hannah Winthrop, 1728–1789, HUM 9, Harvard University Archives, https://nrs.harvard.edu/urn-3:HUL.ARCH:10354447?n=5. Brackets in original.

52.   Winthrop, Annotated almanac, 1759.

53.   Winthrop, Annotated almanac, 1759.

54.   Shipton, *Sibley's Harvard Graduates, Volume IX,* 246.

55.   *A forensic dispute on the legality of enslaving the Africans, held at the public commencement in Cambridge, New-England, July 21st, 1773. By two candidates for the bachelor's degree* (Boston, MA: Printed by John Boyle, for Thomas

Leverett, 1773), 4–5. For the original manuscript, see *Forensic dispute between Theodore Parsons & Eliphalet Pearson: manuscript, 1773,* MS Am 1423, Houghton Library, Harvard University, https://nrs.harvard.edu/urn-3:FHCL.HOUGH :37045020.

The pamphlet does not indicate which position each participant took, but archival evidence points to Eliphalet Pearson having spoken in favor of slavery. See Eliphalet Pearson, "Part of Forensic Dispute," 1773, folder 3, box 1, Eliphalet Pearson Papers, Phillips Academy Archive and Special Collections, Phillips Academy Andover, Andover, Massachusetts, as cited in Peter Galison, "21 July 1773: Disputation, Poetry, Slavery," *Critical Inquiry* 45 (Winter 2019): 380, n. 11.

56.   See *Forensic dispute on legality of enslaving the Africans,* 26–27.

57.   Theophilus Parsons, *Memoir of Theophilus Parsons, Chief Justice of the Supreme Judicial Court of Massachusetts with Notices of Some of His Contemporaries* (Boston, MA: Ticknor and Fields, 1859), 17, https://books.google.com /books?id=9CkrAQAAIAAJ.

58.   Parsons, *Memoir,* 19.

59.   Conrad Edick Wright and Edward W. Hanson, *Sibley's Harvard Graduates,* vol. 18, *Biographical Sketches of Those who Attended Harvard College in the Classes of 1772–1774* (Boston, MA: Massachusetts Historical Society, 1999), 273–275.

60.   Wright and Hanson, *Sibley's Harvard Graduates,* 288–304.

Sidebar: Elmwood: A Complicated History

1.   For a brief biography of Oliver, see Clifford K. Shipton, *Sibley's Harvard Graduates, Volume XIII, 1751–1755: Biographical Sketches of Those Who Attended Harvard College in the Classes 1751–1755 with Bibliographical and Other Notes* (Boston, MA: Massachusetts Historical Society, 1965), 336–344.

2.   Samuel Eliot Morison, a long-standing authority on the early history of Harvard College, notes that public commencement ceremonies were suspended from 1774 to 1781 during the Revolutionary War and Harvard president Samuel Langdon was privately installed so the college could circumvent having to weigh in on Oliver and other royal councilors potential claim to overseer roles. *Three Centuries at Harvard* (Cambridge, MA: Harvard University Press, 1936), 146.

3.   "Thomas Oliver; UK, American Loyalist Claims; 1783," American Loyalist Claims, Series II, Class: AO 13, Piece: 048, The National Archives of the UK, Kew, Surrey, England (from Ancestry.com, online database).

3: The Slavery Economy and Harvard

1.   Foster, *Smalle Beginnings,* 178. See also Gary Staudt, "Slavery and the Early Investment Strategies of Harvard University's Endowment" (master's thesis, Harvard University, 2013).

2.   Foster, *Smalle Beginnings,* 157–158.

3.   Edmund Randolph, "Narrative of the State of New England" (1676), quoted in Peterson, *City-State of Boston,* 154.

4.   Governor William Lord Willoughby to the Privy Council, December 16, 1667, "America and West Indies: December 1667," in *Calendar of State Papers Colonial, America and West Indies: Volume 5, 1661–1668,* ed. W. Noel Sainsbury (London, UK: Her Majesty's Stationery Office, 1880), 520–534, http://www.british-history.ac.uk/cal-state-papers/colonial/america-west-indies/vol5/pp520–534. See also Eric Williams, Capitalism and Slavery (Chapel Hill, NC: The University of North Carolina Press, 1994), 110, quoting also "America and West Indies: December 1667," in *Calendar of State Papers Colonial, America and West Indies,* vol. 5, *1661–1668,* ed. W Noel Sainsbury (London, UK: Her Majesty's Stationery Office, 1880), 520–534.

5.   Larry Gragg, "An Ambiguous Response to the Market: The Early New England-Barbados Trade," *Historical Journal of Massachusetts* 17, no. 2 (Summer 1989): 177.

6.   Edmund Burke, *An account of the European settlements in America: In six parts. I. A short history of the discovery of that part of the world. II. The manners and customs of the original inhabitants. III. Of the Spanish settlements. IV. Of the Portuguese. V. Of the French, Dutch, and Danish. VI. Of the English. Each part contains an accurate description of the settlements in it, their extent, climate, productions, trade, genius and disposition of their inhabitants: the interests of the several powers of Europe with respect to those settlements; and their political and commercial views with regard to each other,* 2 vols. (London, UK: Printed for R. and J. Dodsley in Pall-Mall, 1760), 2:173, https://books.google.com/books?id=6Wg6AAAAcAAJ.

7.   Warren, *New England Bound,* 52.

8.   Hosmer, *Winthrop's Journal,* 2:328.

9.   Sir Charles Whitworth, *State of the Trade of Great Britain in its Imports and Exports Progressively from the Year 1697 also of the Trade to each particular Country, during the above Period, distinguishing each year, in two parts with a Preface and Introduction Setting forth the Articles whereof each Trade consists,* (London, UK: Printed for G. Robinson, etc., 1776), xlviii-xlviv.

10. Governor the Earl of Bellomont to the Council of Trade and Plantations, November 28, 1700, "America and West Indies: November 1700, 26–30," in *Calendar of State Papers Colonial, America and West Indies: Volume 18, 1700,* ed. Cecil Headlam (London, UK: His Majesty's Stationery Office, 1910), accessed March 2, 2022, https://www.british-history.ac.uk/cal-state-papers/colonial /america-west-indies/vol18/pp664–706.

11. Andrés Poey, "A Chronological Table, Comprising 400 Cyclonic Hurricanes Which Have Occurred in the West Indies and in the North Atlantic within 362 Years from 1493 to 1855: With a Bibliographical List of 450 Authors, Books, &c., and Periodicals, Where Some Interesting Accounts May be Found, Especially on the West and East Indian Hurricanes," *The Journal of the Royal Geographical Society of London* 25 (1855): 291–328.

12. John Josselyn, *An Account of Two Voyages to New-England: made during the years 1638, 1663* (1674; reprint, Boston: William Veazie, 1865), 210–211. Peterson, *City-State of Boston,* 113, notes that Massachusetts fishermen sent "refuse fish"—mackerel, which was considered low-grade compared to cod—to the West Indies at low prices to be fed to enslaved people. Warren, *New England Bound,* 55, argues that "New England merchants were by midcentury racializing food: products understood to be beneath English standards were deemed sufficient for enslaved peoples in the West Indies. Rotting fish, however unappetizing to European stomachs, was a relative bargain for the feeding of slaves, for it cost so much less. Colonists could pocket the difference."

13. "Testimony of George Walker of Barbados," quoted in Christopher P. Magra, *The Fisherman's Cause: Atlantic Commerce and Maritime Dimensions of the American Revolution* (New York, NY: Cambridge University Press, 2009), 95.

The West Indies also came to depend on New England's whaling industry. In the 1750s, Nantucket whalers began to sell spermaceti head matter in Rhode Island, where chandlers turned this raw material into candles that were then exported to the Caribbean. By the eve of the American Revolution, over 90% of spermaceti candles in the Caribbean were imported from New England, with Rhode Island alone accounting for around 65% and Boston nearly 20% of the total. James B. Hedges, *The Browns of Providence Plantations: Colonial Years* (Cambridge, MA: Harvard University Press, 1952), 86–122; Alexander Starbuck, *History of the American Whale Fishery from its Earliest Inception to the Year 1876* (Waltham, MA: printed by the author, 1878), 152–153.

Such artificial lighting was essential to Caribbean sugar plantations, enabling them to operate through the night during the harvest period. See, for example, Dunn, *Sugar and Slaves,* 195.

14.   Philip D. Curtin, *The Rise and Fall of the Plantation Complex: Essays in Atlantic History* (New York, NY: Cambridge University Press, 1990), 83.

15.   Richard Vines to John Winthrop, July 19, 1647, in *Winthrop Papers, Volume V, 1645–1649* (Boston, MA: Massachusetts Historical Society, 1947), 172, https://archive.org/details/winthroppapersv5wint/page/n3/mode/2up, as cited in Bernard Bailyn, *The New England Merchants in the Seventeenth Century* (Cambridge, MA: Harvard University Press, 1955), 85.

16.   For an index of sugar prices in Barbados between 1652 and 1694, see Otis Paul Starkey, *The Economic Geography of Barbados: A Study of the Relationships Between Environmental Variations and Economic Development* (New York, NY: Columbia University Press, 1939).

17.   Curtin, *Rise and Fall,* 83.

18.   Stanley L. Engerman and B. W. Higman, "The demographic structure of the Caribbean slave Societies in the eighteenth and nineteenth Centuries," in *General History of the Caribbean,* ed. Franklin W. Knight, vol. 3, *The slave societies of the Caribbean* (New York, NY: Palgrave Macmillan, 2003), 48–50, table 2.1.

19.   John Adams to Robert R. Livingston, 23 June 1783, *Founders Online,* National Archives, accessed February 4, 2022, https://founders.archives.gov/documents/Adams/06-15-02-0025.

20.   Halley, "My Isaac Royall Legacy." It appears likely, as has been written elsewhere, that the Royalls were also involved in the brutal suppression of a planned rebellion of enslaved workers on Antigua. There is, however, some dispute about both whether there was a planned revolt at all, and whether the Royalls were directly involved in the violent crackdown. On the former question, David Barry Gaspar acknowledges that it is "much easier to gauge and authenticate a revolt than a conspiracy to revolt." Yet he concludes there was indeed a plot to rebel. On the latter, the evidence is circumstantial but convincing: the fact that the Royalls would have been compelled to serve in the militia, paired with the fact that among those executed was a driver named Hector, enslaved by the Royalls, gives strong credence to their probable involvement. See David Barry Gaspar, *Bondmen and Rebels: A Study of Master-Slave Relations in Antigua,* (Durham, NC: Duke University Press, 1993), 5–13, 26, 32; and Janet Halley, "When Brands Go Bad: The Rise and fall, and Re-Rise and Re-Fall of Isaac Royall, Jr.," in *Academic Brands: Distinction in Global Higher Education,* eds. Mario Biagioli and Madhavi Sunder (Cambridge University Press, Forthcoming).

21.   See "Documenting Those Enslaved by the Royalls," Royall House and Slave Quarters, accessed January 9, 2022, https://royallhouse.org/slavery/documenting-those-enslaved-by-the-royalls/.

22. See Samuel Francis Batchelder, *Notes on Colonel Henry Vassall: His Wife Penelope Royall, His House at Cambridge, and His Slaves Tony & Darby* (Cambridge, MA: 1917), 74–78, https://books.google.com/books?id=nJYlAQA AMAAJ, and J. L. Bell, *Longfellow House-Washington's Headquarters National Historic Site Historic Resource Study,* (National Park Service, 2012), 31–41, https://www.nps.gov/long/learn/historyculture/upload/Washington-Head quarters-HRS.pdf.

23. This report focuses primarily on families other than the Royalls, about whom much has already been written. Coquillette and Kimball, "Isaac Royall, Jr.: Slave Master, Founder," in *Battlefield of Merit,* 81–88; "HLS Shield Exhibit," especially "The Legacy of Isaac Royall, Jr.," Exhibit Addenda, Harvard Law School, accessed February 4, 2022, https://exhibits.law.harvard.edu /hls-shield-exhibit; and "Slavery," Royall House and Slave Quarters, accessed February 4, 2022, https://royallhouse.org/slavery/ and "The Royalls," Royall House and Slave Quarters, accessed February 4, 2022, https://royallhouse.org /the-royalls/.

24. Quoted in Peterson, *City-State of Boston,* 63; "George Downing to John Winthrop Jr." (August 1645), *Winthrop Papers, Volume V: 1645–1649* (Boston, MA: The Massachusetts Historical Society, 1947), 43, accessed August 30, 2021, https://archive.org/details/winthroppapersv5wint/mode/2up.

25. "George Downing to John Winthrop, Jr.," 43, 44.

26. Larry D. Gragg, "A Puritan in the West Indies: The Career of Samuel Winthrop," *The William and Mary Quarterly* 50, no. 4 (October 1993): 768–786.

27. Gragg, "Puritan in the West Indies," 774, 786; Warren, *New England Bound,* 59.

28. Vere Langford Oliver, *The History of the Island of Antigua, One of the Leeward Caribbees, from the First Settlement in 1635 to the Present Time* (London, UK: Mitchell and Hughes, 1894), 3:251, accessed August 26, 2021, https:// archive.org/details/historyofisland003oliv/.

29. Bremer, *John Winthrop,* 174, and Reg Murphy, "Winthrope's Bay," ArchaeologyAntigua.org, accessed January 13, 2022, https://www.archaeology antigua.org/index.php/winthrope-s-bay. The name, with a slight variation in spelling, is visible on contemporary maps. See "Winthorpes Bay," Google Maps, accessed January 13, 2022, https://goo.gl/maps/KfUHSMUb9Wt52dPs8.

30. The original gift is recorded in an entry dated December 30, 1645: "Extractum Doni Pomarii Sociorum pour Johannem Bulkeleium," box 2, College Books, 1636–1827, College Book 3, 1636–1779, UAI 5.5, Harvard University

Archives, https://nrs.harvard.edu/urn-3:HUL.ARCH:10870587?n=47; transcribed in "Harvard College Records, Part I: Corporation Records, 1636–1750," Colonial Society of Massachusetts, Publications of the Colonial Society of Massachusetts 15 (1895): 205–206.

Both Morison, *Three Centuries of Harvard,* 17, and Manegold, *Ten Hills Farm,* 63, make reference to this gift. As recently as 2008, Harvard University highlighted Winthrop's gift as "the first gift of real estate by alumni" on a website describing the University's endowment: "Harvard's Endowment Funds," The Harvard Guide: Finances, https://www.hno.harvard.edu/guide/finance/index.html (site archived by May 11, 2008).

31. Samuel Winthrop to John Winthrop, 1647, Winthrop Family Papers, Massachusetts Historical Society. Translation published in *Proceedings of the Massachusetts Historical Society, Second Series,* vol. 7 (Boston, MA: Massachusetts Historical Society, 1892), 14–15.

32. Gragg, "Puritan in the West Indies," 778.

33. Gragg, "Puritan in the West Indies," 778; Samuel Winthrop to John Winthrop, Jr., November 1663 and September 1664, Winthrop Family Papers, Massachusetts Historical Society.

34. Samuel Winthrop to John Winthrop, Jr., September 1667, Winthrop Family Papers, Massachusetts Historical Society.

35. Gragg, "Puritan in West Indies," 786.

While Samuel Winthrop's will no longer exists, the property transactions and wills of his widow and children illustrate the wealth they inherited from him. See Oliver, *Island of Antigua,* 3:251–253.

36. See Samuel A. Eliot, *A Sketch of the History of Harvard College and of its Present State* (Boston, MA: Charles C. Little and James Brown, 1848).

37. See Beckert et al., *Harvard and Slavery,* 16.

38. James H. Perkins, *Suffolk County, MA: Probate File Papers,* AmericanAncestors.org, New England Historic Genealogical Society, 2017–2019, (from records supplied by the Massachusetts Supreme Judicial Court Archives, digitized images provided by FamilySearch.org), accessed March 5, 2021; Josiah Quincy, *The History of Harvard University* (Cambridge, MA: John Owen, 1840), 2:428–430, https://books.google.com/books?id=cC4BAAAAYAAJ; Harvard University, *Quinquennial Catalogue, 1636–1915,* 25.

39. *"Our first men": a calendar of wealth, fashion and gentility; containing a list of those persons taxed in the city of Boston, credibly reported to be worth one hundred thousand dollars, with biographical notices of the principal persons,* rev. ed. (Boston, MA: Published by all the Booksellers, 1846), 36, https://books

.google.com/books?id=1FzrR6lOnz8C. See also Michael E. Chapman, "Taking Business to the Tiger's Gate: Thomas Handasyd Perkins and the Boston-Smyrna-Canton Opium Trade of the Early Republic," *Journal of the Royal Asiatic Society Hong Kong Branch* 52 (2012), 7–28.

40. See Mary Jane McClintock Wilson, *Master of Woodland Hill: Benjamin Bussey of Boston, 1757–1842* (Lansing, MI: self-pub., 2006).

41. Charles Warren, *History of the Harvard Law School and Early Legal Conditions in America,* vol. 2 (New York, NY: Lewis Publishing Company, 1908), 283.

42. Quincy, *History of Harvard,* 2:426–427. McLean's will is transcribed in full in Thomas E. Bator and Heidi A. Seely, *The Boston Trustee: The Lives, Laws & Legacy of a Vital Institution* (Jaffrey, NH: David R. Godine, 2015), 139–145.

43. Edward Lurie, *Louis Agassiz: A Life in Science* (Chicago, IL: University of Chicago Press, 1960), 137–138. Lawrence renewed his support for Agassiz's salary in 1853. See Abbott Lawrence to Samuel Atkins Eliot, March 5, 1853, box 10, Corporation papers, 1853–1856, Corporation papers, 2nd series, supplements to the Harvard College Papers, UAI 5.130, Harvard University Archives. After Abbott Lawrence's death, his son affirmed the family's continuing support for Agassiz's salary, until such time as the elder Lawrence's $50,000 bequest could be paid to the University. See James W. Lawrence to William T. Andrews, Esq., November 12, 1855, box 10, Corporation papers, 1853–1856, Corporation papers, 2nd series, supplements to the Harvard College Papers, UAI 5.130, Harvard University Archives.

44. "School Overview: Timeline," Harvard John A. Paulson School of Engineering and Applied Sciences, accessed January 7, 2022, https://www.seas .harvard.edu/about-us/school-overview/timeline.

45. Harvard University, *Dedication of the Thomas Nelson Perkins Room in Massachusetts Hall to the Use of the President and Fellows of Harvard College* (Cambridge, MA: Harvard University Press, 1941), v.

46. Harvard University Press, *Perkins Room,* vi.

47. Harvard University Press, *Perkins Room,* v-vi.

48. Harold Clarke Durrell, "Memoirs of Deceased Members of the New England Historic Genealogical Society: Thomas Nelson Perkins," *The New England Historical and Genealogical Register* 92 (January 1938): 84–85.

49. Carl Seaburg and Stanley Paterson, *Merchant Prince of Boston: Colonel T. H. Perkins, 1764–1854* (1971; repr., Cambridge, MA: Harvard University Press, 2014), 37–44; Benjamin Grande, "Yankees in Haiti: Boston Merchant

Trade in Revolutionary Saint-Domingue" (master's thesis, Tufts University, 2016), 72–105, http://hdl.handle.net/10427/011745.

50. Elizabeth Cary Agassiz was a granddaughter of Thomas Handasyd Perkins. She was also related to the Cushing family, who were business partners of the Perkins and were also a slave-trading family. Thomas Handasyd Perkins's granddaughter, Mary Cary, married Harvard Professor Cornelius Conway Felton who became a President of Harvard University (1860–1862). Felton taught Greek at Harvard (Tutor, 1829–1832; university professor of Greek Literature, 1832–1834; and Eliot Professor of Greek Literature, 1849–1857). See Seaburg and Paterson, *Merchant Prince of Boston*, 433; Lucy Allen Paton, *Elizabeth Cary Agassiz: A Biography* (Boston, MA: Houghton Mifflin Company, 1919), 4, https://books.google.com/books?id=25AAAAAYAAJ; William Richard Cutter, ed., *Genealogical and Personal Memoirs Relating to the Families of the State of Massachusetts*, vol. 4 (New York, NY: Lewis Historical Publishing Company, 1910), 2193, https://books.google.com/books?id=FM8UAAAAYAAJ. Harvard University, *Quinquennial Catalogue, 1636–1915*, 56.

51. Harvard University, *Quinquennial Catalogue, 1636–1915*, 25; "[Meetings of 1823]—Memoir of James Perkins," in *Proceedings of the Massachusetts Historical Society*, vol. 1 (Boston, MA: Massachusetts Historical Society, 1791), 348–71; Samuel A. Eliot, *Harvard College and Its Benefactors* (Boston, MA: C.C. Little and J. Brown, 1846), https://books.google.com/books?id=-Xg7AAAAYAAJ.

52. Quincy, *History of Harvard*, 2:546–548, 564.

53. N. I. Bowditch, *A History of the Massachusetts General Hospital* (Boston, MA: John Wilson & Son, 1851), 416, 432, https://books.google.com/books?id=qg8DAAAAQAAJ.

On its website, Massachusetts General Hospital is described as "the first teaching hospital of Harvard University's new medical school" when it was established. "About Us: The Mass General Difference," Massachusetts General Hospital, accessed November 9, 2021, https://www.massgeneral.org/about/. On the work of Dr. John Collins Warren, first Dean of Harvard Medical School, to found MGH, see Edward Warren, *The Life of John Collins Warren, M. D., Compiled Chiefly from His Autobiography and Journals* (Boston, MA: Ticknor and Fields, 1860), 1:98–102, https://books.google.com/books?id=WccoAQAAMAAJ, and Bowditch, *Massachusetts General Hospital*, 3. Bowditch also lists Harvard among the original subscribers to the fundraising effort for the hospital, see *Massachusetts General Hospital*, 402.

54. Quincy, *History of Harvard,* 2:291, 543. The professorship was renamed after an 1833 bequest by Dr. Joshua Fisher. See Quincy, *History of Harvard,* 2:428, 628 and "Asa Gray at 200: Harvard Professor," Harvard University Herbaria and Libraries, accessed January 21, 2022, https://huh.harvard.edu/book /harvard-professor.

Between them, the three brothers also supported the Astronomical Observatory, the libraries, a fundraising effort to build an exhibition space, and students; see Quincy, *History of Harvard,* 2:401, 488, 592–593, 637, and Eliot, *History of Harvard College,* 182.

55. "[Meetings of 1823]—Memoir of James Perkins."

56. Thomas G. Cary, *Memoir of Thomas Handasyd Perkins; containing Extracts from his Diaries and Letter. With an Appendix* (Boston, MA: Little, Brown, 1856), 223, https://books.google.com/books?id=QKwpAAAAYAAJ; Anna Gardner Fish, "Thomas Handasyd Perkins," Founders, Perkins History Museum, Perkins School for the Blind, accessed August 13, 2021, https://www .perkins.org/founders/#TH-Perkins.

57. Seaburg and Paterson, *Merchant Prince of Boston,* 33–34.

58. Cary, *Perkins,* 5–6; Seaburg and Paterson, *Merchant Prince of Boston,* 33.

59. Robin Blackburn, *The Overthrow of Colonial Slavery, 1776–1848* (New York, NY: Verso, 1988); Laurent Dubois, *Avengers of the New World: The Story of the Haitian Revolution* (Cambridge, MA: The Belknap Press of Harvard University Press, 2004); Carolyn E. Fick, *The Making of Haiti: The Saint Domingue Revolution from Below* (Knoxville, TN: University of Tennessee Press, 1990).

60. Seaburg and Paterson, *Merchant Prince of Boston,* 62.

61. Stanley L. Engerman and B. W. Higman, "The demographic structure of the Caribbean slave societies in the eighteenth and nineteenth centuries," *General History of the Caribbean,* ed. Franklin W. Knight, vol. 3, *The slave societies of the Caribbean* (New York, NY: Palgrave Macmillan, 2007), 60.

62. Sarah Perkins to Eliza Trumbull, Cape François, November 13, 1789, MSS. L 816, box 3, subseries 3, item 3, Perkins Family Papers, 1780–1882, Boston Athenaeum, Massachusetts.

63. Seaburg and Paterson, *Merchant Prince of Boston,* 34; Charles C. Perkins, "Narrative of the Insurrection in St. Domingo, and of a Voyage from Port au Prince to Boston in 1793, by Samuel G. Perkins, communicated, with notes," *Proceedings of the Massachusetts Historical Society,* vol. 2, *Second Series 1885–1886* (Boston, MA: Massachusetts Historical Society, 1886), 305–306.

64. Perkins, "Insurrection in St. Domingo," 307.

65. "The Copartnership, under the firm of Wall, Tardy and Co. of Cape-François," Advertisement, *The Massachusetts Centinel,* June 7, 1786; Seaburg and Paterson, *Merchant Prince of Boston,* 39–40.

66. Seaburg and Paterson, *Merchant Prince of Boston,* 40. In July 1792, Samuel Gardner wrote from St. Domingue to James of going in with a partner to purchase some newly imported enslaved Africans: "a ship arrived from the coast with slaves & we immediately proposed purchasing together, but as I was extremely busy he went on board [and] visited the negroes." He describes boarding the slave ships as part of the normal course of business, and makes it clear that had not been otherwise occupied he would have gone himself. Samuel G. Perkins to James Perkins, July 16, 17, 1792, box 1, item 10, Perkins Family Papers, 1780–1882, MSS. L816, Boston Athenaeum, Massachusetts.

67. See, for example, Captain Josiah Wardwell to Walter Burling, Havana, May 21, 1792, box 2, item 4, Perkins Family Papers, 1780–1882, MSS. L816, Boston Athenaeum, Massachusetts; Samuel G. Perkins to James Perkins, Cape, May 27, 1792, box 2, item 6, Perkins Family Papers, 1780–1882, MSS. L816, Boston Athenaeum, Massachusetts; Captain Josiah Wardwell to Perkins, Burling, & Co., Havana, May 25, 1792, box 2, item 7, Perkins Family Papers, 1780–1882, MSS. L816, Boston Athenaeum, Massachusetts; Captain Josiah Wardwell to Perkins, Burling, & Co., New York, July 5, 1792, box 2, item 30, Perkins Family Papers, 1780–1882, MSS. L816, Boston Athenaeum, Massachusetts; J. Walke to James Perkins, New York, July 6, 1792, box 2, item 31, Perkins Family Papers, 1780–1882, MSS. L816, Boston Athenaeum, Massachusetts; Walter Burling to James Perkins, Cape, July 27, 1792, box 2, item 38, Perkins Family Papers, 1780–1882, MSS. L816, Boston Athenaeum, Massachusetts.

68. Captain Burk to James Yard, "At Sea," June 16, 1792, box 2, item 15, Perkins Family Papers, 1780–1882, Boston Athenaeum, Massachusetts.

69. H. LeMesurier & Co. to James Perkins, Havre, August 31, 1792, box 1, item 3, Perkins Family Papers, 1780–1882, Boston Athenaeum, Massachusetts; John Fuller to Thomas H. Perkins, Philadelphia, September 15, 1790, film A. 842, reel 1, box 1, Thomas Handasyd Perkins Papers, 1789–1892, Massachusetts Historical Society, microfilm.

70. Dubois, *Avengers of the New World;* Fick, *The Making of Haiti;* Michel-Rolph Trouillot, *Silencing the Past: Power and the Production of History* (Boston, MA: Beacon Press, 1995).

71. N. Goldthwait to James Perkins, Turks Island, December 18, 1792, box 1, item 4, Perkins Family Papers, 1780–1882, MSS. L816, Boston Athenaeum, Massachusetts.

72. Seaburg and Paterson, *Merchant Prince of Boston,* 89; Ada Ferrer, *Freedom's Mirror: Cuba and Haiti in the Age of Revolution* (New York, NY: Cambridge University Press, 2014).

73. This man's name is spelled variously both within and across multiple sources. We have chosen to use the name and spelling used in his obituary, printed by the abolitionist newspaper *The Liberator* in 1831. See "DIED [Mousse]," *The Liberator* (Boston, MA), November 5, 1831.

74. "[Meetings of 1823]—Memoir of James Perkins," 358.

75. "DIED [Mousse]," *The Liberator.*

76. Samuel G. Perkins to James Perkins, Cape, May 27, 1792.

77. Samuel Perkins to James Perkins, June 28, 1792, box 2, item 20, Perkins Family Papers, 1780–1882, MSS. L816, Boston Athenaeum, Massachusetts; PB&Co to James Perkins, Cape, August 5, 1792, box 1, item 14, Perkins Family Papers, 1780–1882, MSS. L816, Boston Athenaeum, Massachusetts.

78. Samuel G. Perkins to James Perkins, October 26, 1792, Cape, box 1, item 14, Perkins Family Papers, 1780–1882, MSS. L816, Boston Athenaeum, Massachusetts.

79. Perkins, "Insurrection in St. Domingo," 306, 374–390.

80. Edith Perkins Cunningham, *Owls Nest: A Tribute to Sarah Elliott Perkins* (Cambridge, MA: Riverside Press, 1907), 19, https://books.google.com/books?id=jHAaAAAAYAAJ.

81. Perkins, "Insurrection in St. Domingo," 348, 353.

82. Ralph W. Hidy, "Editor's Foreward," in Seaburg and Paterson, *Merchant Prince of Boston,* vii–viii; *Our First Men,* 35–36; Chapman, "Taking Business to Tiger's Gate."

83. See Martha Bebinger, "How Profits from Opium Shaped 19th-Century Boston," WBUR, July 31, 2017, https://www.wbur.org/news/2017/07/31/opium-boston-history.

84. Quincy, *History of Harvard,* 2:428. In preparing this biographical sketch Quincy consulted Thomas Handasyd Perkins, who composed for Quincy a narrative of his brother's life. Like Quincy's published version, Thomas's sketch praises James's mercantile success in St. Domingo without detailing the nature of the brothers' business. Thomas Handasyd Perkins to Josiah Quincy,

December 13, 1838, Boston, box 3, item 23, Perkins Family Papers, 1780–1882, MSS. L816, Boston Athenaeum, Massachusetts.

85.　Quincy, *History of Harvard,* 2:428–429.

86.　Eliot, *Harvard College and Its Benefactors,* 180; Quincy, *History of Harvard,* 2:412–413.

87.　Quincy, *History of Harvard,* 2:413.

88.　Josiah Quincy, *Considerations relative to the Library of Harvard university, respectfully submitted to the Legislature of Massachusetts* (Cambridge, MA: Charles Folsom, 1833), 5.

89.　Bowditch, *Massachusetts General Hospital,* 430. On the hospital's relationship to the university, see note 53 above.

90.　Quincy, *History of Harvard,* 2:546–548, 583.

91.　Quincy, *History of Harvard,* 2:412, 544–545.

92.　Bertram Zarins, "History of the Massachusetts General Hospital Sports Medicine Service," *The Orthopaedic Journal at Harvard Medical School* 9 (2007): 100, http://www.orthojournalhms.org/volume9/manuscripts/ms13 .pdf.

93.　See "Collection Overview: Scope and Contents," Israel Thorndike Business Records, Hollis for Archival Discovery, Harvard Library, accessed January 7, 2022, https://id.lib.harvard.edu/ead/bak00405/catalog. Also Volume 1, 1781–1788, box 1, folder 2, Israel Thorndike business records, Mss:766 1778–1899, Baker Library Special Collections, Harvard Business School; Volume 1, 1789–1790, box 1, folder 3, Israel Thorndike business records, Mss:766 1778–1899, Baker Library Special Collections, Harvard Business School; Volume 1, 1792, box 15, folder 2, Israel Thorndike business records, Mss:766 1778–1899, Baker Library Special Collections, Harvard Business School; Volume 1, 1795–1796, box 1, folder 11, Israel Thorndike business records, Mss:766 1778–1899, Baker Library Special Collections, Harvard Business School.

94.　Thorndike's brother-in-law and business partner, Moses Brown (AB AM 1768), was also a benefactor of the Divinity School, bequeathing $2,000 to the institution upon his death in 1820. Quincy, *History of Harvard,,* 2:414–415.

95.　"Orders to Nicholas Thorndike from Brown & Thorndike," October 11, 1791, 18460—Correspondence, Historic Beverly, Massachusetts, https:// beverlyhistory.pastperfectonline.com/archive/63CB7150-96A9-40C7-A1E3 -312313391417.

96.　Timothy Kistner, *Federalist Tycoon: The Life and Times of Israel Thorndike* (Lanham, MD: University Press of America, Inc., 2015), 30–31, 49–50.

97. See, for example, "Bill between Nicholas Thorndike and Brown & Thorndike," February 10, 1792, 18483—Bill of Sale, Historic Beverly, Massachusetts, https://beverlyhistory.pastperfectonline.com/archive/E697F9A5-C2A9-4E68-BAB9-270264606260; "Bill of sales by Brown & Thorndike in account of Nicholas Thorndike," February 28, 1792, 18484—Bill of Sale, Historic Beverly, Massachusetts, https://beverlyhistory.pastperfectonline.com/archive/86F5C109-BF6A-4F44-98B1-134304130828; "Update of orders from Nicholas Thorndike in Havanna probably to Brown & Thorndike," May 1, 1793, 18525—Document, Historic Beverly, Massachusetts, https://beverlyhistory.pastperfectonline.com/archive/E9A7A606-DA29-4D59-86C3-974130912571; W. Woodville to Israel Thorndike and John Lovett, December 16, 1801, 12847—Document, Historic Beverly, Massachusetts, https://beverlyhistory.pastperfectonline.com/archive/9ABCA58C-18AB-47F4-900D-950629950107.

98. See Kistner, *Federalist Tycoon,* 41–110, 137–170.

99. Quincy, *History of Harvard,* 2:426.

100. On the total amount received by the hospital, encompassing both McLean's original bequest and residuary income, see Quincy, *History of Harvard,* 2:426, and Bowditch, *Massachusetts General Hospital,* 429. On the hospital's historical relationship to Harvard Medical School, see note 53 above.

For a more in-depth discussion of John McLean's legacies, see Bator and Seely, *Boston Trustee.*

101. Bowditch, *Massachusetts General Hospital,* 419, 429–430.

102. Bowditch, *Massachusetts General Hospital,* 75–76.

103. "History & Progress: Over 200 Years of Treatment, Research, Training and Education," McLean Hospital, accessed, September 24, 2021, https://www.mcleanhospital.org/about/history-progress.

104. Quincy, *History of Harvard,* 2:426.

105. Cyrus Eaton, *Annals of the Town of Warren, with the Early History of St. George's, Broad Bay and the Neighboring Settlements on the Waldo Patent* (Hallowell, ME: Masters, Smith & Co., 1851), 119, https://books.google.com/books?id=qYHc3-EYCygC.

106. *Ship Registers and Enrollments of Boston and Charlestown,* vol. 1, *1789–1795,* compiled by The Survey of Federal Archives Division of Professional and Service Projects, Works Progress Administration (Boston, MA: The National Archives Project, 1942), 11, 34, 43, 47, 61, 103, 138, 152, 185, 203, https://books.google.com/books?id=v-NFAQAAIAAJ.

107. *French Spoliations: A Condensed Report of the Findings of the Court of Claims in Each Case Named in the Amendment Proposed by Senator Lodge to H. R. 19115* (Washington, DC: Government Printing Office, 1912), 9–10, 56–60, 92–93, 101–102, 116–118, 123–124, 146–147, 182–183, https://books.google.com/books?id=ikZHAQAAMAAJ.

108. Warren, *Harvard Law School,* 2:21. Warren's transcription varies slightly but not substantively from the original, primarily in punctuation. See Benjamin Bussey Probate Record, 1842, Norfolk County, Massachusetts, Probate File Papers, 1793–1877, AmericanAncestors.org, New England Historic Genealogical Society, 2019, p. 3, (from records supplied by the Massachusetts Supreme Judicial Court Archives, digitized images provided by FamilySearch .org), accessed March 5, 2021.

109. "Will of Benjamin Bussey," in Bussey Probate Record, 12–13.

110. Warren, *Harvard Law School,* 2:283–284. Bussey also was a Lifetime Subscriber to the fundraising effort for the creation of "the Theological School in Harvard University"—now Harvard Divinity School—and in 1805 he donated $300 to the creation of the Massachusetts Professorship of Natural History, now the Fisher Professor of Natural History. In addition to his support of Harvard University, Bussey was also an early donor to the Massachusetts General Hospital. He is listed among the original subscribers to that institution, with a pledge of $1,000, in Bowditch, *Massachusetts General Hospital,* 412. The receipt issued to Bussey for this donation is held in the University of Michigan archives: James Prince, Treasurer, Receipt for donation to Massachusetts General Hospital, January 3, 1818, box 1, folder 19, Benjamin Bussey Collection, 1767–1872, University of Michigan Library.

111. "Memorial Hall Sculptures," Office for the Arts at Harvard: Memorial Hall / Lowell Hall Complex, accessed October 25, 2021, https://sites.fas.harvard .edu/~memhall/sculptures.html; Shobal Vail Clevenger, *Benjamin Bussey (1757–1842),* 1839, marble, 73 × 51 × 33 cm, Harvard Art Museums, https://hvrd .art/o/305329.

112. Gilbert Stuart, *Benjamin Bussey (1757–1842),* 1809, oil on panel, frame by John Doggett, 101.9 × 86.4 × 9.5 cm (framed), Harvard Art Museums, https:// hvrd.art/o/299878.

113. *Benjamin Bussey's Life* ([Boston, MA?]: B. Bussey, 1841), 4.

114. See Brown University, *Slavery and Justice,* 10, 22.

115. *Benjamin Bussey's Life,* 4. A transcription of the document was published in *The Dedham Historical Register,* vol. 10, no. 3 (Dedham, MA: Dedham Historical Society, 1899), 71–76, https://books.google.com/books?id=fw8MAAAAYAAJ.

For secondary accounts of Bussey's life, in addition to Warren, *Harvard Law School,* see Mary Jane Wilson, "Benjamin Bussey, Woodland Hill, and the Creation of the Arnold Arboretum," *Arnoldia* 64, no. 1 (2005): 2–9, http://arnoldia.arboretum.harvard.edu/pdf/articles/2006-64-1-benjamin -bussey-woodland-hill-and-the-creation-of-the-arnold-arboretum.pdf; Wilson, *Woodland Hill;* and Coquillette and Kimball, *Battlefield of Merit,* 183, n. 32.

116. *French Spoliations,* 7–8, 21–22, 56–60, 75, 89–90, 123–124, and 143–144. A typical voyage carried oxen, barrel hoops and staves, cheese, Indian corn, butter, lard, beef, fish, pork, and potatoes from New Haven, Connecticut, to Martinique in 1798.

Bussey's business correspondence further documents his trade with the West Indies. See, for example, Oliver Putnam to Benjamin Bussey, March 22, 1806, box 1, folder 4, Benjamin Bussey Collection, 1767–1872, University of Michigan Library; William Savage to Oliver Putnam, August 11, 1806, box 1, folder 5, Benjamin Bussey Collection, 1767–1872, University of Michigan Library; and William Savage to Oliver Putnam, October 20, 1806, box 1, folder 5, Benjamin Bussey Collection, 1767–1872, University of Michigan Library.

The finding aid for the Benjamin Bussey Collection at the University of Michigan is available online at https://quod.lib.umich.edu/c/clementsead /umich-wcl-M-1016bus. Noteworthy correspondents include military and political figures, major Boston merchants such as fellow Harvard donors James and Thomas Handasyd Perkins and Israel Thorndike, and an assortment of other prominent people. Material in the collection also illustrates the geographic extent of Bussey's business interests, covering business dealings in Europe, the West Indies, and Mexico, as well as within the United States from Maine in the north to New Orleans, Louisiana, in the south.

117. "Dr. Benjamin Bussey in Acct of an Adventor [sic] in the Brig Providence with Jon.[a] Arnold to New Orleans in the year 1789," June 20, 1796, box 1, folder 1, Benjamin Bussey Collection, 1767–1872, University of Michigan Library.

On tow cloth see for example Gloria Seaman Allen, "'For the People': Clothing Production and Maintenance at Rose Hill Plantation, Cecil County, Maryland," *Historic Alexandria Quarterly* (winter 2003): 4, https://www.alexandriava.gov/uploadedfiles/historic/haq/HistoricAlexandriaQuarterly2003Winter.pdf. Advertisements searching for enslaved people who had run away from their enslavers frequently describe them in tow cloth garments. See Jonathan Prude, "To Look upon the 'Lower Sort': Runaway Ads and the Appearance of Unfree Laborers in America, 1750–1800," *The Journal of American History*

78, no. 1 (June 1991): 145; Lauren Landi, "Reading Between the Lines of Slavery: Examining New England Runaway Ads for Evidence of an Afro-Yankee Culture," Pell Scholars and Senior Theses, 78 (2012): 39–48, https://digitalcommons .salve.edu/pell_theses/78.

118. Contacts in North Carolina, South Carolina, and multiple locations in Georgia are recorded in: Charles Davis to Samuel Howard, May 18, 1802, box 1, folder 3, Benjamin Bussey Collection, 1767–1872, University of Michigan Library; Richard Langdon to Benjamin Bussey, June 26, 1807, box 1, folder 6, Benjamin Bussey Collection, 1767–1872, University of Michigan Library; E. Crane, Jr. to Benjamin Bussey, October 23, 1815, box 1, folder 16, Benjamin Bussey Collection, 1767–1872, University of Michigan Library; and Roswell King to Benjamin Bussey, August 20, 1816, box 1, folder 17, Benjamin Bussey Collection, 1767–1872, University of Michigan Library.

119. Receipt for Charles Davis' passage on the Brig Eleanor, January 2, 1802, box 1, folder 3, Benjamin Bussey Collection, 1767–1872, University of Michigan Library.

120. Charles Davis to Mr. Samuel Howard, May 18, 1802, box 1, folder 3, Benjamin Bussey Collection, 1767–1872, University of Michigan Library.

121. Charles Davis to Mr. Samuel Howard, May 25, 1802, box 1, folder 3, Benjamin Bussey Collection, 1767–1872, University of Michigan Library.

Other correspondence kept Bussey informed of the prices he could expect to receive for various plantation goods in Europe. See, for example, Thos. and A.O. Cremer to Benjamin Bussey, April 28, 1807, box 1, folder 6, Benjamin Bussey Collection, 1767–1872, University of Michigan Library; Wm. Hoskins to Benjamin Bussey, September 18, 1812, box 1, folder 12, Benjamin Bussey Collection, 1767–1872, University of Michigan Library.

122. Jaazaniah Bussey to Benjamin Bussey, January 2, 1793, box 1, folder 1, Benjamin Bussey Collection, 1767–1872, University of Michigan Library; Arch Ewing to Benjamin Bussey, January 25, 1795, box 1, folder 1, Benjamin Bussey Collection, 1767–1872, University of Michigan Library; and Robert Gray to Benjamin Bussey, August 22, 1800, box 1, folder 2, Benjamin Bussey Collection, 1767–1872, University of Michigan Library.

123. See *French Spoliations,* 56–60, 123–124, 143–144.

124. "Schedule A referred to in the annexed account: Sums rec'd by the Executors [1842–1843]," Will of Benjamin Bussey, Bussey Probate Record.

125. "Fay House," Harvard Property Information Resource Center, Harvard University, accessed January 6, 2022, https://harvardplanning.emuseum .com/sites/544/fay-house?ctx=1cb551379ee5a8cd29a91ae8111f07d7e19f685f &idx=0.

126. Josiah Quincy to Benjamin Bussey, July 2, 1824, box 1, folder 22, Benjamin Bussey Collection, 1767–1872, University of Michigan Library. The purchase is confirmed by Suffolk County property records: "Benjamin Bussey to the City of Boston," Massachusetts Land Records, 1620–1986, Suffolk Deeds 1824, vol. 291–292, county courthouses and offices, Massachusetts, image 250 of 681, familysearch.com, accessed September 23, 2021.

127. Compare Carleton Osgood, "A plan of Boston: from actual survey" [Boston, MA?: s.n., 1805?], https://lccn.loc.gov/2011589290, and View of Quincy Market, Boston, Google Maps, accessed October 25, 2021, https://goo.gl/maps/jbFpcZDWf74fgstx8.

128. "Will of Benjamin Bussey," in Bussey Probate Record, 5. Bussey's summer estate in Roxbury is now the site of the Arnold Arboretum. His papers include various correspondence about his interests in Maine—an interest he shared with fellow Harvard donor and Maine landholder Israel Thorndike. The way in which these Harvard donors' land dealings in Maine impacted local Native communities, including the Penobscot and Passamaquoddy, is an important area for future research.

129. Josiah Quincy to Judith Bussey, August 28, 1842, box 1, folder 32, Benjamin Bussey Collection, 1767–1872, University of Michigan Library.

130. E.D. Merrill, "The Atkins Institution of the Arnold Arboretum, Soledad, Cienfuegos, Cuba," *Bulletin of Popular Information,* 4th ser., 8, no. 13 (December 13, 1940): 66, http://arnoldia.arboretum.harvard.edu/pdf/articles/1940-8—the-atkins-institution-of-the-arnold-arboretum-soledad-cienfuegos-cuba.pdf.

131. Ferrer, *Freedom's Mirror.*

132. Rebecca J. Scott, "A Cuban Connection: Edwin F. Atkins, Charles Francis Adams, Jr., and the Former Slaves of Soledad Plantation," *The Massachusetts Historical Review* 9 (2007): 7–34; Rebekah E. Pite, "The Force of Food: Life on the Atkins Family Sugar Plantation in Cienfuegos, Cuba, 1884–1900," *The Massachusetts Historical Review* 5 (2003): 58–93. Slavery was abolished in Cuba in 1886. Rebecca J. Scott, "Gradual Abolition and the Dynamics of Slave Emancipation in Cuba, 1868–86," *The Hispanic American Historical Review* 63, no. 3 (August 1983): 449–477.

133. Louis A. Pérez, *Cuba and the United States: Ties of Singular Intimacy,* 3rd ed. (Athens, GA: University of Georgia Press, 2003), 56–61. See Denise S. Davis-Oyesanya, "E. Atkins and Company and the sugar trade in Cuba" (PhD diss., University of Oklahoma, 1996), 31–64; Marion D. Cahan, "The Harvard Garden in Cuba—A Brief History," *Arnoldia* 51, no. 3 (Fall 1991): 26–27, http://arnoldia.arboretum.harvard.edu/pdf/articles/1991-51-3-the-harvard-garden-in-cuba-a-brief-history.pdf.

134. Scott, "Cuban Connection," 8–9.

135. Scott, "Cuban Connection," 10.

136. Edwin F. Atkins to J. S. Murray, April 25, 1884, vol. 2.5, July 27, 1883–November 29, 1884, Letterbooks, 1878–1912, Correspondence, 1875–1919, Edwin F. Atkins Papers, 1875–1950, Atkins Family Papers, Ms. N-297, Massachusetts Historical Society.

137. See Edwin F. Atkins to J. S. Murray, May 25, 1884, vol. 4.1, April 23, 1884–January 7, 1885, Letterbooks, 1878–1912, Correspondence, 1875–1919, Edwin F. Atkins Papers, 1875–1950, Atkins Family Papers, Ms. N-297, Massachusetts Historical Society. See also Pite, "Force of Food," 61–63. On July 15, 1884, Murray informed Atkins that the Cuban Civil Guard had shot and killed a "runaway negro" employed by a Soledad estate contractor who, under the law, did not have the right to leave the plantation on which he was indentured. Murray described the event as "very disagreeable," but hastened to assure Atkins that "it was no fault of anyone on the estate." Atkins wrote to Murray twice in the following weeks responding to several issues Murray raised in his letter of July 15, 1884. He did not respond to the news of lethal violence against the worker on his property. J. S. Murray to Edwin F. Atkins, July 15, 1884, box 4.1, April 15, 1884–November 15, 1885, J. S. Murray, 1884–1893, Letterbooks, 1884–1916, Soledad Sugar Co. Records, 1884–1916, Atkins Family Papers, Ms. N-297, Massachusetts Historical Society; Edwin F. Atkins to J. S. Murray, July 23 and July 30, 1884, vol. 4.1, April 23, 1884–January 7, 1885, Edwin F. Atkins, 1884–1916, Letterbooks, 1884–1916, Soledad Sugar Co. Records, 1884–1916, Atkins Family Papers, Ms. N-297, Massachusetts Historical Society.

138. J. S. Murray to Edwin F. Atkins, June 19, 1884, box 4.1, April 15, 1884–November 15, 1885, J. S. Murray, 1884–1893, Letterbooks, 1884–1916, Soledad Sugar Co. Records, 1884–1916, Atkins Family Papers, Ms. N-297, Massachusetts Historical Society; see also Kathleen López and Rebekah E. Pite, "Appendix," in "Letters from Soledad in the Atkins Family Papers at the Massachusetts Historical Society," *Massachusetts Historical Review* 9 (2007): 39.

139. Scott, "Cuban Connection," 10, 26.

140. Sven Beckert, Balraj Gill, Jim Henle, and Katherine May Stevens, "Harvard and Slavery: A Short History," in *Slavery and University,* ed. Harris et al., 242.

141. Merrill, "Atkins Institution," 70.

142. Merrill, "Atkins Institution," 66.

143. Liz Mineo, "Between Cuba and Harvard, an uncommon Garden," *Harvard Gazette,* August 1, 2016, https://news.harvard.edu/gazette/story/2016/08/between-cuba-and-harvard-an-uncommon-garden/; Cahan, "Harvard Garden in Cuba" and Jardín Botánico Nacional Universidad de La Habana, accessed February 23, 2022, www.jardinbotanico.co.cu.

144. Beckert, *Empire of Cotton,* x.

145. Harvard University, *Twenty-Second Annual Report of the President of the University at Cambridge to the Overseers Exhibiting the State of the Institution for the Academic Year 1846–47* (Cambridge, MA: Metcalf and Company, printers to the University, 1848), 7–8, https://iiif.lib.harvard.edu/manifests/view/drs:427074853$1i.

146. Abbott Lawrence, "To the Honorable Samuel A. Eliot, Treasurer of Harvard College, Boston, June 27, 1847," in Harvard University, *Twenty-Second Annual Report,* 27–28.

147. Lawrence, "To the Honorable Samuel A. Eliot," in Harvard University, *Twenty-Second Annual Report,* 25. See also Barbara M. Tucker and Kenneth H. Tucker Jr., *Industrializing Antebellum America: The Rise of Manufacturing Entrepreneurs in the Early Republic* (New York, NY: Palgrave Macmillan, 2008).

148. Harvard University, *Twenty-Second Annual Report,* 8.

149. "Lawrence, Abbott (d. 1855)—Will," Suffolk County, Massachusetts, Probate Records, 1636–1899, vol. 153, 1854–1856, digital images, Ancestry.com, accessed April 28, 2021.

150. Tucker and Tucker, *Industrializing Antebellum America,* 161–177.

151. Lawrence to The President and Fellows of Harvard College, Boston, July 19, 1847, box 1, vol. 1, Letterbook, 1847–1865, Abbott Lawrence personal and company correspondence and letterbook, MS Am 3308, Houghton Library, Harvard University; see also Tucker and Tucker, *Industrializing Antebellum America.*

152. Lurie, *Louis Agassiz,* 137–138. Lawrence renewed his support for Agassiz's salary in 1853, see Abbott Lawrence to Samuel Atkins Eliot, March 5, 1853, box 10, Corporation papers, 1853–1856, Corporation papers, 2nd series, supplements to the Harvard College Papers, UAI 5.130, Harvard University Archive. After Abbott Lawrence's death, his son affirmed the family's continuing support for Agassiz's salary, until such time as the elder Lawrence's $50,000 bequest could be paid to the University. See James W. Lawrence to William T. Andrews, Esq., November 12, 1855, box 10, Corporation papers, 1853–1856,

Corporation papers, 2nd series, supplements to the Harvard College Papers, UAI 5.130, Harvard University Archives.

153. Tucker and Tucker, *Industrializing Antebellum America,* 5.

154. On his father's side, Abbott Lawrence Lowell was a 6th-generation Harvard graduate. This line consisted of a minister, a judge, politicians, lawyers, philanthropists, and businessmen associated with such prominent Boston-area institutions as Massachusetts General Hospital, Massachusetts Hospital Life Insurance Company, the Lowell Institute—which invited Louis Agassiz to the United States—and the Boston Museum of Fine Arts. Three of Lowell's patrilineal grandfathers served on the Corporation of Harvard College, while his father served on the Massachusetts Institute of Technology's governing board. His mother's family was similarly wealthy and influential: his grandfather Abbott Lawrence was a businessman and politician, connected to Harvard as an overseer and honorary degree recipient after donating significantly to the establishment of Harvard's Lawrence Scientific School, which Agassiz headed. See Henry Aaron Yeomans, "The Family: The Elder Lowells," chap. 1 in *Abbott Lawrence Lowell, 1856–1943* (Cambridge, MA: Harvard University Press, 1948), and Elizabeth Cary Agassiz, ed., *Louis Agassiz: His Life and Correspondence* (Cambridge, MA: The Riverside Press, 1885; Cambridge, MA: Houghton, Mifflin and Company, 1887), 402–403. See also "Collection Overview: Biographical Note," Papers of Abbott Lawrence Lowell, 1861–1945, 1953, and undated, UAI 15.896, Harvard University Archives, accessed February 17, 2022, https://id.lib.harvard.edu/ead/hua26013/catalog.

155. See Section Four of this report.

156. For a discussion of Abbott Lawrence Lowell's great-grandfather, Massachusetts textile magnate Francis Cabot Lowell, among other members of the Lowell family see Beckert, *Empire of Cotton,* 147–197.

157. Alfred Holt Stone, "The Cotton Factorage System of the Southern States," *The American Historical Review* 20, no. 3 (1915): 557–565; Harold D. Woodman, "The Decline of Cotton Factorage after the Civil War," *The American Historical Review* 71, no. 4 (July 1966): 1219–1236, Walter Johnson, *River of Dark Dreams: Slavery and Empire in the Cotton Kingdom* (Cambridge, MA: The Belknap Press of Harvard University Press, 2013); Beckert, *Empire of Cotton.*

158. Johnson, *River of Dark Dreams,* 244.

159. Abbott Lawrence to Thomas Bancroft, November 6, 1847, and November 29, 1847, and Abbott Lawrence to James M. Crane, October 15, 1847, box 1, vol. 1, Letterbook, 1847–1865, Abbott Lawrence personal and company

correspondence and letterbook, MS Am 3308, Houghton Library, Harvard University.

160. Letters received, William Gray, Atlantic Cotton Mills, 1853–1854, box 21, folder 22, Greenleaf and Hubbard business records, MSS 761 1850–1860 G814, Baker Library Special Collections, Harvard Business School.

161. Maycock and Sullivan, *Building Old Cambridge,* 183; Harvard University, *Quinquennial Catalogue, 1636–1915,* 62.

162. Edward Abbott, *Mrs. James Greenleaf* (Cambridge, MA: The Powell Press, 1903), 12.

163. See Walter Johnson, "Making a World Out of Slaves," chap. 3 in *Soul by Soul: Life inside the Antebellum Slave Market* (Cambridge, MA: Harvard University Press, 1999).

164. See "Collection Overview: Historical Note," Greenleaf and Hubbard Collection, Baker Library, Harvard Business School, accessed February 17, 2022, https://id.lib.harvard.edu/ead/bak00069/catalog.

165. See, for example, Letters received, Samuel Batchelder, York Mfg. Co., 1851–1852, 1856–1859, box 21, folder 4, Greenleaf and Hubbard business records, MSS 761 1850–1860 G814, Baker Library Special Collections, Harvard Business School.

166. Jefferson Davis, Lynda Lasswell Crist, and Mary Seaton Dix, eds., *The Papers of Jefferson Davis,* vol. 6, *1856–1860* (Baton Rouge, LA: Louisiana State University Press, 1989), 547.

167. Thavolia Glymph, "The Second Middle Passage: The Transition from Slavery to Freedom at Davis Bend, Mississippi" (PhD diss., Purdue University, 1994), 9; see also Frank E. Everett Jr., *Brierfield: Plantation Home of Jefferson Davis* (Hattiesburg, MS: University and College Press of Mississippi, 1971).

168. Check stubs, Louisiana State Bank, 1853–1859, box 23, folder 11, pp. 7–10, 13, Greenleaf and Hubbard business records, MSS 761 1850–1860 G814, Baker Library Special Collections, Harvard Business School; "Finding Aid: Biographical Sketches," Payne-Broadwell Family Papers, 1803–1903, The State Historical Society of Missouri, https://files.shsmo.org/manuscripts/columbia/C0983 .pdf.

169. "More on the Life of Jacob U. Payne," New Orleans *Daily Picayune* (March 12, 1900).

170. "Jefferson Davis' Friend Dead: Busy Life of Jacob Upshur Payne, at Whose Home Mr. Davis Died, at an End," *Washington Post,* March 12, 1900.

Sidebar: Darby Vassall and Black Resistance

1.   Harvard University, *Quinquennial Catalogue of the Officers and Graduates of Harvard University, 1636–1890* (Cambridge, MA: John Wilson and Son, 1890), 6, https://books.google.com/books?id=zh9OAAAAMAAJ.

2.   J. L. Bell, *Longfellow House–Washington's Headquarters National Historic Site Historic Resource Study,* (National Park Service, 2012), 16–18, 31, https://www.nps.gov/long/learn/historyculture/upload/Washington-Headquarters-HRS.pdf.

3.   "Darby Vassall," George Washington's Mount Vernon, accessed March 15, 2022, https://www.mountvernon.org/library/digitalhistory/digital-encyclopedia/article/darby-vassall/.

4.   Samuel Francis Batchelder, *Notes on Colonel Henry Vassall (1721–1769): His Wife Penelope, His House at Cambridge, and His Slaves Tony & Darby* (Cambridge, MA: 1917), 71, https://books.google.com/books?id=nJYlAQAAMAAJ.

5.   Bell, *Longfellow House–Washington's Headquarters,* 39.

6.   *Laws of the African Society, Instituted at Boston, Anno Domini 1796* (Boston, MA: Massachusetts Historical Society, 1796); William Cooper Nell, *The Colored Patriots of the American Revolution, with sketches of several Distinguished Colored Persons: to which is added a brief survey of the Condition and Prospects of Colored Americans,* with an introduction by Harriet Beecher Stowe (Boston, MA: Robert F. Walcutt, 1855), https://books.google.com/books?id=Jy8OAAAAIAAJ.

7.   Senate Unpassed 1812, Docket 4522, Digital Archive of Massachusetts Anti-Slavery and Anti-Segregation Petitions, HOLLIS 013622572, IV, Harry Elkins Widener Memorial Library, Harvard University, https://nrs.harvard.edu/urn-3:FHCL:11148848.

8.   "Abiel Smith School," Boston African American National Historic Site Massachusetts, accessed November 17, 2021, https://www.nps.gov/boaf/learn/historyculture/abiel-smith-school.htm.

9.   See, for example, "No Union with Slave Holders!" *The Liberator,* June 14, 1844; "Collections for Expenses of the New England Anti-Slavery Convention, May, 1851 . . ." *The Liberator,* June 13, 1851.

10.   William Cooper Nell included Darby in his 1855 volume *Colored Patriots of the American Revolution,* and penned his obituary in *The Liberator.* See William Cooper Nell, "'Darby Vassall' [Obituary]," *The Liberator,* Nov. 22, 1861.

Wendell Phillips, a Harvard-educated lawyer and prominent white abolitionist, drafted a last will and testament for Darby in 1852: "Vassall, Derby. [Will]. MS. (in Wendell Phillips's hand); Boston, 15 May 1852," box 45,

Wendell Phillips papers, MS Am 1953, (1582), Houghton Library, Harvard University.

11.   Henry Wadsworth Longfellow, journal entry for March 22, 1855, [Journal] A.MS, (unsigned), [v.p.], September 1, 1853–December 31, 1855, vol. 204, Henry Wadsworth Longfellow papers, MS Am 1340, (206), Houghton Library, Harvard University. See also "Lunsford Lane," National Park Service, accessed November 17, 2021, https://www.nps.gov/people/lunsford-lane.htm; and *The Narrative of Lunsford Lane: Formerly of Raleigh, N.C., Embracing an Account of His Early Life, The Redemption, by Purchase of Himself and Family from Slavery, and His Banishment from the Place of His Birth for the Crime of Wearing a Colored Skin* (Boston, MA: self–pub.,1848), https://books.google.com/books ?id=Z2upajdouSwC.

12.   "Petition 36," [Petition of the Colored Citizens of Boston to the Senate and House Representatives of the Commonwealth of Massachusetts], seq. 2000, Acts 1861, c.91, Digital Archive of Massachusetts Anti-Slavery and Anti-Segregation Petitions, HOLLIS 013622572, Harry Elkins Widener Memorial Library, Harvard University, https://nrs.harvard.edu/urn-3:FHCL:10512596?n =200.

13.   Batchelder, *Notes on Colonel Henry Vassall,* 77–78.

Sidebar: Fellow Commoners: Harvard's Colonial Elite

1.   Sidney W. Mintz, *Sweetness and Power: The Place of Sugar in Modern History* (New York, NY: Penguin Books, 1986).

2.   Clifford K. Shipton, *Sibley's Harvard Graduates, Volume VIII: 1726–1730, Biographical Sketches of Those Who Attended Harvard College in the Classes 1726–1730 with Bibliographical and other notes* (Boston, MA: Massachusetts Historical Society, 1951), 521.

Ledger for the Classes of 1723–1731, seq. 274, box 6, Early Records of the Steward, 1649–1812, UAI 71, Harvard University Archives, https://nrs.lib .harvard.edu/urn-3:hul.arch:16501510?n=274. See also entries for James Pitts (seq. 74) and William Hobby (seq. 121).

3.   Craig Wilder, *Ebony & Ivy: Race, Slavery, and the Troubled History of American Universities* (New York, NY: Bloomsbury Press, 2013), 86–87.

4.   Benjamin Peirce, *A History of Harvard University, from its Foundation, in the Year 1636, to the Period of the American Revolution* (Cambridge, MA: Brown, Shattuck, and Company, 1833), 125 (appendix XX).

5.   Janine E. Skerry, "Ancient and Valuable Gifts: Silver at Colonial Harvard," in New England Silver and Silversmithing 1620–1815, ed. Jeannine Falino

and Gerald W.R. Ward (Boston, MA: The Colonial Society of Massachusetts, 2001), 188, https://www.colonialsociety.org/node/1367#en346.

6.　Peirce, *History of Harvard University*, 126.

7.　Skerry, "Ancient and Valuable Gifts."

4: Harvard, Slavery, and Its Legacies before and after the Civil War

1.　For scholarship discussing the many laws, policies, practices, norms, and attitudes that remained as relics of slavery despite its legal prohibition, see generally Leon F. Litwack, *Been in the Storm So Long: The Aftermath of Slavery* (New York, NY: Knopf, distributed by Random House, 1979); Hunter, *To 'joy My Freedom*; Masur, *All the Land*; Foner, *Forever Free*; Franklin, *Reconstruction*; Ariela J. Gross, *What Blood Won't Tell*, 4–5, 9–11, 79–110.

2.　See generally Jacobs, *Courage and Conscience*; Sinha, *Slave's Cause*, 41–44, 67–72, 453–454. These antislavery activists, however, encountered significant resistance, see Cutler, *Boston Gentleman's Mob*. This history is sometimes forgotten; on the complex association between historical memory in discussions of slavery and antislavery, see Minardi, *Making Slavery History*, and Araujo, *Slavery in the Age of Memory*.

3.　Cronin, *Reforming Boston's Schools*, 5, 25–26; Foner, *Reconstruction*, 26; Omori, "Race-Neutral Individualism"; Greenwood, "Community within a Community"; Hill, "Ethnicity and Education."

4.　See U.S. Const. amends. XIII, XIV, XV; see also Foner, *What is Freedom*, chaps. 1–3.

5.　On the white vigilante violence that followed formerly enslaved Blacks when they tried to exercise their newly found freedom, see Foner, *Reconstruction*, 119–123, 425–430; Du Bois, *Black Reconstruction*, 221–230, describes, for example, the insufficient resources given to the Freedmen's Bureau, a federal agency designed to aid the formerly enslaved in the South, as the result of political pushback from Southern whites.

6.　Morison, *Three Centuries of Harvard*, 323.

7.　Morison, *Three Centuries of Harvard*, 322. On the Overseers' aspirations for Harvard during this period, see ibid., 324–331.

8.　"Cambridge Anti-Slavery Society Records now available," The Cambridge Room: Historic tidbits, facts, and notes of interest on Cambridge, Massachusetts brought to you by the Cambridge Public Library's Archivist, updated November 23, 2016, https://thecambridgeroom.wordpress.com/2016/11/23 /cambridge-anti-slavery-society-records-now-available/; Harvard faculty titles and terms confirmed in Harvard University, *Quinquennial Catalogue, 1636–1915*, 104, 108.

9. "No Union with Slave Holders!" *The Liberator* (Boston, MA), June 14, 1844.

10. Massachusetts Anti-Slavery Society Board of Managers, "Officers of the Society," in *Twelfth annual report, presented to the Massachusetts Anti-Slavery Society, by its Board of Managers, January 24, 1844, with an appendix* (Boston, MA: Oliver Johnson, Court Street, 1844). For more on Williams's anti-slavery views and activism, see John R. McKivigan, ed., *The Frederick Douglass Papers, Series Three: Correspondence, Volume 1: 1842–1852* (New Haven, CT: Yale University Press, 2009), 102, n. 15; and Mary Elizabeth Williams Papers, MSS 253, Courtesy of Phillips Library, Peabody Essex Museum, Massachusetts, https://pem.as.atlas-sys.com/repositories/2/resources/644.

11. "Henry Willard Williams, AM, MD," Harvard Medical School Department of Ophthalmology, accessed January 2, 2022, https://eye.hms.harvard .edu/henrywillardwilliams; "Henry Willard Williams Professorship," Harvard Medical School Department of Ophthalmology, accessed January 2, 2022, https://eye.hms.harvard.edu/professorships/williams; Harvard University, *Quinquennial Catalogue, 1636–1915*, 28.

12. Austin Bearse, *Reminiscences of Fugitive-Slave Law Days in Boston* (Boston, MA: W. Richardson, 1880), 3–5; Harvard faculty titles and terms confirmed in Harvard University, *Quinquennial Catalogue, 1636–1915*, 50, 76, 185.

13. Roy E. Finkenbine, "Smith, Joshua Bowen (born 1813), Abolitionists," *American National Biography Online*, Oxford University Press, 2000.

14. See Section Two of this report.

15. Smith appeared frequently in notices in the abolitionist newspaper *The Liberator* and other like-minded periodicals throughout the decades surrounding the Civil War, which frequently noted his involvement with and financial contributions to antislavery work. See, for example, "Pledges," *The Liberator,* June 13, 1856, where Smith was listed as a donor to the Massachusetts Anti-Slavery Society's May 1856 Convention, and "Annual Meeting of the Massachusetts Anti-Slavery Society," *National Anti-Slavery Standard,* February 5, 1870, where he was noted as a councillor of the meeting alongside the well-known abolitionist and Harvard graduate Wendell Phillips.

Smith also appears to have been a colleague of noted Black Bostonian abolitionist and writer William Cooper Nell, who mentioned him as both a source and a co-petitioner in *The Colored Patriots of the American Revolution, with sketches of several Distinguished Colored Persons: to which is added a brief survey of the Condition and Prospects of Colored Americans,* with an introduction by Harriet Beecher Stowe (Boston, MA: Robert F. Walcutt, 1855), https://books.google.com/books?id=Jy8OAAAAIAAJ.

16. Bearse, *Fugitive-Slave Law Days,* 5, and William Henry Siebert, *The Underground Railroad from Slavery to Freedom,* with an introduction by Albert Bushnell Hart (New York, NY: The MacMillan Company, 1898), 437, https://books.google.com/books?id=yspuBhJWS9sC.

17. Bearse, *Fugitive-Slave Law Days,* 6, 36, and Siebert, *Underground Railroad,* 412.

18. Mary Ellen Snodgrass, "Smith, Joshua Bowen," *The Underground Railroad: An Encyclopedia of People, Places, and Operations* (Armonk, NY: Routledge, 2008), 499.

19. "Cambridge Anti-Slavery Society Records," Cambridge Public Library.

20. Eliza Lee Cabot Follen, *The Life of Charles Follen* (Boston, MA: Thomas H. Webb and Company, 1844), 227–237, https://books.google.com/books?id =5zCWAZzVRq4C.

21. John Ware, *Memoir of the Life of Henry Ware Jr.* (Boston, MA: James Munroe and Co, 1846), 361–362. See also Bosco, "Fugitive Slave Act," 228–229; Wilder, *Ebony & Ivy,* 278–280.
 Ware's widow clearly believed her husband had been persecuted by Harvard administration because of his views: In an 1845 exchange with then former Harvard President Josiah Quincy she asked, "if at any time, during [my] husband's connection with the University, he was required by the Corporation to suppress the expression of his opinion upon the subject of slavery as being a condition of holding his Professorship?" Quincy denied that this was the case. "Josiah Quincy to Miss Mary L. Ware, April 22, 1845." Josiah Quincy to Mary L. Ware, April 22, 1845, box 4, Corporation Papers, 1845–46, Corporation Papers, 2nd ser., supplements to the Harvard College Papers, UAI 5.130, Harvard University Archives.

22. "Slavery and Abolition in the Longfellow Archives," Longfellow House Washington's Headquarters, National Park Service, accessed February 4, 2022, https://www.nps.gov/long/learn/historyculture/slavery-related-objects-at -longfellow-nhs.htm.

23. Frederick J. Blue, "The Poet and the Reformer: Longfellow, Sumner, and the Bonds of Male Friendship, 1837–1874," *Journal of the Early Republic* 15, no. 2 (Summer 1995): 280–285.

24. Christoph Irmscher, who has written biographies of both men, characterizes Longfellow as "Agassiz's closest friend." *Louis Agassiz: Creator of American Science* (New York, NY: Houghton Mifflin Harcourt, 2013), 14–15, 18, 21, 25.

25. Henry Wadsworth Longfellow, *Poems on Slavery*, 2nd ed. (Cambridge, MA: J. Owen, 1842), 23–25, https://books.google.com/books?id=DqxcAA AAcAAJ; Christoph Irmscher, *Public Poet, Private Man: Henry Wadsworth Longfellow at 200* (Amherst, MA: University of Massachusetts Press, 2009), 118.

26. "Longfellow and the Fugitive Slave Act," Longfellow House Washington's Headquarters, National Park Service, accessed February 4, 2022, https://www .nps.gov/long/learn/historyculture/henry-wadsworth-longfellow-abolitionist .htm.

27. Henry Wadsworth Longfellow to George Lunt, January 4, 1843, quoted in Irmscher, *Public Poet*, 113.

28. Bosco, "Fugitive Slave Act," 238–239; Irmscher, *Public Poet*, 115–117; "Longfellow and the Fugitive Slave Act," Longfellow House Washington's Headquarters.

29. Henry Wadsworth Longfellow to Charles Sumner, April 20, 1864, quoted in Irmscher, *Public Poet*, 114. Ellipsis in original.

30. Irmscher, *Public Poet*, 116–117; "Josiah Henson," Longfellow House Washington's Headquarters, National Park Service, accessed February 4, 2022, https://www.nps.gov/people/josiah-henson.htm.

31. For more on Darby Vassall, see sidebar in Section Three of this report.

32. Frank Otto Gattell, "Doctor Palfrey Frees His Slaves," *The New England Quarterly* 34, no. 1 (March 1961): 74–75.

33. Gattell, "Doctor Palfrey," 74–77; Frank Otto Gattell, *John Gorham Palfrey and the New England Conscience* (1963; repr., Cambridge, MA and London, UK: Harvard University Press, 2014). A brief overview of Palfrey's life is available at "John Gorham Palfrey: The First Dean of Harvard Divinity School," Harvard Divinity School Library, accessed December 15, 2021, https://guides .library.harvard.edu/hds/john-gorham-palfrey/hds.

34. Josiah Quincy to John Gorham Palfrey, May 25, 1838, unspecified: box 2, Papers of Josiah Quincy, 1811–1874, UAI 15.882, Harvard University Archives.

35. Josiah Quincy to John Gorham Palfrey, May 28, 1838, unspecified: box 2, Papers of Josiah Quincy, 1811–1874, UAI 15.882, Harvard University Archives.

36. Corporation records volume 8, September 26, 1836–August 28, 1847, p. 55, box 8, Harvard University Corporation records: minutes, UAI 5.30, Harvard University Archives.

37. "John Gorham Palfrey," Harvard Divinity School Library; "Palfrey, John Gorham: 1796–1881," United States House of Representatives: History, Art & Archives, accessed February 2, 2022, https://history.house.gov/People/Detail /19319.

38. Gattell, "Doctor Palfrey," 76–84. On the estimated value of the enslaved people Palfrey inherited, see ibid., 80, n. 12, which cites a notarized affidavit sent to Palfrey by his agent: Adam Giffen to John Gorham Palfrey, March 8, 1844, box 6, Giffen, Adam, 12 letters; 1843–1846, 1843–1846, Palfrey Family Papers, MS Am 1704–1704.9, 1704.11–1704.21, MS Am 1704, (355), Houghton Library, Harvard University. The enslaved people who Palfrey freed were: Anna (aged 32) and her four children, Mana (9), Charles (6), Caroline (4), and William (2); Sarah (11); Betsy (30) and her child Ralph (5); Frankey (11); Maria (22) and her child Emily (2); Margery (20) and her infant child; "Little Sam" (27); Amos (61); Clara (55) and her child Amos (9); "Old Sam" (65); Jose (40); and Rose (12).

39. Gattell, "Doctor Palfrey," 80–84. Palfrey advertised for several months in the abolitionist newspaper *The Liberator* to find employment for many of the men and women he freed. See "Liberated Slaves! Employment Wanted," *The Liberator,* April 18, April 25, May 9, and May 16, 1845. Palfrey advertised separately for several additional weeks to find an appropriate place for a man named Samuel, who was "somewhat deficient in intelligence" and thus required "a little more than usual aid and oversight on the part of his employer." See "Place Wanted," *The Liberator,* June 27, July 4, and July 11, 1845.

40. Gattell, *John Gorham Palfrey,* 194–203.

41. See Bosco, "Fugitive Slave Act," 230–242.

42. Palfrey made frequent appearances in the private journals of Harvard Librarian John Langdon Sibley between 1846 and 1881, where Sibley recorded Palfrey socializing with University faculty and administrators well beyond the end of his deanship in 1839 (see for example, May 13, 1846). "John Langdon Sibley's diary (known as Sibley's private journal), 1846–1882 (HUG 1791.72.10)," Harvard University Archives, accessed January 3, 2022, https://wayback.archive -it.org/5488/20170330145830/http://hul.harvard.edu/lib/archives/refshelf /Sibley.htm (archived on March 30, 2017 as part of H-Sites: Harvard Life and Learning collection). During this period, Palfrey's abolitionist writings and speeches were being published for a popular audience. See John Gorham Palfrey, *Papers on the slave power: first published in the "Boston Whig,"* Thomas

Waterman Pamphlet Collection and African American Pamphlet Collection, (Boston, MA: Merrill, Cobb & Co., 1846), https://www.loc.gov/item/06018450/; and *Speech of Mr. Palfrey of Massachusetts on the Political Aspect of the Slave Question, Delivered in the House of Representatives, January 26, 1848* (Washington, DC: J. & C. S. Gideon, 1848), https://books.google.com/books?id =askS-7MbImIC.

43. Gattell, *John Gorham Palfrey,* 191. Citing John Gorham Palfrey, March 17–19, 1850, Journals and Autobiographical Material, Palfrey Family Papers, MS Am 1704–1704.9, 1704.11–1704.21, MS Am 1704.14, Houghton Library, Harvard University.

44. Bosco, "Fugitive Slave Act," 229, citing Caleb Cushing to President [Jared] Sparks, September 8, 1850, MS Sparks 153, Houghton Library, Harvard University. Gattell also cites this letter in reference to Sparks's 1850 visit to Palfrey, see *John Gorham Palfrey,* 191, 318, n. 32.

45. See Nercessian, *Against All Odds,* 7–23, and Scott Podolsky, "Diversity in Leadership: Oliver Wendell Holmes, Racism, and Remembrance," Harvard Medical School, October 29, 2020, https://dicp.hms.harvard.edu/events/2020 /diversity-in-leadership (video available). It is noteworthy that Dean Oliver Wendell Holmes, Sr. opted to respond to the pressure of white petitioners opposed to admission, rather than the many students who spoke out in favor of allowing their Black colleagues to remain enrolled. See, for example, a petition signed by twenty-six Harvard Medical School students in favor of allowing the Black students admission: Petitions and correspondence, re admission of colored students, 11/1850-11/1853, 11/1850-11/1853, oversize-box 7, folder 18, Harvard Medical School, Office of the Dean records, RG M-DE01, Center for the History of Medicine, Francis A. Countway Library of Medicine, Harvard Medical School, http://nrs.harvard.edu/urn-3:HMS .COUNT:16817776?n=2.

In 2020, Harvard Medical School and Harvard School of Dental Medicine students successfully petitioned to have Dean Holmes's name removed from an academic honor society. The organization was renamed in honor of Dr. William Augustus Hinton, an instructor at Harvard Medical School from 1918 to 1949, and Clinical Professor from 1949 to 1950. Dr. Hinton was the first African American appointed a Professor at Harvard University. See "William Augustus Hinton," Harvard Medical School Medical Education, accessed November 15, 2021, https://meded.hms.harvard.edu/william-augustus -hinton.

46. *A Memorial Concerning the Recent History and the Constitutional Rights and Privileges of Harvard College; Presented by the President and Fellows to the*

Legislature, January 17, 1851 (Cambridge, MA: John Bartlett, 1851), https://books.google.com/books?id=2S9cAAAAcAAJ&dq.

47. Gattell, *John Gorham Palfrey,* 203–216.

48. See "Collection Overview: Biographical / Historical," Peabody, Ephraim, 1807–1856, Papers, 1831–1884, bMS 381, Harvard Divinity School Library, Harvard University, accessed November 15, 2021, https://id.lib.harvard.edu/ead /div00381/catalog. Though at least one source refers to Peabody as a Harvard overseer, this does not appear to be the case.

Harvard Treasurer Samuel Atkins Eliot was an active member of King's Chapel, see Henry Wilder Foote, *Annals of King's Chapel, from the Puritan Age of New England to the Present Day,* vol. 2 (Boston, MA: Little, Brown, & Company, 1896), 523–524, https://books.google.com/books?id=Q801AAA AIAAJ.

49. Ephraim Peabody to John Gorham Palfrey, September 29, 1852, Palfrey Family Papers, MS Am 1704–1704.9, 1704.11–1704.21, MS Am 1704, (715), Houghton Library, Harvard University.

50. John Gorham Palfrey to Ephraim Peabody, 1852, Palfrey Family Papers, MS Am 1704–1704.9, 1704.11–1704.21, MS Am 1704.1, (254), Houghton Library, Harvard University.

51. C. G. Loring to Jared Sparks, August 10 and 31, 1853, Jared Sparks letter-books, MS Sparks 153, Houghton Library, Harvard University.

52. "Lemuel Shaw," Commonwealth of Massachusetts; Harvard University, *Quinquennial Catalogue, 1636–1915,* 162. On Lemuel Shaw and the Fugitive Slave Act, see "Biographical Sketch," Lemuel Shaw Papers, Massachusetts Historical Society, accessed November 16, 2021, https://www.masshist.org /collection-guides/view/fa0308. See also Sims's Case, 61 Mass. 285, 7 Cush. 285 (1851).

53. Bosco, "Fugitive Slave Act," 246, citing Board of Overseers, Harvard University, Reports, vol. 9: 1850–1854, UAH 10.54, Harvard University Archives. On Eliot's support for the Compromise of 1850, see Bosco, "Fugitive Slave Act," 233–234.

54. *Historical Register of Harvard University, 1636–1936* (Cambridge, MA: Harvard University Press, 1937), 303, 424, as cited in Bosco, "Fugitive Slave Act," 247.

55. Corydon Ireland, "Blue, gray, and Crimson," *Harvard Gazette,* March 21, 2012, https://news.harvard.edu/gazette/story/2012/03/blue-gray-and-crimson/.

Memorial Hall on Harvard's Cambridge campus was constructed in 1878 as a monument to the Harvard men who died fighting on the side of the

Union. See "Memorial Hall: Historical Notes," Harvard Property Information Resource Center Catalogue, accessed November 15, 2021, https://harvardplanning.emuseum.com/sites/105/memorial-hall?ctx=a2694b0c76a81 085fcaf487c2ba9114fdd72d88a&idx=0.

56. "John Gorham Palfrey," Harvard Divinity School Library.

57. In July 2020, Harvard Medical School students, faculty, and alumni petitioned for the Oliver Wendell Holmes Society to be renamed, citing his "promotion of eugenics and his violence toward Black and Indigenous peoples," see Meera S. Nair, "Harvard Medical and Dental Students Petition to Rename Holmes Society," *Harvard Crimson,* July 12, 2020, https://www.thecrimson .com/article/2020/7/12/holmes-society-petition/.

58. Harvard University, *Quinquennial Catalogue, 1636–1915,* 67.

59. Harvard University, *Quinquennial Catalogue, 1636–1915,* 34, 111.

60. Cohen, "Harvard's Eugenics Era."

61. Oliver Wendell Holmes, *Elsie Venner: A Romance of Destiny* (Boston, MA: Ticknor and Fields, 1861); Josh Doty, "Tricks of the Blood: Heredity and Repair in Oliver Wendell Holmes Sr." chap. 4 in *The Perfecting of Nature: Reforming Bodies in Antebellum Literature* (Chapel Hill, NC: The University of North Carolina Press, 2020); Oliver Wendell Holmes, "The Brahmin Caste of New England," chap. 1 in "The Professor's Story," *The Atlantic Monthly* 5, no. 27 (January 1860): 91–93, https://books.google.com/books?id=BOTqCJ x5RIAC.

62. Daniel J. Kevles, "Francis Galton, Founder of the Faith," chap. 1 in *In the Name of Eugenics: Genetics and the Uses of Human Heredity* (New York, NY: Knopf, 1985).

63. Oliver Wendell Holmes, "Crime and Automatism: With a Notice of Mr. Prosper Despine's Psychologie Naturelle," *The Atlantic Monthly* 35, no. 210 (April 1875): 475.

While later eugenicists would cite hereditary determinism to advocate for sterilization and even euthanasia, Holmes in this paper appears to cite Galton and the inheritance of traits within families to medicalize such behavior and render it amenable to treatment. See also Podolsky, "Diversity in Leadership: Oliver Wendell Holmes, Racism, and Remembrance," Harvard Medical School, October 29, 2020, https://dicp.hms.harvard.edu/events/2020 /diversity-in-leadership (video available).

64. In general, Holmes Sr. has not been referred to as a eugenicist because the term "eugenics" was not coined until 1883, a year after Holmes's retirement from HMS, see James D. Watson and Andrew Berry, *DNA: The Secret of Life,*

(New York, NY: Alfred A. Knopf, 2003), 16. However, scholar Adam S. Cohen classifies Holmes as "an early eugenics advocate," pointing to his coining of and understanding of the "Brahmin caste of New England" and to his published writings speculating about the application of Galton's principles of inheritance to criminality: "If genius and talent are inherited, as Mr. Galton has so conclusively shown . . . why should not deep-rooted moral defects . . . show themselves . . . in the descendants of moral monsters?" See Adam Cohen, *Imbeciles: The Supreme Court, American Eugenics, and the Sterilization of Carrie Buck* (New York, NY: Penguin Press, 2017), 239–240.

65. J. B. S. Jackson, *A Descriptive Catalogue of the Warren Anatomical Museum* (Boston, MA: A. Williams and Company, 1870), 74. For the skull, see ibid., 702 (specimens 3226–3232 and 3233).

66. Likely unbeknownst to the faculty, given the secret nature of the organization, Snowden was also a member of the Boston Vigilance Committee. See Bearse, *Fugitive-Slave Law Days,* 5.

67. Abraham R. Thompson and Joseph Tracy to the Medical Faculty of Harvard College, November 1, 1850, box 4, folder 9, seq. 10, Petitions and correspondence, re admission of colored students, 11/1850-11/1853, Harvard Medical School, Office of the Dean records, RG M-DE01, Center for the History of Medicine, Francis A. Countway Library of Medicine, Harvard Medical School, https://iiif.lib.harvard.edu/manifests/view/drs:51163619$10i; Nercessian, *Against All Odds,* 7–8.

68. Nercessian, *Against All Odds,* 9.

69. Nercessian, *Against All Odds,* 10,11.

70. C. A. Robertson et al. to the Medical Faculty of Harvard College, [January 3, 1851?], box 4, folder 9, seq. 1, Petitions and correspondence, re admission of colored students, 11/1850-11/1853, Harvard Medical School, Office of the Dean records, RG M-DE01, Center for the History of Medicine, Francis A. Countway Library of Medicine, Harvard Medical School, https://iiif.lib .harvard.edu/manifests/view/drs:51163619$1i.

71. Nercessian, *Against All Odds,* 12–13.

72. Nercessian, *Against All Odds,* 14.

73. The Medical Faculty of Harvard College to Abraham R. Thompson, [c. December 26, 1850], box 4, folder 9, seq. 3, Petitions and correspondence, re admission of colored students, 11/1850-11/1853, 11/1850-11/1853, Harvard Medical School, Office of the Dean records, RG M-DE01, Center for the History of Medicine, Francis A. Countway Library of Medicine, Harvard Medical School, https://iiif.lib.harvard.edu/manifests/view/drs:51163619$3i.

74. Harvard University, *Quinquennial Catalogue, 1636–1915,* 34, 111.

75. Jackson, *Warren Anatomical Museum,* iii, v.

76. Harvard University, *Quinquennial Catalogue, 1636–1890,* 32.

77. Harvard University, *Quinquennial Catalogue, 1636–1915,* 34.

78. Louis Agassiz and Elizabeth Cary Agassiz, *A Journey in Brazil* (Boston, MA: Ticknor and Fields, 1868), https://books.google.com/books?id=TN08 AAAAcAAJ.

79. "Radcliffe: From College to Institute," Harvard Radcliffe Institute, accessed August 16, 2021, https://www.radcliffe.harvard.edu/about-the-institute /history.

80. Harvard University, *Quinquennial Catalogue, 1636–1890,* 32.

81. Will of Alexander Agassiz, Probate Record Books (1900–1916), and Probate Docket Books (1901–1916), Suffolk County, Massachusetts, Probate Record Book, vol. 960–970, 1910, digital images, Ancestry.com, accessed February 8, 2022.

  Alexander's will also designates bequests of books and scientific apparatus to the Lawrence Scientific School and various museums at Harvard, as well as $50,000 for the American Academy of Arts and Sciences in Boston (now Cambridge) and $50,000 for the National Academy of Sciences at Washington, DC.

82. The Lowell Institute was founded in 1846 as an educational institution in Boston. It was endowed by a substantial bequest from John Lowell, Jr. to support the Institute's activities, including free public lectures by experts. "Lowell Institute," *The Boston Recorder* 31, no. 29 (July 16, 1846): 114. See also Margaret W. Rossiter, "Benjamin Silliman and the Lowell Institute: The Popularization of Science in Nineteenth-Century America," *The New England Quarterly* 44, no. 4 (1971): 602–626.

83. Irmscher, *Louis Agassiz,* 80. Agassiz was already well known among Boston and Harvard scientists associated with the Boston Society of Natural History, where Jeffries Wyman referenced Agassiz's work at the society's February 1843 meeting; see Boston Society of Natural History, Proceedings of the Boston Society of Natural History. Boston etc.: Boston Society of Natural History, 1841–1844, vol. 1, 100.

84. Irmscher, *Louis Agassiz,* 44–51.

85. Phillip Sloan, "The Gaze of Natural History," chap. 5 in *Inventing Human Science: Eighteenth-Century Domains,* ed. Christopher Fox, Roy Porter, and Robert Wokler (Berkeley and Los Angeles, CA: University of California Press,

1995), 112–151; Mary P. Winsor, *Reading the Shape of Nature: Comparative Zoology at the Agassiz Museum* (Chicago, IL: University of Chicago Press, 1991).

86. Nancy Stepan, *Picturing Tropical Nature* (Ithaca, NY: Cornell University Press, 2001), 16.

87. Stepan, *Picturing Tropical Nature,* 13–18.

88. James Poskett, *Materials of the Mind: Phrenology, Race, and the Global History of Science, 1815–1920* (Chicago, IL: Chicago University Press, 2019), 3–13.

89. Today, the Morton Cranial Collection is held by the University of Pennsylvania Museum of Archaelogy and Anthropology. In 2020, in response to student protests, the collection was removed from public display. In 2021, the university announced that it was beginning a process of repatriating or reburying the remains of the individuals in the collection. See Christopher D. E. Willoughby, "Medicine, Racism, and the Legacies of the Morton Skull Collection," *History of Anthropology Review* 45 (2021), https://histanthro .org/news/observations/medicine-racism-and-the-legacies-of-the-morton -skull-collection/, and Jill DiSanto, "Penn Museum Announces the Repatriation of the Morton Cranial Collection," *Penn Today,* April 13, 2021, https:// penntoday.upenn.edu/news/penn-museum-announces-repatriation-morton -cranial-collection.

90. Brian Wallis, "Black Bodies, White Science: Louis Agassiz's Slave Daguerreotypes," *American Art* 9, no. 2 (Summer 1995): 39–61; Louis Agassiz, "Transcript of letter to R. M. Agassiz et al. [Boston], December 2, 1846," Louis Agassiz Correspondence and Other Papers, MS Am 1419, Houghton Library, Harvard University, https://iiif.lib.harvard.edu/manifests/view/drs:12 379926$326i.

91. Agassiz, "Transcript of letter to R. M. Agassiz et al. [Boston], December 2, 1846."

92. Agassiz visited scientists and research institutions like Yale, Columbia, and Princeton before stopping in Philadelphia where he observed the Morton skulls. His encounter with African American hotel workers occurred in Philadelphia following his meeting with Morton. Agassiz, "Transcript of letter to R. M. Agassiz et al. [Boston], December 2, 1846," esp. seq. 335–336. See also Stephen Jay Gould, *The Mismeasure of Man,* revised and expanded ed. (New York: NY: W.W. Norton & Company, 1996), 76–77.

93. Agassiz, "Transcript of letter to R. M. Agassiz et al. [Boston], December 2, 1846," seq. 335–336; see Gould, *Mismeasure of Man,* 76–77.

94. Gould, *Mismeasure of Man,* 74.

95. *Proceedings of the Boston Society of Natural History,* vol. 3, *1848–1851* (Cambridge, MA: Printed for the Society by Bolles and Houghton, 1851), 36–37.

96. Molly Rogers, *Delia's Tears: Race, Science, and Photography in Nineteenth-Century America* (New Haven, CT: Yale University Press, 2010), 202–205.

97. Louis Agassiz, "Geographical Distribution of Animals," *The Christian Examiner and Religious Miscellany* 48, no. 2, 4th ser., 13 (March 1850): 181–204, https://books.google.com/books?id=CgEZAAAAYAAJ. For the quote, see p. 181.

98. Agassiz, "Geographical Distribution of Animals," 181.

99. Louis Agassiz, "The Diversity of the Origin of the Human Races," *The Christian Examiner and Religious Miscellany* 49, no. 1, 4th ser., 14 (July 1850): 110–145, https://books.google.com/books?id=XwEZAAAAYAAJ. For the quote, see p. 143.

100. Scott Podolsky and colleagues at Harvard Medical School provided valuable input to the discussion of this intellectual history. See also William Stanton, *The Leopard's Spots: Scientific Attitudes toward Race in America, 1815–1859* (Chicago, IL: University of Chicago Press, 1960); Thomas F. Gossett, *Race: The History of an Idea in America* (New York, NY: Schocken Books, 1963); Bruce Dain, *A Hideous Monster of the Mind: American Race Theory in the Early Republic* (Cambridge, MA: Harvard University Press, 2002); Ibram X. Kendi, *Stamped from the Beginning: The Definitive History of Racist Ideas in America* (New York, NY: Bold Type Books, 2016).

101. Elizabeth Cary Agassiz, "Letters to Louis Agassiz, 1849–1850," Papers of Elizabeth Cabot Cary Agassiz, 1838–1920 (inclusive), 1838–1908 (bulk), A-3, 9, Schlesinger Library, Harvard Radcliffe Institute.

102. See Bosco, "Fugitive Slave Act."

103. Agassiz, "Diversity of Origins," 112.

104. Agassiz, "Diversity of Origins," 142.

105. Elizabeth Cabot Cary to her mother, April 15–16, "Letters from South Carolina, Washington, New Orleans, etc., 1851–1852," folder 10, seq. 29, Elizabeth Cary Agassiz Papers, 1838–1920, A-3, Schlesinger Library, Harvard Radcliffe Institute, https://iiif.lib.harvard.edu/manifests/view/drs:10431489$29i. See also Rogers, *Delia's Tears,* 205.

106. Gregg Hecimovich, "The Life and Times of Alfred, Delia, Drana, Fassena, Jack, Jem, and Renty," chap. 2 in *To Make Their Own Way in the World: The Enduring Legacy of the Zealy Daguerreotypes,* ed. Ilisa Barbash, Molly Rogers, and Deborah Willis (Cambridge, MA: Peabody Museum Press, Aperture, 2020), 106–108. See also *Make Their Own Way,* 279–280.

107. See the book review of *Make Their Own Way,* Parul Sehgal, "The First Photos of Enslaved People Raise Many Questions About the Ethics of Viewing," *New York Times,* September 29, 2020, https://www.nytimes.com/2020/09 /29/books/to-make-their-own-way-in-world-zealy-daguerreotypes.html.

108. Hecimovich, "Life and Times."

109. In 1859, Agassiz presented his entire collection—including human remains, animal specimens, fossils, and more—to the Trustees. He estimated that he spent more than $10,000 of his own money—derived at least in part from the salary he received from the University, paid until 1855 by Abbott Lawrence and funded for some time thereafter by Lawrence's bequest to the University—in collecting and preserving the specimens, see Museum of Comparative Zoology, *Report of the Committee of the Overseers of Harvard College appointed to visit The Lawrence Scientific School during the year 1860; together with The Reports Submitted by the professors* (Cambridge, MA: Welch, Bigelow, and Company, 1873), 45–46.

110. [Louis] Agassiz to Harriot Pinckney Holbrook, Monday 25, [1852?], Louis Agassiz Correspondence and Other Papers, MS Am 1419, Houghton Library, Harvard University.

111. Harvard University, *Twenty-Sixth Annual Report of the President of Harvard University to the Overseers on the state of the university for the academic year 1850–1851* (Cambridge, MA: Metcalf and Company, printers to the University, 1852), 5–7, https://iiif.lib.harvard.edu/manifests/view/drs:42 7074869$1i.

112. "An Extraordinary Importation from South Africa," *The Boston Evening Transcript,* September 28, 1860.

Christopher D. E. Willoughby provided valuable input on race science at Harvard Medical School generally and on the story of Sturmann in particular, based on research for "Skull Collecting, Medical Museums, and the International Dimensions of Racial Science," chap. 5 in *Masters of Health: Racial Science and Slavery in U.S. Medical Schools* (Chapel Hill, NC: University of North Carolina Press, forthcoming fall 2022).

113. "An Extraordinary Importation from South Africa," *The Boston Evening Transcript.*

114. "Amusements—Boston Aquarial and Zoological Garden," *The Boston Evening Transcript,* October 3, 1860.

115. "Amusements—The Aquarial Gardens," *The Boston Evening Transcript,* October 3, 1860.

116. "Amusements—Boston Aquarial and Zoological Garden," *The Boston Evening Transcript*.

117. Walter Clarence, *The aborigines of South Africa, now on exhibition at the Boston Aquarial and Zoölogical Gardens in Central Court, Washington Street: giving a brief description of the southern portion of the African continent, and a sketch of the early life of each individual specimen of the nomadic tribes* (Boston, MA: Printed for Cutting & Butler by J. P. Plumer, 1860).

118. "Amusements—Boston Aquarial and Zoological Garden," *The Boston Evening Transcript*.

119. "Specimens of the South African Tribes," *New York Tribune*, January 5, 1861; "Advertisement," *New York Herald*, January 3, 1861. See also Matthew Smith Miller, "Surely his mother mourns for him: Africans on exhibition in Boston and New York, 1860–1861," (AB thesis, Harvard University, 2011).

120. Sturmann's name has been transcribed with a variety of different spellings. Here we are using the spelling that appears in the first Boston Evening Transcript announcement of the exhibition: "An Extraordinary Importation from South Africa." It is likely that the names reported were not only printed inaccurately, but were in at least some cases assigned stage names.

121. "Suicide at the Aquarial Gardens," *The Boston Evening Transcript*, April 29, 1861.

122. "Amusements—Boston Aquarial and Zoological Gardens," *The Boston Evening Transcript*, April 30, 1861.

123. Jeffries Wyman, "Observations on the Skeleton of a Hottentot," *The Anthropological Review* 3, no. 11 (October 1865): 330–335.

124. Wyman, "Observations on the Skeleton of a Hottentot," 334.

125. Wyman, "Observations on the Skeleton of a Hottentot," 333.

126. Jackson, *Warren Anatomical Museum*, 702.

127. Winsor, "'In the Prime of His Admirable Manhood,'" chap. 1 and "'I Have Been Disappointed in My Collaborators,'" chap. 2 in *Reading the Shape of Nature;* Irmscher, *Louis Agassiz*.

128. Louis Agassiz's letters on the collections of specimens for the museum can be found in Alexander Agassiz, "Agassiz letter books, 1859–1910," vol. 4, Alexander Agassiz and Louis Agassiz letters, June 18, 1866–July 30, 1868, Spec. Coll. MCZ F890, Ernst Mayr Library, Museum of Comparative Zoology, Harvard University, https://nrs.harvard.edu/urn-3:FMUS.MCZ:2709033.

129. In her biography of Louis, Elizabeth wrote that their marriage "connected him by the closest ties with a large family circle," including his brother-in-law, future Harvard President Cornelius Felton (president, 1860–1862; faculty, 1832–1860; tutor, 1829–1832), quoted in Irmscher, *Louis Agassiz*, 278. Elizabeth was the granddaughter of wealthy merchant Thomas Handasyd Perkins (see Section Three of this report), and her family ties included her namesakes, the prominent Boston (and Harvard) families the Cabots and the Carys. See "Collection Overview: Biography," Papers of the Cabot family, 1786–2013, A-99, Schlesinger Library, Radcliffe Institute, Harvard University, accessed February 10, 2022, https://id.lib.harvard.edu/ead/schoo131/catalog; "Biographical Sketch," Thomas Greaves Cary Papers, 1832–1885, accessed February 10, 2022, https://www.masshist.org/collection-guides/view/fa0339.

130. Irmscher, *Louis Agassiz*, 297–308.

131. Irmscher, *Louis Agassiz*, 297.

132. Irmscher, *Louis Agassiz*, 298–300.

133. "Agassiz letter books, 1859–1910," Museum of Comparative Zoology, Harvard University.

134. Stepan, *Picturing Tropical Nature*.

135. Stepan, *Picturing Tropical Nature;* Dain Borges, "'Puffy, Ugly, Slothful and Inert': Degeneration in Brazilian Social Thought, 1880–1940," *Journal of Latin American Studies* 25, no. 2 (May 1993): 235–256.

136. Christoph Irmscher, "Mr. Agassiz's 'Photographic Saloon'," chap. 7 in *Make Their Own Way*, ed. Barbash et al., 205, 208–209.

137. Agassiz and Agassiz, *Journey in Brazil*, 251–252; Irmscher, "Mr. Agassiz's 'Photographic Saloon'," 215–216.

138. Agassiz and Agassiz, *Journey in Brazil*, ix-x.

139. See Elizabeth Cary Agassiz to Sallie and Emma, January 6, 1868, seq. 87, folder 17, Letters to Mrs. Cary, Sally and Emma while they were in Europe, 1867–1868, Elizabeth Cary Agassiz Papers, 1838–1920, A-3, Schlesinger Library, Radcliffe Institute, Harvard University, https://nrs.lib.harvard.edu/urn-3:rad .schl:2026876?n=87.

See also Irmscher, *Louis Agassiz*, 297: "In 1868, Elizabeth Agassiz published *A Journey in Brazil*, a vivid account of her husband's research trip to Brazil . . . Here there was no more ventriloquizing for Agassiz. He was no longer her mask; instead, he had become her topic."

140. Harvard biologist and historian Stephen Jay Gould, who held an Alexander Agassiz Professorship of Zoology, wrote that Elizabeth "expurgated

without indication" racist passages in the collection of Louis Agassiz's correspondence that she edited and published in 1885. Gould published many of these passages, see *Mismeasure of Man,* 77, quote on 79. See also Agassiz, *Louis Agassiz.*

Agassiz biographer Christoph Irmscher also presents evidence that Elizabeth revised her husband's correspondence prior to publication, citing multiple letters that Louis Agassiz wrote to Samuel Gridley Howe, a member of the American Freedmen's Inquiry Commission, in which Agassiz sought to convince Howe of the dangers of miscegenation. Irmscher, *Louis Agassiz,* 245–251, 390, n. 61.

141. Agassiz and Agassiz, *Journey in Brazil,* 49.

142. Agassiz and Agassiz, *Journey in Brazil,* 481.

143. Sollors et al., eds., *Blacks at Harvard,* 2. Scott graduated from the Cambridge Latin School in 1894. See Helen Fuller, "The Valedictory," *The Cambridge Tribune,* June 30, 1894, https://cambridge.dlconsulting.com/cgi-bin/cambridge?a=d&d=Tribune18940630-01.2.29. Radcliffe was chartered as a degree-granting institution the same year. See "Radcliffe: From College to Institute," Harvard Radcliffe Institute.

144. Samuel Eliot Morison is quoted in the section on Charles William Eliot on "History of the Presidency," Office of the President, Harvard University, accessed May 25, 2021, https://www.harvard.edu/president/history.

145. On Eliot's election to the presidency: Henry James, *Charles W. Eliot, President of Harvard University, 1869–1909,* vol. 1 (Boston, MA and New York, NY: Houghton Mifflin Company, 1930), 194–195; Edwin C. J. T. Howard, George L. Ruffin, and Robert Tanner Freeman graduated from the medical, law, and dental schools respectively in 1869. See Sollors et al., eds., *Blacks at Harvard.*

146. Sollors et al., eds., *Blacks at Harvard,* 2–3; Synnott, *The Half-Opened Door,* 48.

147. Sollors et al., eds., *Blacks at Harvard,* 6. Eliot himself was Grant's dental patient.

148. Harvard University, *Quinquennial Catalogue, 1636–1915,* 846.

149. See, for example, Louis R. Harlan, *Booker T. Washington: The Wizard of Tuskegee, 1901–1915* (New York, NY: Oxford University Press, 1983).

150. Harlan, *Booker T. Washington, 1901–1915,* vii-viii.

151. "A Plea for His Race: Booker T. Washington Tells about the Efforts of the Negro," *The Atlanta Constitution* September 19, 1895. Reprinted in Louis R.

Harlan, ed., *The Booker T. Washington Papers,* vol. 3, *1889–1895* (Urbana, IL: University of Illinois Press, 1974), 586.

152. Harlan, *Booker T. Washington, 1901–1915,* 33.

153. Harlan, *Booker T. Washington, 1901–1915,* 50–51.

154. See *Address of Booker T. Washington: delivered at the alumni dinner of Harvard University Cambridge, Mass., after receiving the honorary degree of "Master of Arts"* (Boston, MA: B. T. Washington, 1896), PDF, https://www.loc.gov/resource/lcrbmrp.t0f13/.

155. Sollors et al., *Blacks at Harvard,* xviii. Nathaniel Southgate Shaler, who once served as Louis Agassiz's assistant, became dean of the Lawrence Scientific School in 1891. See Irmscher, *Louis Agassiz,* 263–265; David N. Livingstone, "Science and Society: Nathaniel S. Shaler and Racial Ideology," *Transactions of the Institute of British Geographers* 9, no. 2 (1984): 181–210. Henry Eustis, who died in 1885, also served as dean of the Lawrence Scientific School, see "Prof. Henry Lawrence Eustis," *Harvard Crimson,* January 13, 1885, https://www.thecrimson.com/article/1885/1/13/prof-henry-lawrence-eustis-on-sunday.

156. Cohen, "Harvard's Eugenics Era."

157. See Section Three of this report.

158. William Morton Wheeler, "The Bussey Institution, 1871–1929," chap. 31 in *The Development of Harvard University since the Inauguration of President Eliot, 1869–1929,* ed. Samuel Eliot Morison (Cambridge, MA: Harvard University Press, 2013), 513–514. After William Castle's retirement in 1936 and the death of another primary faculty member in 1938, the Massachusetts Department of Public Health acquired the property and the Institution's operations effectively merged with the Division of Biological Sciences in the 1960s. See Karl Sax, "The Bussey Institution: Harvard University Graduate School of Applied Biology: 1908–1936," *The Journal of Heredity* 57, no. 5 (September 1966): 178.

159. William Ernest Castle to Charles W. Eliot, March 8, 1907, and March 7, 1908, unspecified: box 80, Castle, William Ernest, 1905–1908, Records of the President of Harvard University, Charles W. Eliot, UAI 5.150, Harvard University Archives. On Eliot's involvement in convincing Castle to remain at Harvard, see J. A. Weir, "Harvard, Agriculture, and the Bussey Institution," *Genetics* 136, no. 4 (April 1994): 1227–1231.

160. Harvard University, *Quinquennial Catalogue of the Officers and Graduates of Harvard University,* 1636–1920 (Cambridge MA: Harvard University, 1920), 108, https://books.google.com/books?id=aQpLAQAAMAAJ.

Sargent is also the namesake of the Sargent College of Health and Rehabilitative Sciences at Boston University, which acquired the Sargent School of Physical Training in 1929, see "Our History," Boston University College of Health and Rehabilitative Sciences: Sargent College, accessed February 9, 2022, https://www.bu.edu/sargent/about-us/our-history/.

161. Josiah Royce and Charles William Eliot, *Dudley Allen Sargent: fiftieth anniversary, 1869–1919* (Cambridge, MA: Sargent School for Physical Education, 1919?), 6.

Sargent's project also brings to mind the history of "posture photographs" at Ivy League and Seven Sisters institutions well into the twentieth century, but further research is necessary to determine the ways in which these efforts were connected. See, for example, Ron Rosenbaum, "The Great Ivy League Nude Posture Photo Scandal," *New York Times,* January 15, 1995, https://nyti.ms/3hYy4uE.

162. Dudley Allen Sargent, "Physical Education in Relation to Race Improvement," (speech, Race Betterment Conference, Battle Creek, MI, January 6–10, 1918), GV342 Sa73pei Sargent, D.A., Relation of Physical Education to Race Improvement, 1914, box 11, Papers of Dudley Allen Sargent, HUG 1768.4, Harvard University Archives.

163. Preliminary forms for 17600–17854, box 29, Records of the Department of Physical Education: anthropometric measurements of Harvard students, 1860–1920, UAV 689.270.1, Harvard University Archives; Class of 1860–1865, box 1, Records of the Department of Physical Education: anthropometric measurements of Harvard students, 1860–1920, UAV 689.270, Harvard University Archives; Dudley Allen Sargent, Anthropometric Apparatus with Directions for Measuring and Testing the Principal Physical Characteristics of the Human Body, 2nd ed. (Cambridge, MA: self pub., 1887), https://books.google.com/books?id=mphAAQAAIAAJ; Ledyard W. Sargent, ed., *Dudley Allen Sargent: an autobiography* (Philadelphia, PA: Lea & Febiger, 1927); Dudley Allen Sargent, *Handbook of Developing Exercises* (Boston, MA: Rand, Avery, & Co., 1882), https://books.google.com/books?id=uCEAAAAYAAJ.

164. "Du Bois, W. E. B. (William Edward Burghardt), 1868–1963, Anthropometric chart, 1888." W. E. B. Du Bois Papers, MS 312, Special Collections and University Archives, University of Massachusetts Amherst Libraries, http://credo.library.umass.edu/view/full/mums312-b237-i156 and Anthropometric chart and photograph of W.E.B. Du Bois, #3129, box 9, Records of the Department of Physical Education: anthropometric measurements of Harvard students, 1860–1920, UAV 689.270.7p, Harvard University Archives.

165. "Collection Organization," Dudley Allen Sargent measurement cards from schools and organizations other than Harvard, 1880–1920, HUG 1768.60, Harvard University Archives, accessed February 9, 2022, https://id.lib.harvard.edu/ead/hua02003/catalog.

166. See Dudley Allen Sargent, "The Physical Characteristics of the Athlete," *Scribner's Magazine* 2, no. 5 (November 1887): 541–561, with an extract reprinted in *Harvard Crimson,* November 8, 1887, accessed March 9, 2022, https://www.thecrimson.com/article/1887/11/8/the-physical-characteristics-of-the-athlete/. See also Peter Cryle and Elizabeth Stephens, "The Object of Normality: Composite Statues of the Statistically Average American Man and Woman, 1890–1945," chap. 7 in *Normality: A Critical Genealogy* (Chicago, IL: University of Chicago Press, 2017).

167. Dudley Allen Sargent, "Is War a Biological Necessity?" *American Physical Education Review* 20, no. 3 (March 1915): 142.

168. For example, at a 1914 conference Sargent discussed concerns about "race suicide" due to declining birth rates in some countries because, as he explained it, "inferior races and individuals tend to multiply more rapidly than the superior races." Sargent, "Physical Education in Relation to Race Improvement." See also Dudley Allen Sargent, "The Physical Development of Women," *Scribner's Magazine* 5, no. 2 (February 1889).

169. James, *Charles W. Eliot, 1869–1909,* vol. 1:xv

170. "Mixture of Kindred Races," *San Francisco Chronicle,* March 23, 1909, unspecified: box 222, folder 279, Race Blending, Records of the President of Harvard University, Charles W. Eliot, UAI 5.150, Harvard University Archives.

171. "President Eliot Believes Intermarriage of Races Is Bad for All Concerned," *Post* (St. Louis, MO), n.d., unspecified: box 222, folder 279, Race Blending, Records of the President of Harvard University, Charles W. Eliot, UAI 5.150, Harvard University Archives.

172. "Aroused By Eliot Attack on Races," *Traveller* (Boston, MA), March 8, 1909, unspecified: box 222, folder 279, Race Blending, Records of the President of Harvard University, Charles W. Eliot, UAI 5.150, Harvard University Archives.

173. "Mixture of Kindred Races," *San Francisco Chronicle,* March 23, 1909, unspecified: box 222, folder 279, Race Blending, Records of the President of Harvard University, Charles W. Eliot, UAI 5.150, Harvard University Archives.

174. "He makes Cupid laugh," illustration, unknown newspaper, n.d., unspecified: box 222, folder 279, Race Blending, Records of the President of Harvard University, Charles W. Eliot, UAI 5.150, Harvard University Archives.

175. William Monroe Trotter to Charles W. Eliot, April 28,1909, unspecified: box 114, Race, 1909, Records of the President of Harvard University, Charles W. Eliot, UAI 5.150, Harvard University Archives.

176. Charles W. Eliot to William Monroe Trotter, April 30, 1909, unspecified: box 114, Race, 1909, Records of the President of Harvard University, Charles W. Eliot, UAI 5.150, Harvard University Archives.

177. Charles W. Eliot to William Monroe Trotter, April 30, 1909. In an earlier speech at the Tuskegee Normal and Industrial Institute, Eliot explained his conviction that political and social equality are unrelated, saying: "For social equality rests on natural or instinctive likes and dislikes, affinities and repulsions, which no political institutions have ever been able to control." See What Uplifts a Race and What Holds It Down, unspecified: box 220, folder 180, Records of the President of Harvard University, Charles W. Eliot, UAI 5.150, Harvard University Archives.

178. Charles W. Eliot to William Monroe Trotter, April 30, 1909.

179. William Monroe Trotter to Charles W. Eliot, May 1, 1909, unspecified: box 114, Race, 1909, Records of the President of Harvard University, Charles W. Eliot, UAI 5.150, Harvard University Archives.

180. Charles W. Eliot, *Public opinion and sex hygiene: an address delivered at the fourth International congress on school hygiene, at Buffalo, New York, August 27th, 1913* (New York, NY: The American Federation for Sex Hygiene, 1913).

181. Paul A. Lombardo, "When Harvard Said No to Eugenics: The J. Ewing Mears Bequest, 1927," *Perspectives in Biology and Medicine* 57, no. 3 (Summer 2014): 379.

182. See Oscar Riddle, "Biographical Memoir of Charles Benedict Davenport, 1866–1944," in *Biographical Memoirs, Volume XXV—Fourth Memoir* (Washington, DC: National Academy of Sciences of the United States of America, 1947), 83–84, http://www.nasonline.org/publications/biographical -memoirs/memoir-pdfs/davenport-charles.pdf; "Galton's Children: Charles B. Davenport," Center for the History of Medicine at Countway Library, Harvard Medical School, accessed February 9, 2022, https://collections.count way.harvard.edu/onview/exhibits/show/galtonschildren/galton-s-children /charles-b—davenport.

183. Riddle, "Charles Benedict Davenport," 83–84; Cohen, *Imbeciles,* 111–112.

184. "Galton's Children: Charles B. Davenport," Harvard Medical School.

185. Cohen, *Imbeciles,* 112.

186. C. B. Davenport, "The Effects of Race Intermingling," *Proceedings of the American Philosophical Society* 56, no. 4 (1917), 368. See also Morris Steggerda, "Charles Benedict Davenport (1866–1944); The man and his contributions to physical anthropology," American Journal of Physical Anthropology 2, no. 2 (June 1944): 167–185.

187. "Background Note," Charles Benedict Davenport Papers, American Philosophical Society Library, accessed February 1, 2022, https://search.amphilsoc .org/collections/view?docId=ead/Mss.B.D27-ead.xml.

188. L. C. Dunn, *William Ernest Castle, 1867–1962: A Biographical Memoir* (Washington DC: National Academy of Sciences, 1965), 36–37, http://www .nasonline.org/publications/biographical-memoirs/memoir-pdfs/castle -william-e.pdf.

189. Dunn, "William Ernest Castle," 51–52; Wheeler, "The Bussey Institution," 513.

   After Castle's retirement, the Massachusetts Department of Public Health acquired the property and the Institution's operations effectively merged with the Division of Biological Sciences in the 1960s. See Sax, "The Bussey Institution," 178.

190. Dunn, "William Ernest Castle," 60, 63; Garland E. Allen, "The Eugenics Record Office at Cold Spring Harbor, 1910–1940: An Essay in Institutional History," *Osiris* 2 (1986): 232.

191. Lombardo, "When Harvard Said No to Eugenics," 378, 380.

192. Cohen, "Harvard's Eugenics Era."

193. W. E. Castle, *Genetics and Eugenics: A Text-book for students of biology and a reference book for animal and plant breeders* (Cambridge, MA: Harvard University Press, 1916), https://books.google.com/books?id=R5LPAAAAMAAJ.

194. Castle, "The Possibility and Prospects of Breeding a Better Human Race," chap. 27 in *Genetics and Eugenics.* See also Cohen, "Harvard's Eugenics Era."

195. Castle, *Genetics and Eugenics,* 235.

196. Castle, *Genetics and Eugenics,* 258–259.

197. Cohen, *Imbeciles,* 10. Philip R. Reilly, "Eugenics and Involuntary Sterilization: 1907–2015," *Annual Review of Genomics and Human Genetics* 16

(August 2015): 351–368; Black women were especially subject to these procedures in the latter half of the twentieth century.

198. Reilly, "Eugenics and Involuntary Sterilization," 355.

199. Allen, "Eugenics Record Office."

200. Egbert Klautke, "'The Germans are beating us at our own game': American eugenics and the German sterilization law of 1933," *History of the Human Sciences* 29, no. 3 (July 1, 2016): 25–43.

201. Allen, "Eugenics Record Office," and Garland E. Allen, "Science Misapplied: The Eugenics Age Revisited," *Technology Review* 99, no. 6 (August 1996): 22–31.

202. Stefan Kühl, *The Nazi Connection: Eugenics, American Racism, and German National Socialism* (New York, NY: Oxford University Press, 1994); Klautke, "'The Germans are beating us at our own game'," 28.

203. Allen, "Science Misapplied."

Sidebar: Alberta V. Scott: First Black Graduate of Radcliffe College

1. "Albert V. Scott," Cambridge USA, accessed March 14, 2022, https://www.cambridgeusa.org/listing/alberta-v.-scott

2. Anna Russo, "Scott, Alberta Virginia," Oxford African American Studies Center, May 31, 2013, accessed March 14, 2022.

3. Russo, "Scott, Alberta Virginia."

4. Sarah L. Burks, *Alberta Scott House: 28 Union Street, Cambridge, Mass. 02139* (Cambridge, MA: Cambridge Historical Commission, 2021), 11, https://www.cambridgema.gov/-/media/Files/historicalcommission/pdf/chcmeetingfiles/L134_prelim_report.pdf.

5. Russo, "Scott, Alberta Virginia."

6. Burks, *Alberta Scott House,* 11.

7. "RADCLIFFE'S COLORED GRADUATE.: MISS ALBERTA SCOTT CAMBRIDGE WILL TEACH HER BRETHREN IN THE SOUTH-FAVORITE AMONG FELLOW STUDENTS. NEWTON CLUB'A FOURTH." *Boston Daily Globe* (1872–1922), June 23, 1898.

8. Burks, *Alberta Scott House,* 11.

9. "Who We Are," Association of Black Harvard Women, accessed March 14, 2022, https://abhwomen.org/avs-leadership-academy.

10. "Our Namesakes," Greener Scott Scholars, accessed March 14, 2022, https://greenerscottscholars.org/

Sidebar: Richard T. Greener: First Black Graduate of Harvard College

1.   "Richard T. Greener," Cambridge USA, accessed March 14, 2022, https://www.cambridgeusa.org/listing/richard-t.-greener.

2.   "Richard T. Greener Memorial," University of South Carolina, accessed March 14, 2022, https://sc.edu/greener.

3.   Katherine Reynolds Chaddock, *Uncompromising Activist: Richard Greener, First Black Graduate of Harvard College* (Baltimore, MD: Johns Hopkins University Press, 2017), 2.

4.   Chaddock, *Uncompromising Activist,* 13–16, 19.

5.   Chaddock, *Uncompromising Activist,* 24–25.

6.   Chaddock, *Uncompromising Activist,* 27, 31.

7.   Chaddock, *Uncompromising Activist,* 29–30.

8.   Chaddock, *Uncompromising Activist,* 30.

9.   Chaddock, *Uncompromising Activist,* 26, 29.

10.   Chaddock, *Uncompromising Activist,* 30.

11.   Chaddock, *Uncompromising Activist,* 27.

12.   Chaddock, *Uncompromising Activist,* 35

13.   Chaddock, *Uncompromising Activist,* 46–48.

14.   Chaddock, *Uncompromising Activist,* 57.

15.   Chaddock, *Uncompromising Activist,* 79.

16.   Chaddock, *Uncompromising Activist,* 128

5: Segregation, Marginalization, and Resistance at Harvard

1.   Lovett, *Black Colleges and Universities,* 4–5; Urban and Wagoner, Jr., *American Education,* 167–168.

2.   See Roberts v. City of Boston, 59 Mass. 198, 5 Cush. 198 (1849). Some whites did support racially mixed schools. Senator Sumner fought for years racially integrated schools and argued before the Massachusetts Supreme Judicial Court on behalf of plaintiff Sarah Roberts. Donald, *Charles Sumner and the Coming of the Civil War,* 4, 151. He asserted: "The separation of the schools, so far from being for the benefit of both races, is an injury to both." See *Roberts,* 59 Mass. at 204.

Chief Justice Lemuel Shaw, who wrote the opinion, was a Harvard alumnus, fellow, and overseer. See "Lemuel Shaw," Commonwealth of Massachusetts. He wrote: "The [Boston Primary School] committee . . . have come to the conclusion, that the good of both classes of school will be best promoted, by maintaining the separate primary schools for colored and for white children, and we can perceive no ground to doubt, that this is the honest result of their experience and judgement." See *Roberts,* 59 Mass. at 209 (1850). Even philanthropists who aided schools supported the practice of racial segregation and systematically provided less funding to southern Black schools. See Urban and Wagoner, Jr., *American Education,* 166–171.

3.   See Carleton Mabee, "A Negro Boycott to Integrate Boston Schools," *New England Quarterly* 41, no. 3 (September 1968): 341–361.

4.   Plessy v. Ferguson, 163 U.S. 537, 552 (1896) (Harlan, J., dissenting) coined the oft-quoted phrase "separate but equal"; see also *Plessy,* 544–545 (discussing *Roberts*); Ficker, "*Roberts* to *Plessy.*"

5.   For a discussion on racial segregation in elementary and secondary education, see Urban and Wagoner, Jr., *American Education,* 165–168; for HBCUs, see generally Lovett, *Black Colleges and Universities.*

6.   See Lovett, *Black Colleges and Universities,* xii-xiii; Anderson, *Education of Blacks,* 239, 248–249; Allen et al., "Historically Black Colleges and Universities," 263, 267.

7.   There was little support for mixed schools anywhere in the North. See Urban and Wagoner, Jr., *American Education,* 165; Sollors et al., eds., *Blacks at Harvard,* 1–4; West, "Harvard and the Black Man."

8.   Synnott, *The Half-Opened Door,* 38; Karabel, *The Chosen,* 41–42, 49–50. See also "Harvard and the Battle Over Restriction," chap. 3 in ibid.

9.   See "Collection Overview: The Lowell Presidency," Records of the President of Harvard University, Abbott Lawrence Lowell, Hollis for Archival Discovery, February 25, 2022, https://id.lib.harvard.edu/ead/hua03003/catalog.

10.   "At a Meeting of the Faculty of Arts and Sciences, January 17, 1911," box 1, folder 15, Admission—New Plan for Records of the President of Harvard University, Abbott Lawrence Lowell, [Series 1909–1914] UAI 5.160, Harvard University Archives. The addition of the approved course route for admission became known as the "New Plan of Admission." For confirmation that the New Plan was implemented in the 1910–1911 school year, see Harvard University, "Appendix—Report of the Chairman of the Committee on Admission," *Reports of the President and the Treasurer of Harvard College 1912–1913* (Cambridge, MA: Harvard University, 1914), 254–261, https://nrs.harvard.edu/urn-3:HUL.ARCH:30013263?n=256.

11.   Lowell viewed the shift away from admission only by exam as a means to "make Harvard as national as possible." Abbott Lawrence Lowell to Andrew

Carnegie, January 19, 1911, and Andrew Carnegie to Abbott Lawrence Lowell, January 20, 1911, box 1, folder 15, Admission—New Plan for Records of the President of Harvard University, Abbott Lawrence Lowell, [Series 1909–1914], UAI 5.160, Harvard University Archives.

12.   Andrew Carnegie to Abbott Lawrence Lowell, January 19, 1911, Harvard University Archives; Abbott Lawrence Lowell to Andrew Carnegie, January 20, 1911, Harvard University Archives.

13.   Synnott, *The Half-Opened Door,* 56–57; Karabel, *The Chosen,* 52.

14.   Synnott, *The Half-Opened Door,* 58, 61.

15.   To identify Jewish students, this 1922 Statistical Report used a three-tiered "J1, J2, J3" system, marking the level of certainty of a given individual's Jewishness. Records consulted included admission forms, registration cards, bursar office records, and senior class albums, and involved looking at a student's birthplace, school, home address, and parents' vocations and names (including the mother's family name in case the family had changed their name) see Synnott, *The Half-Opened Door,* 93–95. The statistical report is included in Limitation of Numbers, box 197, folder 387, Admission to Harvard College— Report of Committee on Methods of Sifting Candidates, Records of the President of Harvard University, Abbott Lawrence Lowell, [Series 1925–1928], UAI 5.160, Harvard University Archives.

16.   [Abbott Lawrence] Lowell to Henry James, November 3 and 6, 1925, Limitation of Numbers, box 227197, folder 184387, Admission to Harvard College—Report of Committee on Methods of Sifting Candidates, Records of the President of Harvard University, Abbott Lawrence Lowell, [Series 1925–1928], UAI 5.160, Harvard University Archives, quoted in Synnott, *The Half-Opened Door,* 108. Henry James, the son of William James and nephew of the novelist Henry James, served as a Harvard overseer and the chairman of the Special Committee on the Size of the Freshman Class, which oversaw this review of the admissions process.

17.   Synnott, *The Half-Opened Door,* 109–110.

18.   Synnott, *The Half-Opened Door,* 107–108.

19.   On the use of such tactics, particularly interviews and character assessments, by public universities against African American students, see Tomiko Brown-Nagin, *Civil Rights Queen: Constance Baker Motley and the Struggle for Equality* (New York, NY: Pantheon, 2022), 91–93, 95–96, 100–04, 115–17, 152–53, 155–56, 157.

20.   See Morton Keller and Phyllis Keller, *Making Harvard Modern: The Rise of America's University* (New York, NY: Oxford University Press, 2001), 60–63.

21. Synnott, *The Half-Opened Door,* 38, 40, 47, 207–208, 220; Sollors et al., eds., *Blacks at Harvard,* 2–3.

22. Keller and Keller, *Making Harvard Modern,* 61.

23. Synnott, *The Half-Opened Door,* 47. The University did not keep records identifying students by race for much of its history. As a result, scholars, left to rely on scattered surveys, limited governmental documents, and class book photographs, have struggled to accurately document the Black presence at Harvard.

24. Synnott, *The Half-Opened Door,* 207–209.; Keller and Keller, *Making Harvard Modern,* 60–61.

25. Synnott, *The Half-Opened Door,* 47; Sollors et al., eds., *Blacks at Harvard,* xxi-xxiii; Perkins, "African American Female Elite," 728–729.

26. [Abbott Lawrence] Lowell to Charles B. Davenport, April 12, 1913, box 2, unspecified: folder 34, American Breeders' Association, Records of the President of Harvard University, Abbott Lawrence Lowell, 1909–1933: folder lists, UAI 5.160, Harvard University Archives.

27. [Abbott Lawrence] Lowell to LeBaron B. Colt, March 21, 1922, box 174, unspecified: folder 1077, Immigration, Restriction of Records of the President of Harvard University, Abbott Lawrence Lowell, 1909–1933: folder lists, UAI 5.160, Harvard University Archives.

28. [Abbott Lawrence] Lowell to Sidney L. Gulick, August 28, 1918, box 105, unspecified: folder 399, Immigration, Records of the President of Harvard University, Abbott Lawrence Lowell, 1909–1933: folder lists, UAI 5.160, Harvard University Archives.

29. Painter, "Jim Crow at Harvard: 1923"; Sollors et al., eds., *Blacks at Harvard,* xxi–xxiii; Synnott, *The Half-Opened Door,* 49–50.

30. Knox's great-aunt Harriet Jacobs authored the famous memoir *Incidents in the Life of a Slave Girl* (Boston, MA: self pub., 1861). In the late nineteenth century, Jacobs lived in Cambridge and ran boarding houses that served Harvard students and faculty, including Harvard Law School Dean Christopher Langdell. See Jean Fagan Yellin, "Harriet Jacobs's Family History," *American Literature* 66, no. 4 (December 1994): 765–767; Jean Fagan Yellin, *Harriet Jacobs: A Life* (New York, NY: Basic Civitas Books, 2004), 222.

31. See Sollors et al., *Blacks at Harvard,* 195–227. Five Black freshmen were admitted to the school in the fall of 1921. While residence in the freshman halls was required except in special circumstances, just three of the five admitted Black freshman applied for dormitory residence and only one was

granted it. See Raymond Pace Alexander, "Voices from Harvard's Own Negroes," *Opportunity* 1, no. 3 (March 1923): 29–31.

32. See the letter from petitioning Harvard alumni to the President and Fellows of Harvard College in 1922, "Memorial to the Corporation" box 171, unspecified: folder 981, Freshman Dormitories, Records of the President of Harvard University, Abbott Lawrence Lowell, 1909–1933: folder lists, UAI 5.160, Harvard University Archives.

33. Alexander, "Voices from Harvard's Own Negroes." See also Lewis, *Du Bois* (2000), 88–89.

Edwin Jourdain, Jr.'s son Spencer Jourdain—also a Harvard graduate—has chronicled the experiences of his father and other Black students at Harvard in this era in the family memoir *The Dream Dancers: An American Reflection Upon Past, Present and Future.* He describes his father's activism during the Dormitory Crisis in vol. 1, *New England Preservers of the Dream, 1620–1924* (Evanston, IL: Shorefront Press, 2016), 214–226.

34. "Memorial to the Corporation" (1922), Harvard University Archives.

35. [Abbott Lawrence] Lowell to Frederick L. Allen, October 22, 1921, box 171, folder 981, Freshman Dormitories, Records of the President of Harvard University, Abbott Lawrence Lowell, [Series 1919–1922] UAI 5.160, Harvard University Archives.

There had been incidents, before and after the freshman halls becoming mandatory in 1914, when students objected to their roommates or hall neighbors based on race. The administration always responded with alternative accommodations. See, for example, Richard E. Stifel to S. B. R. Briggs, July 22, 1910, box 12, folder 366, Dormitories—General Correspondence Records of the President of Harvard University, Abbott Lawrence Lowell, [Series 1909–1914] UAI 5.160, Harvard University Archives, and N. S. Davis to Abbott Lawrence Lowell, October 6, 1915, box 57, folder 70a, Freshman Halls. Records of the President of Harvard University, Abbott Lawrence Lowell, [Series 1914–1917] UAI 5.160, Harvard University Archives.

36. One other Black student, Euclid P. Ghee, one year behind Jourdain, was also permitted to live in the freshman halls. See "NEGRO GRADUATE PROTESTS: Says University Forsakes Freedom for Race Oppression," *New York Times,* January 13, 1923, https://nyti.ms/3LouWpE.

37. Andrew Schlesinger, *Veritas: Harvard College and the American Experience,* (Chicago, IL: I.R. Dee, 2005), 162.

38. "NEGRO GRADUATE PROTESTS," *New York Times.*

39. President Lowell to Arthur Warner, November 12, 1921, box 171, folder 981, Freshman Dormitories, Records of the President of Harvard University, Abbott Lawrence Lowell, [Series 1919–1922] UAI 5.160, Harvard University Archives.

40. For untitled and undated drafts addressing "the negro question," c. October 1922, see Freshman Dormitories, box 171, folder 981, Records of the President of Harvard University, Abbott Lawrence Lowell, [Series 1919–1922] UAI 5.160, Harvard University Archives.

41. R. C. Benchley to [Abbott Lawrence] Lowell, June 15, 1922, box 171, unspecified: folder 981, Freshman Dormitories, Records of the President of Harvard University, Abbott Lawrence Lowell, 1909–1933: folder lists, UAI 5.160, Harvard University Archives. Concerning the racial makeup of the committee, see Wolters, "The New Negro on Campus," 199 and Louis Marshall, "Alfred Jaretzki," *Publications of the American Jewish Historical Society* 31 (1928): 266–268.

42. Wolters, "The New Negro on Campus," 199.

43. "Memorial to the Corporation" (1922), Harvard University Archives.

44. Painter, "Jim Crow at Harvard: 1923," 628–634.

45. Schlesinger, *Veritas,* 165. In his initial response, Lowell explained his view of the compulsory nature of the freshman halls as a special case and wrote, "I am sure you will understand why, from the beginning, we have not thought it possible to compel men of different races to reside together." Bruce's response to Lowell was one of "shock" that such a well-cultivated young man as his son would be discriminated against for his race alone. "Not race, but culture, I had supposed, is the basis of sound nationality," wrote Bruce. See Harvard Alumni Association and Associated Harvard Clubs, "Colored Students at Harvard," *Harvard Alumni Bulletin* 25, no. 16 (January 18, 1923): 456–457. See also "Colored Students in the Freshman Halls," *Harvard Alumni Bulletin* 25, no. 18 (February 1, 1923): 527–533.

46. "NEGRO GRADUATE PROTESTS," *New York Times.*

47. "Attacks Harvard On Negro Question," *New York Times.*

48. Wolters, "The New Negro on Campus," 201.

49. Harvard Alumni Association and Associated Harvard Clubs, "Negroes in the Freshman Halls," *Harvard Alumni Bulletin* 25, no. 28 (April 12, 1923): 830.

50. Synnott, *The Half-Opened Door,* 48.

51. Keller and Keller, *Making Harvard Modern*, 61.

52. Synnott, *The Half-Opened Door*, 49.

53. Courtney Suciu, "The NAACP's Anti-Lynching Campaign," *ProQuest* (blog), February 13, 2019, https://about.proquest.com/en/blog/2019/the-naacps-anti-lynching-campaign/.

54. The scholar William Leo Hansberry was also a member of the class of 1921. So too was Edward O. Gourdin, though he was in Paris competing at the Olympics on this date. See Daphne Abeel, "Edward Orval Gourdin: Brief Life of a Breaker of Barriers, 1897–1966," *Harvard Magazine*, November 1997, https://harvardmagazine.com/sites/default/files/html/1997/11/vita.html.

The Cambridge Chronicle reported on a Klan meeting in North Cambridge in October 1922. See "The Ku Klux Klan Holds Meeting in North Cambridge, Tuesday Night," *The Cambridge Chronicle*, October 7, 1922, https://cambridge.dlconsulting.com/?a=d&d=Chronicle19221007-01.2.2.

55. *Boston Herald*, June 18, 1924, as quoted in *Harvard College Class of 1921: Report of the Triennial Reunion Report, June 1924*, p. 33, Secretary's Reports, Class Material, Class of 1921, HUD 321.4, Harvard University Archives.

A similar incident occurred at Princeton the same year. See John S. Weeren. "Shades of the Ku Klux Klan: The Class of 1920's 'Fiery Fourth'," *The Princeton University Library Chronicle* 71, no. 1 (Autumn 2009): 89–98.

56. *The Twenty-First Gun* 2, no. 2 (May 6, 1927): 7, Class Material, Class of 1921, HUD 321.4, Harvard University Archives.

57. See, for example, *Harvard Lampoon* 84, no. 9 (January 18, 1923), box 17, The Harvard Lampoon, HUK 510 Copy A, Harvard University Archives, and "Klan Fills Cambridge With Horrible Manifestations—Opposes Quinn for Mayor—Names Kopey Its Klandidate," *Harvard Crimson*, November 1, 1923, https://www.thecrimson.com/article/1923/11/1/klan-fills-cambridge-with-horrible-manifestations-opposes/.

58. "The Krimson K. K. K.," *Harvard Crimson*, October 22, 1923, https://www.thecrimson.com/article/1923/10/22/the-krimson-k-k-k-pto/; "Ku Klux Klan At Harvard Awaits Moment To Strike," *Harvard Crimson*, October 22, 1923; James Weldon Johnson to President and Board of Overseers of Harvard University, October 23, 1923, telegram, box 201, folder 507, Ku Klux Klan, Records of the President of Harvard University, Abbott Lawrence Lowell, UAI 5.160, Harvard University Archives. See also "More Facts Appear On Harvard Klan: Some Klansmen Seeking to Reorganize in University—College Rulings an Obstacle—Evasion Likely," *Harvard Crimson*, October 25, 1923, https://www.thecrimson.com/article/1923/10/25/more-facts-appear-on-harvard-klan/;

"Kollegiate Klansman," *Harvard Crimson,* October 25, 1923, https://www.the crimson.com/article/1923/10/25/kollegiate-klansmen-pdefinite-information -that-harvard/.

59. See Sollors et al., *Blacks at Harvard,* xxx.

60. Synnott, *The Half-Opened Door,* 47; on his exclusion from the glee club and social marginalization, see W. E. B. Du Bois, "A Negro Student at Harvard," 439–458.

61. Harvard University, *Quinquennial Catalogue of the Officers and Graduates, 1636–1930* (Cambridge, MA: Harvard University Press, 1930), 87.

62. See Samuel Eliot Morison, "A Memoir and Estimate of Albert Bushnell Hart." *Proceedings of the Massachusetts Historical Society* 77 (1965): 34–35, 44–45, 47.

63. Albert Bushnell Hart, *Slavery and Abolition, 1831–1841* (New York, NY: Harper & Brothers Publishers, 1906), xv, https://books.google.com/books?id =73x1AAAAMAAJ.

64. Hart, *Slavery and Abolition,* 120.

65. Hart, *Slavery and Abolition,* 145.

66. Hart, *Slavery and Abolition,* 100.

67. Albert Bushnell Hart, *School History of the United States* (New York, NY: American Book Company, 1918), 253, https://books.google.com/books?id =gYUUAAAAYAAJ.

68. Hart, *School History,* 252.

69. Hart, *Slavery and Abolition,* 94.

70. Albert Bushnell Hart, *The Southern South* (New York, NY: Appleton and Company, 1910), 214, https://books.google.com/books?id=0SUUAAAAYAAJ.

71. Hart, *The Southern South,* 186.

72. See Lewis, *Du Bois* (1993), 100–155.

73. Du Bois, W.E.B., 1890, box 120 VT, Student Folders, ca. 1890–1995 (inclusive), UAIII 15.88.10, Harvard University Archives.

74. Lewis, *Du Bois* (1993), 113; Jacqueline Goggin, "Countering White Racist Scholarship: Carter G. Woodson and *The Journal of Negro History,*" *The Journal of Negro History* 68, no. 4 (Fall 1983): 356.

75. W. E. B. Du Bois, "Enforcement of the Slave Trade Laws," in *The Annual Report of the American Historical Association for the Year 1891* (Washington, DC: Government Printing Office, 1892), 163–174, https://digitalcommons.law.ou .edu/indianserialset/5323/. The *American Historical Review,* the association's

flagship journal, was not launched until 1895. See Morison, "Albert Bushnell Hart," 34.

76. Hart, *The Southern South*, 325.

77. Hart, *The Southern South*, 105.

78. Hart, *The Southern South*, 134.

79. Albert Bushnell Hart, "The Outcome of the Southern Race Question," *The North American Review* 188, no. 632 (1908): 50.

80. Hart, *The Southern South*, 136.

81. Albert Bushnell Hart, "Remedies for the Southern Problem," *The Independent,* January-June 1905, 994.

82. Hart, *The Southern South*, 189.

83. Du Bois, "A Negro Student at Harvard," 443.

84. Du Bois, "A Negro Student at Harvard," 439.

85. Du Bois, "A Negro Student at Harvard," 441. This sentiment is challenged to at least some degree by an account of Robert Morse Lovett, whom he called "perhaps the closest white student friend I made at Harvard." See W. E. B. *The Autobiography of W. E. B. Du Bois: A Soliloquy on Viewing My Life from the Last Decade of Its First Century* (New York, NY: International Publishers, 1968), 278.

86. Du Bois, "A Negro Student at Harvard," 441.

87. Bruce A. Kimball, "'This Pitiable Rejection of a Great Opportunity': W. E. B. Du Bois, Clement G. Morgan, and the Harvard University Graduation of 1890," *The Journal of African American History* 94, no. 1 (Winter 2009): 12. Kimball notes that Du Bois was at the time enrolled in Peabody's course, "Ethics of Social Reform." On Peabody, see "Francis Greenwood Peabody," Harvard Divinity School Library, accessed February 1, 2022, https://library.hds.harvard.edu/exhibits/hds-20th-century/peabody.

88. Kimball, "'Pitiable Rejection', 12–14. Morgan was allowed to speak at Class Day, the day before Commencement.

89. Du Bois, *Autobiography,* 418.

90. Du Bois, "A Negro Student at Harvard," 453. While this professor may be speaking by conjecture, Du Bois's racial makeup was known to Harvard through Dudley Allen Sargent's intake forms. See [measurement card and photograph of W. E. B. Du Bois], #3129, box 9, Records of the Department of Physical Education: anthropometric measurements of Harvard students, 1860–1920, UAV 689.270.7p, Harvard University Archives.

91. Lewis, *Du Bois* (1993), 82.

92. On Fisk, see "Fisk University Accreditation," Fisk University, accessed January 7, 2022, https://www.fisk.edu/about/accreditation/. Saran Donahoo and Wynetta Y. Lee, "The Adversity of Diversity: Regional Associations and the Accreditation of Minority-Serving Institutions," chap. 19 in *Understanding Minority-Serving Institutions,* ed. Marybeth Gassman, Benjamin Baez, and Caroline Sotello Viernes Turner (New York, NY: State University of New York Press, 2008), discusses the historical exclusion of HBCUs by accrediting organizations. The Southern Association of Colleges and Schools (SACS)—the regional accreditor for 80% of HBCUs—had "both written and unwritten policies denying membership to HBCUs" until the 1930s, when they began granting limited accreditation to some HBCUs without permitting them full membership. SACS only began granting HBCUs full membership in 1956, see Donahoo and Lee, "The Adversity of Diversity," 294.

In one instance, an HBCU was denied accreditation based on "the quality and size of its library, the lack of advanced degrees among its faculty, and the low salary scales for members of its faculty who had advanced training, experience and responsibilities"—in other words, because of the lack of funding and high educational achievement that were systematically denied to educational organizations serving Black communities. James D. Anderson, "Philanthropy, the State and the Development of Historically Black Public Colleges: The Case of Mississippi," *Minerva* 35, no. 3 (September 1997): 300.

93. Lewis, *Du Bois* (1993), 81–82.

94. Lewis, *Du Bois* (1993), 82–84, 96–97, 100.

95. Lewis, *Du Bois* (1993), 84. This home, at 20 Flagg St., is identified with a historical marker and is part of Cambridge's African American Heritage Trail, accessed February 2, 2022, https://www.cambridgema.gov/historic/cambridge history/historicmarkers#aaht.

96. Lewis, *Du Bois* (1993), 103; Du Bois, "A Negro Student at Harvard," 454; Du Bois, W. E. B., Student Folder, Harvard University Archives.

97. Du Bois, *Autobiography,* 278.

98. Harvard Club of New York City to W. E. B. Du Bois, November 17, 1942, W. E. B. Du Bois Papers, MS 312, Special Collections and University Archives, University of Massachusetts Amherst Libraries, http://credo.library.umass.edu /view/full/mums312-b098-i060.

99. W. E. B. Du Bois to Harvard Club of New York City, December 16, 1942, W. E. B. Du Bois Papers, MS 312, Special Collections and University Archives,

University of Massachusetts Amherst Libraries, http://credo.library.umass.edu /view/full/mums312-b098-i061.

100. See "Harvard Club of New York membership card, ca. 1900," W. E. B. Du Bois Papers, MS 312, Special Collections and University Archives, University of Massachusetts Amherst Libraries, https://credo.library.umass.edu /view/full/mums312-b158-i029. Despite the title of this archival record, the object does not in fact appear to be a permanent membership card.

101. Shaler, Dean of the Lawrence Scientific School from 1891 to 1906, wrote, "The African and European races must remain distinct in blood . . . It is their duty to remain apart." See Livingstone, "Science and Society," 193.

102. Lewis, *Du Bois* (1993), 154–155.

103. W. E. B. Du Bois. "Harvard and the South: a commencement part, ca. 1891," W. E. B. Du Bois Papers, MS 312, Special Collections and University Archives, University of Massachusetts Amherst Libraries, 1, 10–11, http://credo .library.umass.edu/view/full/mums312-b230-i012.

104. Du Bois. "Harvard and the South," 10.

105. Du Bois, "Harvard and the South," 15

106. W. E. B. Du Bois to Albert Bushnell Hart, April 15, 1918, W. E. B. Du Bois Papers, MS 312, Special Collections and University Archives, University of Massachusetts Amherst Libraries, http://credo.library.umass.edu/view/full /mums312-b011-i339.

107. Kimball, "Pitiable Rejection," 16; Perkins, "African American Female Elite," 720. See also Lewis, *Du Bois* (2000), 90–91, 99–100.

108. Lewis S. Gannett to W. E. B. Du Bois, March 3, 1922, W. E. B. Du Bois Papers, MS 312, Special Collections and University Archives, University of Massachusetts Amherst Libraries, http://credo.library.umass.edu/view/full /mums312-b019-i274; W. E. B. Du Bois to Lewis S. Gannett, March 13, 1922, W. E. B. Du Bois Papers, MS 312, Special Collections and University Archives, University of Massachusetts Amherst Libraries, http://credo.library.umass.edu /view/full/mums312-b019-i279; W. R. Valentine to W. E. B. Du Bois, May 11, 1922, W. E. B. Du Bois Papers, MS 312, Special Collections and University Archives, University of Massachusetts Amherst Libraries, http://credo.library .umass.edu/view/full/mums312-b020-i205.

109. Lewis, *Du Bois* (2000), 90.

110. Lewis, *Du Bois* (2000), 100.

111. See Mark V. Tushnet, *The NAACP's Legal Strategy against Segregated Education, 1925–1950* (Chapel Hill, NC: University of North Carolina Press, 1987); McNeil, *Groundwork.*

112. McNeil, *Groundwork,* 200–201.

113. McNeil, *Groundwork,* 53. See also "This Fight . . . Is Not an Isolated Struggle," chap. 10 in ibid. Notably, Dean Roscoe Pound and Professor Felix Frankfurter encouraged and mentored Houston.

114. "Department of African and African American Studies Timeline," Harvard University, accessed February 4, 2022, https://hwpi.harvard.edu/files/aaas /files/department_of_african_and_african_american_studies_timeline.pdf.

115. Lani Guinier, "My Father's Undergraduate Years at Harvard College," *The Journal of Blacks in Higher Education* 21 (Autumn 1998): 104–105. Eugenia Guinier to Howard Dodson, n.d., box 1, folder 2, Eugenia Guinier— "Recollections and Insights into Ewart G. Guinier," Ewart Guinier papers, 1910–1989, Sc MG 420, Schomburg Center for Research in Black Culture, New York Public Library.

116. Ewart Guinier and Susan Gordon, "Trapped at Harvard," unpublished manuscript, p. 1–2, 6, 10–11, box 1, folder 9, Autobiographical, Ewart Guinier papers, 1910–1989, Sc MG 420, Schomburg Center for Research in Black Culture, New York Public Library.

117. Guinier and Gordon, "Trapped at Harvard," p. 2–3, 10–11, New York Public Library.

118. Eugenia Guinier to Howard Dodson, n.d., Ewart Guinier papers, New York Public Library.

119. Guinier and Gordon, "Trapped at Harvard," p. 4, New York Public Library.

120. "The Nobel Peace Prize 1950: Ralph Bunche—Biographical," The Nobel Prize, accessed January 11, 2022, https://www.nobelprize.org/prizes/peace/1950 /bunche/biographical/.

121. Guinier and Gordon, "Trapped at Harvard," p. 5–6, New York Public Library.

122. Guinier and Gordon, "Trapped at Harvard," p. 6, New York Public Library.

123. Guinier and Gordon, "Trapped at Harvard," p. 8, New York Public Library.

124. Guinier and Gordon, "Trapped at Harvard," p. 9, New York Public Library.

125. Guinier and Gordon, "Trapped at Harvard," p. 11, New York Public Library.

126. Eugenia Guinier to Howard Dodson, n.d., Ewart Guinier papers, New York Public Library. See also "Biographical / Historical Information," *Ewart Guinier Papers, 1910–1989,* New York Public Library Archives and Manuscripts, accessed February 4, 2022, https://archives.nypl.org/scm/20650.

127. "Biographical / Historical Information," *Ewart Guinier Papers, 1910–1989,* New York Public Library.

128. See Ethan Bronner, "Lani Guinier Joins Faculty Of Law School At Harvard," *New York Times,* January 24, 1998, https://nyti.ms/30I1eCg. For many years before Guinier's appointment, Derrick Bell, the first Black professor appointed to the Harvard Law School faculty, and students staged protests seeking greater faculty diversity. See, for example, Fox Butterfield, "Harvard Law Professor Quits Until Black Woman is Named," *New York Times,* April 24, 1990, https://nyti.ms/30D2x5t.

129. Like the history of women at Harvard, generally, the history of women of color at Harvard and Radcliffe has seldom been a subject of description or analysis. See Ulrich, *Yards and Gates,* 147; Ulrich, "Harvard's Womanless History"; Jane Knowles, "Access, Equal Access, and Beyond: A Brief History of Radcliffe College," *Radcliffe Quarterly* 72, no. 3 (September 1986): 3–5, https://iiif.lib.harvard.edu/manifests/view/drs:427992496$113i; Sally Schwager, "Taking Up the Challenge: The Origins of Radcliffe" in *Yards and Gates,* 96.

130. Ulrich, "Yards and Gates," 323; see also Drew Gilpin Faust, "Mingling Promiscuously: A History of Women and Men at Harvard" in *Yard and Gates,* 317–327.

131. Perkins, "African American Female Elite," 718–744, quote on 729.

132. Knowles, "Access, Equal Access, and Beyond."

133. Sollors et al., eds., *Blacks at Harvard,* 2.

134. Knowles, "Access, Equal Access, and Beyond."

135. Perkins, "African American Female Elite," 729.

136. See Perkins, "African American Female Elite," 728–729.

137. "Eva Dykes, Transcript," Interviews of the Black Women Oral History Project, 1976–1981, OH-31; T-32, Schlesinger Library, Harvard Radcliffe Institute, https://nrs.harvard.edu/urn-3:RAD.SCHL:10041689; Sollors et al., *Blacks at Harvard,* 169. See also note 92 above on HBCU accreditation.

138. Muriel Spence, "Minority Women at Radcliffe: Talent, Character, Endurance," *Radcliffe Quarterly* (Cambridge, Mass., Radcliffe College, Sept. 1986), 20. Accessed November 13, 2021. https://iiif.lib.harvard.edu/manifests/view/drs:427992496$130i.

139. Spence, "Minority Women at Radcliffe," 20.

140. "Eva Dykes, Transcript," Harvard Radcliffe Institute, ii, 7–12; Caroline Bond Day, "The Pink Hat: A Sketch," *Opportunity: A Journal of Negro Life* 4, no. 48 (December 1926): 379–380.

141. "Eureka," *The Crusader* 4, no. 3 (May 1921): 21, https://www.marxists.org /history/usa/pubs/crusader/v4n03-may-1921-crusader-r.pdf.

142. For a detailed biography see "Eva Dykes, Transcript," Harvard Radcliffe Institute, i-iii. Dykes was also profiled in Sollors et al., *Blacks at Harvard*, 160–167.

143. "Eva Dykes, Transcript," Harvard Radcliffe Institute, i-iii, 6, 21.

144. "Who Was Eva B. Dykes," Eva B. Dykes Library, Oakwood University, accessed February 4, 2022, https://library.oakwood.edu/index.php/aboutus /who-was-eva-b-dykes.

145. "The Aeolians," Oakwood University, accessed November 13, 2021, https://oakwood.edu/the-aeolians/.

146. Eva B. Dykes, "Preface," in *The Negro in English Romantic Thought, or A Study of Sympathy for the Oppressed* (Washington, DC: Associated Publishers, Inc. 1942).

147. Otelia Cromwell, Lorenzo Dow Turner, and Eva Beatrice Dykes, *Readings from Negro Authors, for Schools and Colleges* (New York: Harcourt, Brace and company, 1931).

148. Eva B. Dykes, "Philip Henry Lotz, *Rising Above Color*," *The Journal of Negro History* 29, no. 2 (April 1944): 223–224.

149. Dykes, "Philip Henry Lotz," 224.

150. On Du Bois as Day's mentor, see Anastasia C. Curwood, "Caroline Bond Day (1889–1948): A Black Woman Outsider Within Physical Anthropology," *Transforming Anthropology* 20, no. 1 (April 2012): 81.

151. Hooton's legacy as a proponent of some eugenics theories is disputed. It seems clear that he did not wholly subscribe to the belief that "undesirable" inheritable traits were inherently tied to race. Rather, he explicitly stated that he "desire[d] emphatically to dissociate the finding of his science from the acts of human injustice which masquerade as 'racial measures' or 'racial movements' or even 'racial hygiene,'" and argued that, "Anthropologists have found as yet no relationship between any physical criterion of race and mental capacity, whether in individuals or in groups." Earnest A. Hooton, "Plain Statements about Race," *Science* 83, no. 2161 (May 29, 1936): 512. On Hooton's views on race, see Curwood, "Caroline Bond Day," 82; Eugene Giles, "Two faces of

Earnest A. Hooton," Supplement, *American Journal of Physical Anthropology* 149, no. S55 (November 2012): 105–113.

152. See "Caroline Bond Day," in *Blacks at Harvard,* ed. Sollors et al., 169; "Collection Overview: Biographical Sketch," Caroline Bond Day papers, 993–21; 994–22, Peabody Museum Archives, Hollis for Archival Discovery, Harvard University, accessed November 14, 2021, https://id.lib.harvard.edu/ead/pea00032/catalog.

153. "Caroline Bond Day," in *Blacks at Harvard,* ed. Sollors et al., 169.

154. "Biographical Sketch," *Caroline Bond Day Papers,* Harvard University; Sollors et al., *Blacks at Harvard,* 169, 181.

155. Caroline Bond Day, "Race Crossings in the United States," reprinted in *Blacks at Harvard,* ed. Sollors et al., 184–185.

156. Curwood, "Caroline Bond Day," 82.

157. Curwood, "Caroline Bond Day," 80, 82.

158. Caroline Bond Day, *A study of some Negro-white families in the United States,* with a foreword and notes on the anthropometric data by Earnest A. Hooton (Cambridge, MA: Peabody Museum of Harvard University, 1932).

159. Day's work commands considerable respect today, while at the same time being critiqued as a product of its time in its efforts to demonstrate the capability of African Americans to conform to the respectable, middle-class social norms defined by white Americans. See Curwood, "Caroline Bond Day," 85–86, and Heidi Ardizzone, "'Such fine families': photography and race in the work of Caroline Bond Day," *Visual Studies* 21, no. 2 (October 2006): 106–132.

160. Lani Guinier, *The Tyranny of the Meritocracy: Democratizing Higher Education in America* (Boston, MA: Beacon Press, 2015), 136–137.

161. Synnott, *The Half-Opened Door,* 207; Karabel, *The Chosen,* 400–401; Smith, *The Harvard Century,* 230–268.

162. Karabel, *The Chosen,* 7.

163. Synnott, *The Half-Opened Door,* 202–203.

164. Synnott, *The Half-Opened Door,* 204.

165. Keller and Keller, *Making Harvard Modern,* 62.

166. Synnott, *The Half-Opened Door,* 205; Keller and Keller, *Making Harvard Modern,* 34–35, 293–294.

167. Synnott, *The Half-Opened Door,* 205–207; Keller and Keller, *Making Harvard Modern,* 294–297.

168. Kent Garrett and Jeanne Ellsworth, *The Last Negroes At Harvard: The Class of 1963 and the 18 Young Men Who Changed Harvard Forever* (Boston, MA: Houghton Mifflin Harcourt, 2020), 21–23. See also Karabel, *The Chosen,* 379.

169. Synnott, *The Half-Opened Door,* 207–208.

170. Synnott, *The Half-Opened Door,* 207–208; Lawrence E. Eichel, "The Crisis of 1969," *Blacks at Harvard,* ed. Sollors et al., 379–400; "Department of African and African American Studies Timeline," Harvard University.

171. Synnott, *The Half-Opened Door,* 208.

172. Sollors et al., *Blacks at Harvard,* xxvii. Notably, in 1963, Harvard's Student Council on Undergraduate Activities denied recognition to the Harvard African and Afro-American Club on the basis that its membership policy was discriminatory. That decision was overturned after an outcry. Keller and Keller, *Making Harvard Modern,* 286.

173. Sollors et al., *Blacks at Harvard,* xxviii.

174. Synnott, *The Half-Opened Door,* 208.

175. Michael E. Xie, "Harvard's Goaltender: William R. Fitzsimmons, '67," *The Harvard Crimson,* May 22, 2017, https://www.thecrimson.com/article /2017/5/22/fitzsimmons-profile-1967, and Matteo Wong, "Changemaker in Admissions: David L. Evans made a difference for 50 years," *Harvard Magazine,* September-October 2020, https://www.harvardmagazine.com/2020/09 /jhj-changemaker-in-admissions.

176. Keller and Keller, *Making Harvard Modern,* 350.

177. Columbia University, Stanford University, and the University of Pennsylvania. See Brief of Columbia University et al. as Amici Curiae Supporting Petitioner, Regents of the University of California v. Bakke, 438 U.S. 265 (1978) (No. 76-811) [hereinafter Brief of Columbia University et al. for the Petitioner]. The brief also noted the support of several other institutions. See ibid., at 7 (listing Brown University, Massachusetts Institute of Technology, and Duke University, among others). The Association of American Law Schools, which included Harvard Law School, also submitted an amicus brief. See Brief for the Association of American Law Schools as Amicus Curiae Supporting Petitioner, Regents of the University of California v. Bakke, 438 U.S. 265 (1978) (No. 76-811).

178. See Brief of Columbia University et al. for the Petitioner, *Bakke,* 438 U.S. 265 (1978) (No. 76-811).

179. Affirmative action based on sex and race is described as "important differential lens providers," see Erwin N. Griswold, "Some Observations on the 'Defunis' Case," Columbia Law Review 75, no. 3 (April 1975): 512–519.

180. Brief of Columbia University et al. for the Petitioner, *Bakke*, 438 U.S. 265 (1978) (No. 76-811).

181. See *Bakke*, 438 U.S. 265, 316–19 (1978).

182. See *Bakke*, 438 U.S. 265, 321–34 (1978); see also Nick Anderson, "How Harvard set the model for affirmative action in college admissions," *Washington Post*, June 21, 2016, https://www.washingtonpost.com/news/grade-point/wp /2016/06/21/how-harvard-set-the-model-for-affirmative-action-in-college -admissions/.

183. For the argument that race is a "critical component" in admissions programs for higher education, see Brief of the Association of American Law Schools et al. as Amici Curiae Supporting Petitioners, Texas v. Hopwood, 533 U.S. 929 (2001) (No. 00-1609).

184. For the argument that although the case was about a law school, its far-reaching implications could have problematic impacts on the medical profession because racial diversity in medical schools enhanced healthcare, see Brief of the Association of American Medical Colleges et al. as Amici Curiae Supporting Appellees, Hopwood v. Texas, 78 F.3d 932 (5th Cir. 1996) (No. 98-50506).

185. See Brief of Harvard University et al. as Amici Curiae Supporting Respondents, Grutter v. Bollinger, 539 U.S. 306 (2003) (Nos. 02-241 and 02-516). For the argument that the "diversity rationale" accepted in *Bakke* was not distinguished by Adarand Constructors v. Pena, 515 U.S. 200 (1995), see Brief of Judith Areen et al. as Amici Curiae Supporting Appellants, Grutter v. Bollinger, 247 F.3d 631 (2001) (No. 01-1447).

186. See Grutter v. Bollinger, 539 U.S. 306, 308, 330, 335–338 (2003).

187. See Grutter v. Bollinger, 539 U.S. 306, 330 (2003). The book was also heavily relied upon by other amicus submissions to the Court. See, for example, Brief of Amherst et al. as Amici Curiae Supporting Respondents, Grutter v. Bollinger, 539 U.S. 306 (2003) (Nos. 02-241 and 02-516).

188. See Marcia G. Synnott, "The Evolving Diversity Rationale in University Admissions: From Regents v. Bakke to the University of Michigan Cases," *Cornell Law Review* 90, no. 2 (January 2005): 463, 487–495, https://scholarship .law.cornell.edu/cgi/viewcontent.cgi?article=2986&context=clr.

189. See Brief of Brown University et al. as Amici Curiae Supporting Respondents, Fisher v. University of Texas at Austin, 570 U.S. 297 (2013) (No. 11-345); for an outline of Harvard's legal involvement in admissions cases, see also "Harvard Makes the Case of Diversity," News, *Harvard Magazine*, August 14, 2012.

190. See Brief for Respondents, Fisher v. University of Texas at Austin, 570 U.S. 297 (2013) (No. 11-345).

191. See Brief of Dean Robert Post and Dean Martha Minow as Amici Curiae Supporting Respondents, Fisher v. University of Texas at Austin, 570 U.S. 297 (2013) (No. 11-345).

192. Students for Fair Admissions, Inc. v. President and Fellows of Harvard College, 980 F.3d 157 (2020) (No. 19-2005).

193. Camille G. Caldera, Delano R. Franklin, and Samuel W. Zwickel, "Federal Judge Rules Harvard's Admissions Policies Do Not Discriminate Against Asian American Applicants," *The Harvard Crimson,* October 2, 2019, https://www.thecrimson.com/article/2019/10/2/admissions-suit-decision/.

194. Caldera et al., "Federal Judge Rules."

195. Daniel J. Hemel, "Summers Unveils Financial Aid Initiative," *The Harvard Crimson,* February 27, 2004, https://www.thecrimson.com/article/2004/2/27/summers-unveils-financial-aid-initiative-parents/.

196. "Harvard increases financial aid to low-income students," *The Harvard Gazette,* September 1, 2011, https://news.harvard.edu/gazette/story/2011/09/harvards-record-166-million-financial-aid-program-will-increase-aid-to-low-income-students-and-provide-a-new-financial-aid-calculator-for-students-and-families/.

197. For more on financial aid, see "Financial Aid," Harvard College, accessed February 17, 2022, https://college.harvard.edu/financial-aid. In March 2022, the University announced that beginning in the 2022–2023 academic year, families with annual incomes of up to $75,000 (up from $65,000) will be expected to contribute nothing to the cost of their child's education.

198. For the "I, Too, Am Harvard" campaign, see Bethonie Butler, "'I, Too, Am Harvard': Black students show they belong," *Washington Post,* March 5, 2014, https://www.washingtonpost.com/blogs/she-the-people/wp/2014/03/05/i-too-am-harvard-black-students-show-they-belong; see also "Presidential Task Force on Inclusion and Belonging," Harvard University.

199. See Nate Herpich, "Sherri Ann Charleston named chief diversity and inclusion officer: Diversity and higher ed expert joins Harvard from UW-Madison," *Harvard Gazette,* June 22, 2020, https://news.harvard.edu/gazette/story/2020/06/sherri-ann-charleston-named-chief-diversity-and-inclusion-officer; Nate Herpich, "Fresh strides in equity, diversity, inclusion, and belonging: Sherri Charleston reflects on her 1st year, outlines new five-year strategic model," *Harvard Gazette,* October 20, 2021, https://news.harvard.edu

/gazette/story/2021/10/sherri-charleston-on-1st-year-as-diversity-and-inclusion
-chief.

Sidebar: The Klan on Campus?

1.   Equal Justice Initiative, *Lynching in America: Confronting the Legacy of Racial Terror*, 3rd ed. (Montgomery, AL: self–pub., 2017), 14, https://eji.org/wp
-content/uploads/2005/11/lynching-in-america-3d-ed-110121.pdf.

2.   David J. Goldberg, "Unmasking the Ku Klux Klan: The Northern Movement against the KKK, 1920–1925," *Journal of American Ethnic History* 15, no. 4 (Summer 1996): 33.

3.   Mark Paul Richard, "The Ku Klux Klan in 1920s Massachusetts," *Historical Journal of Massachusetts* 47, no. 1 (Winter 2019): 5

4.   "A Mobilization of Americans," *Harvard Crimson*, February 25, 1922, https://www.thecrimson.com/article/1922/2/25/a-mobilization-of-americans
-pthe-harvard/.

"Ku Klux Klan At Harvard Awaits Moment To Strike," *Harvard Crimson*, October 22, 1923.

"More Facts Appear On Harvard Klan: Some Klansmen Seeking to Reorganize in University—College Rulings an Obstacle—Evasion Likely," *Harvard Crimson*, October 25, 1923, https://www.thecrimson.com/article
/1923/10/25/more-facts-appear-on-harvard-klan.

"Kollegiate Klansman," *Harvard Crimson*, October 25, 1923, https://www
.thecrimson.com/article/1923/10/25/kollegiate-klansmen-pdefinite-information
-that-harvard.

5.   "Harvard Klan Grows In Popularity, Says University Paper," *The Fiery Cross*, Indiana State Edition, November 2, 1923.

6.   "Harvard Warned of a Coming Klan Drive And Assault on Discrimination Bar," *The New York Times*, October 23, 1923, https://nyti.ms/3v8FOR8.

7.   Equal Justice Initiative, *Lynching in America*, 53–54

8.   James Weldon Johnson to President and Board of Overseers of Harvard University, October 23, 1923, telegram, box 201, folder 507, Ku Klux Klan, Records of the President of Harvard University, Abbott Lawrence Lowell, UAI 5.160, Harvard University Archives. See also "Negro Protests Klan at Harvard," *The New York Times*, October 24, 1923, https://nyti.ms/3LUjyB6.

9.   George B. Burch, "A Terrible Night," *Harvard Crimson*, October 25, 1923, https://www.thecrimson.com/article/1923/10/25/a-terrible-night-pbthe-crimson
-invites. For more on popular opinions on chapel, see "Popularizing Chapel,"

Harvard Crimson, November 5, 1923, https://www.thecrimson.com/article
/1923/11/5/popularizing-chapel-psome-one-at-dartmouth.

J. N. Leonard, "Johnny Harvard and the Klan," *Harvard Crimson*, October 25, 1923, https://www.thecrimson.com/article/1923/10/25/johnny-harvard
-and-the-klan-pto.

10. "Grow Old Along With Me—," *Harvard Crimson*, November 23, 1923,
https://www.thecrimson.com/article/1923/11/23/grow-old-along-with-me
-pthe.

11. "From an Older Brother," *Harvard Crimson*, November 23, 1923.

12. For scholarship on racism and humor, see, for example, Stuart Hall, "The
Whites of Their Eyes: Racist Ideologies and the Media" in *Selected Writings on
Race and Difference*, ed. Paul Gilroy and Ruth Wilson Gilmore (Durham, NC:
Duke University Press, 2021) and Michael Omi, "In Living Color: Race and
American Culture," in *Cultural Politics in Contemporary America*, ed. Ian Angus
and Sut Jhally (London, UK: Routledge, 1989), 121.

6: Conclusion and Recommendations to the
President and Fellows of Harvard College

1.   In fact, no obligation to remedy harms of slavery exists in American law;
recent litigation seeking such remedies has been unsuccessful. See, for example,
In re African-American Slave Descendants Litigation, 304 F. Supp. 2d. 1027
(N.D. Ill. 2004) holding that plaintiffs' attempt to bring remedial claims based
on slavery more than a century after the end of the Civil War and the formal
abolition of slavery failed, "consistent with the position taken by numerous
courts which have considered the issue over the last century. In the content
most pertinent here—higher education—the US Supreme Court has upheld
race-conscious admissions policies meant to increase access for "underrepre-
sented minorities," including people of African origin who may be descended
from enslaved people; but the rationale the Court recognized for such policies was a compelling interest in "diversity," rather than remedying vestiges of
past discrimination or slavery. See *Bakke* for upholding race as one factor
among many in admissions to promote an interest in educational benefits of
diversity. Justice Marshall argued in a separate opinion that the lingering effects of slavery justified race-conscious admissions in higher education; no
other justice joined his opinion, see *Bakke*, 438 US at 387–402 (Marshall, J.);
Grutter v. Bollinger, 539 US 306 (2003). Many scholars have criticized the non-
compensatory, diversity-based justification for affirmative action. See Tomiko
Brown-Nagin, "Elites, Social Movements, and the Law: The Case of Affirmative Action," *Columbia Law Review* 105, no. 5 (June 2005): 1436, 1453–1463;

see also ibid., n. 69, noting that Columbia University President Lee Bollinger questioned whether Bakke's diversity rationale was a "powerful enough" argument in support of affirmative action and believed *Brown v. Board of Education* and the harms of state-mandated segregation should instead be the starting point for public debate.

2.   *Harvard University's Community Engagement in the City of Boston*, April 26, 2021, and other relevant reports are available online. See "Reports & Publications," Harvard in the Community, accessed February 7, 2022, https://community.harvard.edu/reports.

3.   See, for example, Thai Jones, "Slavery reparations seem impossible. In many places, they're already happening," *Washington Post*, Jan. 31, 2020, https://www.washingtonpost.com/outlook/2020/01/31/slavery-reparations-seem-impossible-many-places-theyre-already-happening.

4.   For relevant literature, see Wilder, *Ebony and Ivy*; Richard J. Cellini, "University Slavery Reparations: Pathways through the Bramble Bush," (paper, Slavery and the Universities Workshop, Warren Center for Studies in American History, Harvard University, Cambridge, MA, September 29, 2021), 8–9.

5.   For a thoughtful discussion of these matters in different but relevant global contexts, see Martha Minow, *Between Vengeance and Forgiveness: Facing History after Genocide and Mass Violence* (Boston, MA: Beacon Press, 1998), particularly chap. 5.

6.   Rachel L. Swarns, "Is Georgetown's $400,000-a-Year Plan to Aid Slave Descendants Enough?" *New York Times*, October 30, 2019, https://www.nytimes.com/2019/10/30/us/georgetown-slavery-reparations.html.

7.   These recommendations define "descendant communities" broadly, given the breadth of the harms described in this report. With the exception of Recommendation 4, the concept of descendants is not limited to enslaved people with ties to the University through ownership by University affiliates.

8.   Harvard already engages in community service in Boston and in Massachusetts and has ties with state and local educational institutions that could be expanded in ways that address problems with racially disproportionate impacts linked to slavery and its legacies such as hunger and food insecurity, mass incarceration, and housing access inequity. See *Harvard University's Community Engagement* (April 26, 2021), and Harvard University, *Harvard in Massachusetts: Facts & Impact*, February 23, 2021, https://community.harvard.edu/files/comm/files/2020_facts_impact_a.pdf.

There also is precedent for engagement with the West Indies. Harvard, through HBS, recently developed an educational partnership with UWI.

See "Historic Agreement between The UWI Five Islands Campus and Harvard Business School," *Antigua Newsroom*, October 25, 2021, https://antiguanews room.com/historic-agreement-between-the-uwi-five-islands-campus-and -harvard-business-school/. Notably, as a part of its reparative efforts for its entanglements with slavery, Glasgow University also established a partnership with UWI.

9. The Cambridge-Harvard Summer Program served 300+ students, and the Crimson Summer Academy aided 69 underserved high school students from 20 Boston, Cambridge, and Somerville schools in fiscal year 2020, see The Crimson Summer Academy at Harvard University, accessed January 10, 2022, https://www.crimsonsummer.harvard.edu/index.php. The language about the new non-profit is taken from the University's initial statement about the sale of edX, see "Update on edX," Office of the President, Harvard University, accessed January 10, 2022, https://www.harvard.edu/president/news/2021 /update-on-edx/. The social goals of the new endeavor are also described, see Nate Herpich, "Harvard and MIT-led nonprofit to tackle longstanding inequities in education," *Harvard Gazette*, June 29, 2021, https://news.harvard.edu /gazette/story/2021/06/edx-acquired-by-education-technology-company-2u/.

10. Harvard Medical School, the Paulson School of Engineering and Applied Sciences, the Graduate School of Arts and Sciences, the Faculty of Arts and Sciences, Harvard Business School, Harvard Graduate School of Education, Harvard Kennedy School, and Harvard Radcliffe Institute all have engaged in partnerships with HBCUs that permit faculty and students of Harvard and of HBCUs to collaborate with and learn from one another.

11. Harvard University Presidential Task Force on Inclusion and Belonging, "Pursuing Excellence on a Foundation of Inclusion," accessed February 1, 2022, https://inclusionandbelongingtaskforce.harvard.edu/files/inclusion/files /harvard_inclusion_belonging_task_force_final_report_full_web_180327.pdf.

Appendix A: List of Human Beings Enslaved by Prominent Harvard Affiliates

1. Wendy Warren, *New England Bound: Slavery and Colonization in Early America* (New York: Liveright Publishing Corporation, 2016), 32. Warren cites, in this passage, C. N. Degler, "Slavery and the Genesis of American Race Prejudice," *Comparative Studies in Society and History* 2, no. 1 (October 1959): 54–55; Margaret Ellen Newell, "Indian Slavery in Colonial New England," chap. 2 in *Indian Slavery in Colonial America,* edited and with an introduction by Alan Gallay (Lincoln, NE: University of Nebraska Press, 2009), 34;

Edmund S. Morgan, *The Puritan Family: Religion and Domestic Relations in Seventeenth-Century New England* (New York, NY: Harper and Row, 1966), 109; and suggests that readers see also Linda M. Heywood and John K. Thornton, "'Canniball Negroes,' Atlantic Creoles, and the Identity of New England's Charter Generation," *African Diaspora* 4, no. 1 (2011): 79–80. See also Lorenzo Johnston Greene, *The Negro in Colonial New England, 1620–1776* (New York, NY: Columbia University Press; P. S. King & Staples, ltd., 1942), 168; Richard S. Dunn, *Sugar and Slaves: The Rise of the Planter Class in the English West Indies, 1624–1713* (Chapel Hill, NC: University of North Carolina Press, 1972), 228; Allegra di Bonaventura, *For Adam's Sake: A Family Saga in Colonial New England* (New York, NY: Liveright Publishing Corporation, 2013), 17; Margaret Ellen Newell, *Brethren by Nature: New England Indians, Colonists, and the Origins of American Slavery* (Ithaca, NY: Cornell University Press, 2015), 12–13.

2. See Section Six of this report.

3. Harvard University, *Quinquennial Catalogue of the Officers and Graduates of Harvard University, 1636–1915* (Cambridge, MA: Harvard University Press, 1915), 120, https://books.google.com/books?id=JiNOAAAAMAAJ.

In this document, all pre-1752 dates have been updated to the New Style system following the Gregorian calendar, in which the calendar year runs from January 1 to December 31. See "The 1752 Calendar Change," Colonial Records & Topics, Connecticut State Library, accessed February 17, 2022, https://libguides.ctstatelibrary.org/hg/colonialresearch/calendar.

4. "Buildings / Sites," Harvard Property Information Resource Center, Harvard University, https://harvardplanning.emuseum.com/sites/list.

Table A.1

1. While not given the title of President, Nathaniel Eaton was the first leader appointed at Harvard College. See Harvard University, *Quinquennial Catalogue, 1636–1915*, 54; Samuel Eliot Morison, *Three Centuries of Harvard, 1636–1936* (1936; 13th repr. Cambridge MA: Belknap Press of Harvard University Press, 2001), 7–10.

2. John Winthrop, *The History of New England from 1630 to 1649*, vol. 1, ed. James Savage (Boston, MA: Little, Brown and Company, 1853), 310–311, n. 1, https://books.google.com/books?id=KIarrcIX7QAC. Winthrop's description of the Moor was reprinted in John Langdon Sibley, *Biographical Sketches of Graduates of Harvard University in Cambridge, Massachusetts*, vol. 1, *1642–1658* (Cambridge, MA: Charles William Sever, 1873), 5, https://books.google.com/books?id=SRZSAQAAMAAJ.

3.   On the brass markers, see Susan E. Maycock and Charles M. Sullivan, *Building Old Cambridge: Architecture and Development* (Cambridge, MA: MIT Press, 2016), 8, figure 1.7.

4.   *Diary of Cotton Mather, 1681–1708,* Collections of the Massachusetts Historical Society, 7th ser., vol. 7 (Boston, MA: Massachusetts Historical Society, 1911), 22, 203, https://books.google.com/books?id=lFWl8_xp9MoC& newbks=1.

5.   Will of Increase Mather, *Suffolk County, MA: Probate File Papers, AmericanAncestors.org,* New England Historic Genealogical Society, 2017–2019, from records supplied by the Massachusetts Supreme Judicial Court Archives, digitized images provided by FamilySearch.org, accessed February 15, 2022.

6.   See Christie McDonald and Karl M. Aspelund, eds., *Increase: What's in a Name? The Man, His Legacy, and the Naming of Mather House, Catalogue of an Exhibition in the SNLHTC Gallery, Mather House, February–May 2017* (Cambridge, MA: self–pub., 2017), https://mather.harvard.edu/files/mather/files /increasemather_e-book_web.pdf.

7.   *Records of the Church of Christ at Cambridge in New England, 1632–1830: Comprising the Ministerial Records of Baptisms, Marriages, Deaths, Admission to Covenant and Communion, Dismissals and Church Proceedings,* copied and ed. Stephen Paschall Sharples, (Boston, MA: Eben Putnam, 1906), 96, https:// books.google.com/books?id=RoLJh2dqZcgC; Benjamin Wadsworth, Diary, 1725–1736, box 1, seq. 126, Papers of Benjamin Wadsworth, UAI 15.868, Harvard University Archives, https://iiif.lib.harvard.edu/manifests/view /drs:14299446$56i; Diary of Henry Flynt, 1723–1747, seq. 86, HUG 1399.18, Harvard University Archives, https://iiif.lib.harvard.edu/manifests/view /drs:46676980$86i; Benjamin Wadsworth Diary, 1725–1736, 1670–1737, box 1, seq. 26, Papers of Benjamin Wadsworth, UAI 15.868, Harvard University Archives, https://iiif.lib.harvard.edu/manifests/view/drs:14299446$126i; Harvard University Faculty of Arts and Sciences, Official Minutes, September 24, 1725–March 3, 1752, box 8, vol. 12, seq. 102 and 137, Early Faculty minutes, 1725–1806, UAIII 5.5, Harvard University Archives, https://iiif.lib.harvard.edu /manifests/view/drs:46760183$1i.

8.   See Christina Pazzanese, "To Titus, Venus, Juba, and Bilhah," *Harvard Gazette,* April 6, 2016, https://news.harvard.edu/gazette/story/2016/04/to-titus -venus-bilhah-and-juba/; and "Wadsworth House Plaque Dedication," Office of the President, Harvard University, accessed February 4, 2022, https://www .harvard.edu/president/speeches-faust/2016/wadsworth-house-plaque -dedication/.

9. *Church of Christ at Cambridge*, 109; and Wadsworth, Diary, 1725–1736, Harvard University Archives, seq. 39, https://iiif.lib.harvard.edu/manifests /view/drs:14299446$39i.

10. *Vital Records of Cambridge Massachusetts to the Year 1850*, vol. 2, *Marriages and Deaths*, Compiled by Thomas W. Baldwin (Boston, MA: New England Historic Genealogical Society, 1915), 441–442, https://books.google.com/books ?id=lc8UAAAAYAAJ; "Diary of Rev. Edward Holyoke, 1709–1768," *The Holyoke Diaries, 1709–1856*, with an introduction and annotations by George Francis Dow (Salem, MA: The Essex Institute, 1911), 37, 44, https://archive.org/details /holyokediaries00dowg/page/n7/mode/2up.

11. See note 12 above.

12. Lewis Morey Hastings, "The Streets of Cambridge: Some Account of Their Origin and History," in *The Cambridge Historical Society Publications XIV: Proceedings for the Year 1919* (Cambridge, MA: Cambridge Historical Society, 1925), 65, https://books.google.com/books?id=558yAQAAMAAJ.

13. "Diary of Rev. Edward Holyoke," 18, 22, 23, 25. Although Bilhah is never explicitly referred to in the diaries as either as a servant or as "negro," the editor identifies her as a servant and her name—which is drawn from the Hebrew Bible—is clear evidence of her status. Biblical names were common among both enslaved and free African Americans during the period of enslavement. And while white colonists also frequently used biblical names as well, Bilhah—a maid given by her mistress to the mistress's husband to bear children for him when his wife could not (Gen. 1:1–8)—was the kind of name frequently used for enslaved women. John C. Inscoe notes that, in the Southern United States, "those names commonly used by slaves that were rarely used by southern whites, whether drawn from African, Biblical, classical, or other sources, outnumber those names shared by both groups," see "Carolina Slave Names: An Index to Acculturation," *The Journal of Southern History* 49, no. 4 (November 1983): 527–554.

14. "Diary of Rev. Edward Holyoke," 25.

15. Dinah is identified as a servant in multiple Holyoke family households, and there is substantial evidence that she was enslaved. She first appears in President Edward Holyoke's diary in January 1757, when Holyoke recorded her weight alongside that of the other members of his household as part of an annual ritual. Dinah weighed just over 51 pounds, indicating that she was a child but obviously not a newborn. She appears several more times in President Holyoke's diaries. In one instance, Holyoke records Dinah accompanying Mary Landman to Boston "in order for Piscataway"—Holyoke notes Molly's last name but does not give one for Dinah; enslaved people typically were not

recognized as having family names in this period. After President Holyoke's death in 1769, Dinah reappears in his daughter-in-law's Mary Holyoke's household "scowering" the house and the pewter in two separate entries in 1780, and then disappears until yet another family member notes her death in 1818. Dinah's disappearance from the family record after 1780 is consistent with the end of slavery in Massachusetts as a result of several court cases in 1781. One other enslaved person—identified by the editor as a "negro servant"—left the Holyoke family around this time: Mary Holyoke noted on December 14, 1781, "Cato left us to live in Boston." See "Index," *Holyoke Diaries,* 195; "Diary of Rev. Edward Holyoke," 17, 18, 20, 22, 26; "Diary of Mrs. Mary (Vial) Holyoke, *1760–1800,*" *Holyoke Diaries,* 103, 105, 106, 111; "Diary of Margaret Holyoke, Daughter of Dr. Augustus and Mary (Vial) Holyoke, *1801–1823,*" *Holyoke Diaries,* 169; on the end of slavery in Massachusetts, see "Massachusetts Constitution and the Abolition of Slavery," Mass.gov, accessed December 1, 2021, https://www.mass.gov/guides/massachusetts-constitution-and-the-abolition -of-slavery.

Like Bilhah, Dinah is never identified as being of African or Indigenous descent. Also like Bilhah, Dinah is a biblical name frequently assigned to enslaved women. See Newbell Niles Puckett, *Black Names in America: Origins and Usage,* edited by Murray Heller (Boston, MA: G. K. Hall, 1975), and Inscoe, "Carolina Slave Names: An Index to Acculturation."

The scant records leave Dinah's life open to interpretation. One scholar has posited, given Dinah's age when she first appears in the diaries, that she may have been Bilhah's daughter. Another has speculated that the trip with Molly Landman in 1762 may have been a permanent departure, thus rendering the Dinah in later family diaries another individual. See Jane Kamensky, "The View from 1764," in *The Philosophy Chamber: Art and Science in Harvard's Teaching Cabinet, 1766–1820,* ed. Ethan W. Lasser (New Haven, CT: Yale University Press, 2017), 6, and Christina J. Hodge, "'A Sharp White Background': Enslavement and Privilege at Eighteenth-Century Harvard College," *Historical Archaeology* 55, no. 4 (2021): 470.

16. *Vital Records of Cambridge,* 2:805.

17. Hastings, "The Streets of Cambridge," 62.

Table A.2

1.   Throughout the colonial era and well into the nineteenth century, the University did not control the appointment of Overseers: The colonial and later the state legislature determined membership. Generally, all Governors, Deputy Governors, and Lieutenant Governors were automatically Harvard

Overseers by virtue of their positions, along with magistrates and ministers from Cambridge and the surrounding towns. After 1780, the list also included various members of the state legislature. Harvard and the Legacy of Slavery researchers have not reviewed the full list of Overseers in the 17th and 18th centuries to identify all of those who were slaveholders; this is an important area for future research. For a full description of the permutations of the Board of Overseers in the seventeenth, eighteenth, and nineteenth centuries, see Harvard University, *Quinquennial Catalogue, 1636–1915*, 13–17.

2. Harvard University, *Quinquennial Catalogue, 1636–1915*, 13.

3. Newell, *Brethren by Nature*, 40–41, 79, describes this woman's enslavement and later escape from Winthrop's household. See also C. S. Manegold, *Ten Hills Farm: The Forgotten History of Slavery in the North* (Princeton, NJ: Princeton University Press, 2010), 42. As Governor of the Massachusetts Bay Colony during the Pequot War, Winthrop also decided what to do with the estimated hundreds of Indigenous people taken prisoner by soldiers of the Massachusetts Bay colony during the war. He oversaw the distribution of women and children as slaves to English colonists, as well as the shipment of captives to the West Indies for sale to the sugar planters there. See Manegold, *Ten Hill Farm*, 41–43; for a more detailed account, see Newell, "'David's warre': The Pequot War and the Origins of Slavery in New England," chap. 1, "'I doe not see how wee can thrive untill wee get into a stock of slaves': Slavery in the Puritan Atlantic World," chap. 2, and Indians we have received into our houses": Pequot War Captives in New England Households, *Brethren by Nature*.

4. "About," Winthrop House, Harvard College, accessed January 25, 2022, https://winthrop.harvard.edu/about.

5. "Memorial Hall Sculptures," Office for the Arts at Harvard: Memorial Hall / Lowell Hall Complex, accessed March 23, 2022, https://sites.fas.harvard .edu/~memhall/sculptures.html.

6. Charles Osgood, *John Winthrop (1588–1649)*, c. 1840–1850, oil on canvas, 76.2 × 63.5 cm, Harvard Art Museums, https://hvrd.art/o/304798.

7. Manegold, *Ten Hills Farm*, 42; see Roger Williams to John Winthrop, August 1639, in Glenn W. LaFantasie, ed., *The Correspondence of Roger Williams*, vol. 1, *1629–1653*, assisted by Robert S. Cocroft et al., revised from an unpublished manuscript ed. Bradford F. Swan (Hanover, RI and London, UK: Brown University Press / University of New England Press, 1988), 199–200. cited in Newell, *Brethren by Nature*, 79, where the Rhode Island founder in a letter to Winthrop described these children as sons.

8.   Newell, *Brethren by Nature,* 66, documents at least three women and two men entering Winthrop's household after the Pequot War; this number presumably includes the wife of Mononotto, leaving an additional two women as well as the two men. She further describes Winthrop's 1639 will in which he left his property on Governor's Island and the enslaved Indigenous people who labored there to his son Adam. See also Francis J. Bremer, *John Winthrop: America's Forgotten Founding Father* (New York: Oxford University Press, 2003), 318.

9.   Harvard University, *Quinquennial Catalogue, 1636–1915,* 13. See also Sibley, *Biographical sketches of graduates of Harvard, 1642–1658,* 1–2, esp. n. 1.

10.   Josiah Quincy, *The History of Harvard University* (Cambridge, MA: John Owen, 1840), 1:172.

11.   Newell, *Brethren by Nature,* 33–35, 93. Israel Stoughton played a prominent role in the Pequot War, commanding soldiers from the Massachusetts Bay Colony in the slaughter or capture and enslavement of hundreds of members of the Pequot tribe in what is now southern New England. Pequot women and children who survived the war were divided among Indigenous tribes allied with the English colonists and among English settlers in New England, while adult men were shipped to the West Indies and traded to English planters in exchange for cotton, tobacco, and African slaves. See also James Savage, Richard S. Dunn, and Laetitia Yeandle, eds., *The Journal of John Winthrop, 1630–1649* (Cambridge, MA: Harvard University Press, 1996), 225–228, 246.

12.   "Stoughton Hall: Site Name History," Harvard Property Information Resource Center, Harvard University, accessed March 14, 2022, https://harvard planning.emuseum.com/sites/954/stoughton-hall; Quincy, *History of Harvard,* 1:172–180.

13.   Newell, Brethren by Nature, 93–94, asserts that Dorcas is the "Blackamore maid" held up as a sign of the colonists' success in Christianizing their servants in New Englands first fruits: in respect, first of the conversion of some, conviction of divers, preparation of sundry of the Indians, 2. of the progresse of learning, in the colledge at Cambridge in Massachusetts Bay. With divers other speciall matters concerning that country (London, UK: R. O. and G. D. for Henry Overton, 1643), 10–11. On April 13, 1641, John Winthrop recorded in his journal that, "A negro maid, servant to Mr. Stoughton of Dorchester [. . .] was received into the church and baptized." Journal of John Winthrop, 347. "Dorcas ye Blackmore" is identified as becoming a member of the church on April 16, 1641, in Records of the First Church of Dorchester in New

England, 1636–1734 (Boston, MA: George H. Ellis, 1891), 5, https://books.google.com/books?id=o-xzW5V-AzoC.

14.   Harvard University, *Quinquennial Catalogue, 1636–1915,* 13, names Endicott as an Overseer by virtue of his role as Deputy Governor of the colony in 1642, and further notes that, from 1642 until 1697, the overseers were comprised of "the *Governor* and *Deputy Governor*" along with local magistrates and elders. Endicott served as governor, deputy governor, or assistant governor of the colony for all but one year from 1629 until his death in 1665, see "Biographical Sketches: John Endicott," Guide to the Collection, Endicott Family Papers:1612–1958, Massachusetts Historical Society, accessed March 10, 2022, https://www.masshist.org/collection-guides/view/fa0021.

15.   Hugh Peter to John Winthrop, July 15, 1637, Winthrop Family Papers 3:450, Massachusetts Historical Society, accessed March 8, 2022, https://www.masshist.org/publications/winthrop/index.php/view/PWF03d354. Hugh Peter received a young woman (see below), so the "younge boy" he requested in his letter must have been for Endicott.

16.   Sibley, *Graduates of Harvard University, 1642–1658,* 1–2, esp. n. 1; Harvard University, *Quinquennial Catalogue, 1636–1915,* 13.

17.   Hugh Peter to John Winthrop, July 15, 1637, Massachusetts Historical Society; *Records and Files of the Quarterly Courts of Essex County Massachusetts,* vol. 1, *1636–1656* (Salem, MA: The Essex Institute, 1911), 11, https://books.google.com/books?id=7Boi57UNjuUC; Hugh Peter to John Winthrop, September 4, 1639, Winthrop Family Papers, vol. 4, Massachusetts Historical Society, accessed March 10, 2022, https://www.masshist.org/publications/winthrop/index.php/view/PWF04d132; *Records of the Court of Assistants of the Colony of the Massachusetts Bay, 1630–1692,* vol. 2 (Boston, MA: County of Suffolk, 1904), 95, https://books.google.com/books?id=I70VAQAAIAAJ, all cited in Newell, *Brethren by Nature.*

18.   Leverett would have been an Overseer of the College by virtue of his role as Governor of the colony from 1673 to 1679. John Leverett Papers, Massachusetts Historical Society, accessed March 14, 2022, https://www.masshist.org/features/saltonstall/john-leverett.

19.   Leverett was directly and extensively involved in the mass enslavement of Indigenous people during King Philip's War. He recruited mercenaries to fight on behalf of the Massachusetts Bay Colony in King Philip's War with promises of "captives and plunder." In September 1676, Leverett issued a certificate declaring New England's Indigenous peoples—including noncombatant women and children—enslavable. By the end of the war, there were

roughly 2,000 captive Natives in New England households—a number that does not include those sold to plantations in the West Indies or in markets on the other side of the Atlantic. Governor Leverett's Certificate, September 12, 1676, Photostats, Massachusetts Historical Society, Boston, cited in Newell, *Brethren by Nature,* 141, 150–151, 159.

20. "Leverett House: Site Name History," Harvard Property Information Resource Center, Harvard University, accessed March 14, 2022, https:// harvardplanning.emuseum.com/sites/940/leverett-house; "Collection Overview: Biography (Early Life and Career)," Papers of John Leverett 1652–1724, 1730, UAI 15.866, Harvard University Archives, accessed March 14, 2022, https://hollisarchives.lib.harvard.edu/repositories/4/resources/4298; "John Leverett," History of the Presidency, Harvard Office of the President, accessed March 14, 2022, https://www.harvard.edu/president/history/#1700s.

21. John Langdon Sibley, *Biographical sketches of graduates of Harvard University in Cambridge, Massachusetts, Volume 2, 1659–1677* (Cambridge, MA: Charles William Sever, University Bookstore, 1881), 166–188.

22. "History," Dudley Community, accessed January 14, 2022, https://dudley .harvard.edu/history; Dean Dudley, *Supplement to the History and Genealogy of the Dudley Family* (self pub., 1898), 8, https://books.google.com/books?vid =HARVARD:32044014585277.

23. Both the unnamed girl and Peter are listed among "Indians" who died in Roxbury in *Vital Records of Roxbury Massachusetts to the End of the Year 1849,* vol. 2, *Marriages and Deaths,* Compiled by Thomas W. Baldwin (Salem, MA: The Essex Institute, 1926), 680, https://books.google.com/books?id=Apwl AQAAMAAJ, cited in Wayne Tucker, "Joseph Dudley, Brill the Enslaved Coachman, and Enslaved Indians," The Dudley Family of Roxbury & Their Enslaved People, Eleven Names Project, accessed August 28, 2021, https:// eleven-names.com/2021/08/18/judge-paul-dudley/. With thanks to the Hon. Byron Rushing for bringing this history to the attention of the Harvard and the Legacy of Slavery team.

24. *Diary of Samuel Sewall, 1674–1729, Vol. II, 1699/1700–1714,* Collections of the Massachusetts Historical Society, vol. 6, 5th ser. (Boston, MA: Massachusetts Historical Society, 1879), 371, https://books.google.com/books?id =hbsTAAAAYAAJ; *Diary of Samuel Sewall, 1674–1729, Vol. II, 1699/1700–1714,* Collections of the Massachusetts Historical Society, vol. 7, 5th ser. (Boston, MA: Massachusetts Historical Society, 1882), 9, 232, 248, https://books.google .com/books?id=y7sTAAAAYAAJ; Will of Rebecca Dudley, *Suffolk County, MA: Probate File Papers, AmericanAncestors.org,* New England Historic Genealogical Society, 2017–2019, (from records supplied by the Massachusetts

Supreme Judicial Court Archives, digitized images provided by Family Search.org), cited in Wayne Tucker, "Joseph Dudley."

25. Mather would have been appointed an Overseer by virtue of his position as the Minister of the North Church in Boston, after the composition of the Overseers reverted in 1707 to the original 1642 rules: "The *Governor* and *Deputy Governor* for the time being, and all the *magistrates* of this jurisdiction, together with the *teaching elders* of the six next adjoining towns, viz. Cambridge, Watertown, Charlestown, Boston, Roxbury, and Dorchester. . . ." See Harvard University, *Quinquennial Catalogue,* 13. See also John Langdon Sibley, *Biographical Sketches of Graduates of Harvard University in Cambridge, Massachusetts, Volume III, 1678–1689* (Cambridge, MA: Charles William Sever, University Bookstore, 1885), 20, 21.

26. *Diary of Cotton Mather, 1681–1708,* 22, 203. Historians believe that this is the same enslaved person named in Increase Mather's 1723 will as "The Spaniard." See Henry W. Haynes, "Cotton Mather and His Slaves," *Proceedings of the American Antiquarian Society* (Oct. 1889), 191–192, https://www.americanan tiquarian.org/proceedings/48057585.pdf.

27. See McDonald and Aspelund, *Increase: What's in a Name?.*

28. After 10 years of servitude, Mather permitted Onesimus to purchase a "Negro-lad" to replace himself in Mather's household. Thereafter, Mather wrote, Onesimus was permitted to "Enjoy and Employ his whole Time for his own purposes"—except for a variety of services that he was still required to perform for Mather's family, including bringing in firewood every night, shoveling at the Mather home after "great snows," and generally being on call when the family deemed his services necessary to them. See *Diary of Cotton Mather, 1681–1708,* 363; *Diary of Cotton Mather, 1709–1724,* Collections of the Massachusetts Historical Society, 7th ser., vol. 8 (Boston, MA: Massachusetts Historical Society, 1912), 363.

29. *Diary of Cotton Mather, 1709–1724,* 384.

30. *Diary of Cotton Mather, 1709–1724,* 477, 562.

31. *Church of Christ at Cambridge,* 79; "First Church Timeline," First Church in Cambridge, accessed January 14, 2022, https://www.firstchurchcambridge .org/first–church–timeline/.

First Church in Cambridge functioned as the official church for the University until 1814, when the Corporation and Overseers voted to create and maintain a "Society for religious instruction, worship and ordinances on the Lord's day" within Harvard. See *Church of Christ in Cambridge,* 394–395; Morison, *Three Centuries of Harvard,* 201–202.

Harvard "held a partial right of ownership" in the second, third, and fourth meetinghouses built for the use by the Church of Christ (today's First Church) from the Second Meetinghouse constructed in 1651 until the Fourth, to which it contributed one-seventh of the cost of construction in the mid-eighteenth century. Each of these meetinghouses stood near the site occupied since 1925 by Lehman Hall in Harvard Yard. See Maycock and Sullivan, *Building Old Cambridge,* 615–616.

32.   *Church of Christ at Cambridge,* 59, 183, 184.

33.   Hastings, "The Streets of Cambridge," 41, 64; Maycock and Sullivan, *Building Old Cambridge,* 178–180.

34.   William Thaddeus Harris, *Epitaphs from the Old Burying-ground in Cambridge, with Notes* (Cambridge, MA: John Owen, 1845), 48, https://books .google.com/books?id=wrXW6T1MeKUC.

35.   Harris, *Epitaphs,* 48.

36.   Samuel A. Eliot, *A Sketch of the History of Harvard College and of its Present State* (Boston, MA: Charles C. Little and James Brown, 1848), 172.

37.   Cecil Headlam, ed., *Calendar of State Papers, Colonial Series. America and West Indies. 1706–1708. June. Preserved in the Public Record Office* (London, UK: Her Majesty's Stationery Office, 1916; repr. Vaduz, Liechtenstein: Kraus Reprint Ltd., 1964), 262, https://books.google.com/books?id=nIMwAQAAMAAJ, cited in Wayne Tucker, "Paul Dudley: Pirates, Epic Grift, and a Baptism," Dudley Family of Roxbury.

38.   "History," Dudley Community; Dudley, *Genealogy of the Dudley Family,* 8.

39.   Walter Eliot Thwing, *History of the First Church in Roxbury Massachusetts, 1630–1904* (Boston, MA: W. A. Butterfield, 1908), 143, https://books .google.com/books?id=MarbrrRJusYC, cited in Tucker, "Paul Dudley."

40.   *Church of Christ at Cambridge,* 124; "First Church Timeline."

41.   *Church of Christ at Cambridge,* 108.

42.   This William Brattle (AM 1722) was the son of the Reverend William Brattle (AM 1680) described above.

43.   Clifford K. Shipton, *Sibley's Harvard Graduates,* vol. 7, *1722–1725* (Boston, MA: Massachusetts Historical Society, 1945), 13.

The Hopkins Trust was established in the 1710s with a bequest from benefactor Edward Hopkins (listed below) and administered primarily for the benefit of Harvard College. See Charles Pickering Bowditch, *An Account of the Trust Administered by the Trustees of the Charity of Edward Hopkins* (1889), https://books.google.com/books?id=jAcAAAAAYAAJ.

44. *Church of Christ at Cambridge,* 97.

45. John Singleton Copley, *William Brattle (1706–1776),* 1756, oil on canvas, 128 × 102.5 cm, Harvard Art Museums, https://hvrd.art/o/227540.

46. Hastings, "The Streets of Cambridge," 41, 64; Maycock and Sullivan, *Building Old Cambridge,* 178–180.

47. *Church of Christ at Cambridge,* 109.

48. Clifford K. Shipton, *Sibley's Harvard Graduates,* vol. 5, *Biographical Sketches of Those Who Attended Harvard University, 1701–1712* (Cambridge, MA: Harvard University Press, 1937), 637.

49. *Church of Christ at Cambridge,* 109, 110.

50. *Church of Christ at Cambridge,* 109.

51. Shipton, *Sibley's Harvard Graduates, 1701–1712,* 227.

52. Shipton, *Sibley's Harvard Graduates, 1701–1712,* 227. On the Hopkins Foundation see Bowditch, *Charity of Edward Hopkins.*

53. *Vital Records of Cambridge,* 2:806.

54. *Church of Christ at Cambridge,* 109, 111.

55. *Church of Christ at Cambridge,* 111.

56. *Church of Christ at Cambridge,* 109.

57. *Church of Christ at Cambridge,* 171.

58. "August 21, 1757," Diary of Ebenezer Storer, 1749–1764, p. 73, Mss C 2004, R. Stanton Avery Special Collections, New England Historic Genealogical Society, Congregational Library and Archives, accessed August 25, 2021, https://congregationallibrary.quartexcollections.com/Documents/Detail/ebenezer-storer-diary-1749-1764/32130?item=32232.

59. In 1771, Storer served as the executor of his mother Mary Storer's estate when she died in Boston. The first thing listed on her probate inventory is "A negro man named London," valued at £20. In 1761, London was one of three enslaved people inherited by Mary upon her husband's death. There is no will included in the probate record, and it is unclear how Ebenezer Storer, in his role as executor, disposed of London—whether by sale, by distributing him to one of Mary's heirs, or by taking ownership of London himself. See Mary Storer Probate Record, *Suffolk County, MA: Probate File Papers,* American-Ancestors.org, New England Historic Genealogical Society, 2017–2019, (from records supplied by the Massachusetts Supreme Judicial Court Archives, digitized images provided by FamilySearch.org), accessed August 25, 2021; Ebenezer Storer Probate Record, *Suffolk County, MA: Probate File Papers,* AmericanAncestors.org, New England Historic Genealogical Society, 2017–2019,

(from records supplied by the Massachusetts Supreme Judicial Court Archives, digitized images provided by FamilySearch.org), accessed August 25, 2021.

60. *The Manifesto Church: Records of the Church in Brattle Square, Boston, with Lists of Communicants, Baptisms, Marriages and Funerals, 1699–1872* (Boston, MA: The Benevolent Fraternity of Churches, 1902), 184, 185, 187, 189, https:// books.google.com/books?id=Iufi5eVXCGoC. Cato first appears in the 1764 will of Thomas Hancock, John's uncle and guardian. Thomas Hancock was also a benefactor of Harvard College, leaving £1000 in his will to fund the Hancock Professorship of Hebrew and Other Oriental Languages. Will of Thomas Hancock, *Suffolk County, MA: Probate File Papers,* AmericanAncestors.org, New England Historic Genealogical Society, 2017–2019, (from records supplied by the Massachusetts Supreme Judicial Court Archives, digitized images provided by FamilySearch.org), accessed April 2, 2021. The will stipulates that Cato should be manumitted when he turns 30.

Cato also appeared in Lydia Hancock's 1777 will in which she stipulates that he should receive 6 pounds, 13 shillings, and 4 pence from her estate "at the time he shall become free by my late husband's will." Will of Mrs. Lydia Hancock, *Suffolk County, MA: Probate File Papers,* AmericanAncestors.org, New England Historic Genealogical Society, 2017–2019, (from records supplied by the Massachusetts Supreme Judicial Court Archives, digitized images provided by FamilySearch.org), accessed April 2, 2021. As John and Lydia Hancock shared a home, Cato and the other enslaved people named in Lydia Hancock's will lived in John Hancock's house up to the time of her death. See William M. Fowler, *The Baron of Beacon Hill* (Boston, MA: Houghton Mifflin Company, 1980), 77.

61. *Manifesto Church,* 185; Pamela Athearn Filbert, "Curiouser and Curiouser," Vita Brevis: A resource for family history from AmericanAncestors .org by the New England Historic Genealogical Society, February 25, 2019, https://vitabrevis.americanancestors.org/2019/02/curiouser/.

62. Will of Mrs. Lydia Hancock, AmericanAncestors.org.

63. Will of Mrs. Lydia Hancock, AmericanAncestors.org.

64. Will of Mrs. Lydia Hancock, AmericanAncestors.org.

65. Where documents refer to more than one enslaved person but do not specify a number, we have counted two enslaved people for the purposes of the overall number reported elsewhere by the committee.

66. From Thomas Hubbard's will, quoted in Clifford K. Shipton, *Sibley's Harvard Graduates,* vol. 6, *1713–1721* (Boston, MA: Massachusetts Historical Society, 1942), 494.

67. Oliver was an overseer by virtue of his position as lieutenant governor of the Massachusetts Bay Colony. See note 22 above.

68. "Thomas Oliver UK Loyalist Claims, 1783," American Loyalist Claims, Series II: Class: AO 13, Piece: 048, electronic record, The National Archives of the UK (retrieved from American Loyalist Claims, 1776–1835, AO 12–13, Ancestry.com).

69. Clifford K. Shipton, *Sibley's Harvard Graduates, Volume XIII, 1751–1755: Biographical Sketches of Those Who Attended Harvard College in the Classes 1751–1755 with Bibliographical and Other Notes* (Boston, MA: Massachusetts Historical Society, 1965), 336.

Table A.3

1. Hannibal had three children who were baptized at First Church. We have not included them here because research to date has not uncovered their mother's identity, whether she was enslaved, or by whom, nor has it uncovered whether and by whom the children were enslaved.

2. *Church of Christ at Cambridge,* 109, 145; *Vital Records of Cambridge,* 2:442.

3. Diary of Henry Flynt, 1723–1747, seq. 264, Harvard University Archives, https://iiif.lib.harvard.edu/manifests/view/drs:46676980$264i.

4. John Greenwood, *Henry Flynt (1675–1760),* c. 1749–1750, oil on canvas, 87 cm × 77.2 cm × 5.7 cm (framed), Harvard Art Museums, https://hvrd.art /o/304644.

5. *Church of Christ at Cambridge,* 109.

6. *Vital Records of Cambridge,* 2:441.

7. John Winthrop, Annotated almanac, 1759, box 5, vol. 4, seq. 5, Papers of John and Hannah Winthrop, 1728–1789, HUM 9, Harvard University Archives, https://iiif.lib.harvard.edu/manifests/view/drs:45560269$5i.

8. See "About," Winthrop House, Harvard College, accessed January 25, 2022, https://winthrop.harvard.edu/about.

9. John Singleton Copley, *John Winthrop (1714–1779),* 1773, oil on canvas, 155.6 cm × 121.3 cm × 11.4 cm (framed), Harvard Art Museums, https://hvrd .art/o/299882.

10. Hastings, "The Streets of Cambridge," 68. The square is across Mt. Auburn Street from the former site of Professor Winthrop's house on the corner of Mt. Auburn and what is now John F. Kennedy St. See Maycock and Sullivan, *Building Old Cambridge,* 138, figure 3.35.

11. "Historic Markers," Cambridge Historic Commission, accessed January 20, 2022, https://www.cambridgema.gov/historic/cambridgehistory/historic markers.

12. Winthrop, Annotated almanac, Harvard University Archives.

Table A.4

1. Historian Wendy Warren identifies Thomas Danforth as an enslaver in *New England Bound* (154), citing *An Historic Guide to Cambridge,* which notes that, in his will, Danforth declared "that the negro man Philip ffeild *[Ed. note: Ffeild in table]* should serve Mr. Foxcroft four years, and then be a free man." See *An Historic Guide to Cambridge,* compiled by members of the Hannah Winthrop Chapter of the National Society of the Daughters of the American Revolution (Cambridge, MA: self pub., 1907), https://books.google.com /books?id=ckIVAAAAYAAJ.

2. This Andrew Bordman was the fourth member of his family to serve as a steward. He was also brother-in-law to University President Benjamin Wads worth. After his death, his son became the fifth and final Bordman to serve in the role. See Clifford K. Shipton, *Sibley's Harvard Graduates,* vol. 4, *Biographical Sketches of Those Who Attended Harvard University, 1690–1700* (Cambridge, MA: Harvard University Press, 1933), 19, 84; Harvard University, *Quinquennial Catalogue of the Officers and Graduates of Harvard University, 1636–1890* (Cambridge, MA: John Wilson and Son, 1890), 56, https://books.google.com/books ?id=zh9OAAAAMAAJ.

3. Deed of sale, January 1, 1716 / 7, box 2, folder 3, Papers of the Bordman family, 1686–1837, HUGS 1228, Harvard University Archives, https://iiif.lib .harvard.edu/manifests/view/drs:52823945$1i.

4. Maycock and Sullivan, Building Old Cambridge, 123, 759, 765.

5. Harris, *Epitaphs,* 90.

6. Notebook, 1686–1741, box 3, Papers of the Bordman family, 1686–1837, HUG 1228, Harvard University Archives, https://iiif.lib.harvard.edu/manifests /view/drs:52760842$61i. See also *Church of Christ at Cambridge,* 145.

7. Notebook, 1686–1741, Harvard University Archives; Harris, *Epitaphs,* 90.

8. Notebook, 1686–1741, Harvard University Archives.

9. Notebook, 1686–1741, Harvard University Archives.

10. Notebook, 1686–1741, Harvard University Archives.

11. *Church of Christ at Cambridge,* 109.

12. *Vital Records of Cambridge*, 2:442. Elizabeth Bordman was the widow of Steward Andrew Bordman (II) and the mother of Steward Andrew Bordman (III). See *Vital Records of Cambridge to the Year 1850*, vol. 1, *Births,* compiled by Thomas W. Baldwin (Boston, MA: New England Historic Genealogical Society, 1914), 73, https://books.google.com/books?id=SMscZFWeblsC.

13. Shepard Congregational Society, *The Manual of the First Church in Cambridge (Congregational), Corner of Garden and Mason Streets, Cambridge, Massachusetts* (Boston, MA: Press of Samuel Usher, 1900), 30, https://books .google.com/books?id=mQAFEN3KfGsC.

Hastings was steward of Harvard College in 1767, when student Samuel Phillips wrote a letter to his parents that described taking a meal in the College kitchens "among the Negros." Given that Hastings is documented in First Church records as having enslaved a man named Cato as early as 1761, and that an enslaved child born in Hastings' household several years after this letter was also named Cato—presumably after his father—it seems likely that the adult Cato was one of the Black workers Phillips mentions in his letter. Samuel Phillips 5th to father Samuel Phillips the 4th, December 4, 1767, box 1, folder 21, Phillips family collection, Phillips Academy Archives and Special Collections, Andover, Massachusetts, https://phillipsacademy archives.net/collections/phillips-family-papers/samuel-phillips-5th-to-father -samuel-phillips-the-4th/.

14. "Jonathan Hastings House," Cambridge and the American Revolution, History Cambridge, accessed January 21, 2022, https://historycambridge.org /Cambridge–Revolution/Hastings%20House.html.

15. *Church of Christ at Cambridge*, 172, 224, 226.

16. *Church of Christ at Cambridge*, 233.

17. *Church of Christ at Cambridge*, 234.

Table A.5

1. See Bowditch, *Charity of Edward Hopkins.*

2. Edward Hopkins probate record, Connecticut State Library, Probate Packets, Hopkins, Deborah-Hosmer, S, 1641–1880, Ancestry.com, Connecticut Wills and Probate Records, 1609–1999.

3. See Bowditch, *Charity of Edward Hopkins,* and "Biographical / Historical" note, II: Hopkinton Records, 1700–ca. 1880s, Records of the Trustees of the Charity of Edward Hopkins, HUY 26, Harvard University Archives, accessed October 13, 2021, https://id.lib.harvard.edu/ead/c/hua47010c00016/catalog.

4. Josiah Quincy, *History of Harvard,* 1:406–407.

5.   Peterson, *City-State of Boston,* 130–133. See also Newell, *Brethren by Nature,* 142, 145, 168–170.

6.   "Notable Alumni," The Boston Latin School, accessed November 9, 2021, https://www.bls.org/m/pages/index.jsp?uREC_ID=203830&type=d&pREC _ID=404406.

7.   Harvard University, *Quinquennial Catalogue, 1636–1915,* 22.

8.   Clifford K. Shipton, *Sibley's Harvard Graduates,* vol. 8, *1726–1730* (Boston, MA: Massachusetts Historical Society, 1951), 509–510.

9.   *Church of Christ at Cambridge,* 109.

10.   Hastings, "The Streets of Cambridge," 68.

11.   *Edmund Trowbridge,* ca. 1730–1740, oil on canvas, 113.8 cm × 87.1 cm, National Portrait Gallery, https://npg.si.edu/object/npg_H-AAA__194_.

12.   *Church of Christ at Cambridge,* 203.

13.   *Church of Christ at Cambridge,* 203.

14.   Elise Lemire, *Black Walden: Slavery and Its Aftermath in Concord, Massachusetts* (Philadelphia, PA: University of Pennsylvania Press, 2009), 114–115; Will of John Cuming, *Middlesex County, MA: Probate File Papers, 1648–1871,* AmericanAncestors.org, New England Historic Genealogical Society, 2014, (from records supplied by the Massachusetts Supreme Judicial Court Archives, digitized images provided by FamilySearch.org); Quincy, *History of Harvard,* 2:423–424; Thomas Francis Harrington, *The Harvard Medical School: A History, narrative, and documentary,* edited by James Gregory Mumford, 3 vols. (New York, NY: Lewis Publishing Company, 1905), 1:271–272.

15.   Lemire, *Black Walden,* esp. 19–21, 126–127.

16.   Lemire, *Black Walden,* esp. 41, 126–127.

17.   Will of Thomas Hancock, AmericanAncestors.org.

18.   Will of Thomas Hancock, AmericanAncestors.org.

19.   "Documenting Those Enslaved by the Royalls," Royall House and Slave Quarters, accessed January 9, 2022, https://royallhouse.org/slavery/documenting -those-enslaved-by-the-royalls/. See also Janet Halley, "My Isaac Royall Legacy," *Harvard BlackLetter Law Journal* 24 (2008): 130–131, http://www.law.harvard .edu/faculty/jhalley/cv/24.Harvard.Blackletter.117.pdf.

20.   Robert Feke, *Isaac Royall and family,* 1741, oil on canvas, 56.1875 in × 77.75 in, Harvard Law School Library, https://images.hollis.harvard.edu /permalink/f/100kie6/HVD_VIAolvwork598105. See also "The Legacy of Isaac Royall, Jr.," Exhibit Addenda, Harvard Law School, accessed February 4, 2022, https://exhibits.law.harvard.edu/hls-shield-exhibit.

21.　See Royall House and Slave Quarters, accessed January 9, 2022, https://royallhouse.org/.

22.　Daniel R. Coquillette and Bruce A. Kimball, *On the Battlefield of Merit: Harvard Law School, the First Century* (Cambridge, MA: Harvard University Press, 2015), 81–82.

23.　The Perkins brothers (James, Thomas Handasyd, and Samuel Gardner) bought and sold enslaved human beings to turn a profit. In the 1780s and 1790s, they ran a mercantile house in St. Domingue that brought foodstuffs and timber from New England to the Caribbean for sale; purchased enslaved people directly off of ships and in the markets in St. Domingue for sale on other Caribbean islands; and purchased sugar, coffee, and other products produced by enslaved people in the Caribbean for sale in the U.S. and Europe. All three brothers spent time in St. Domingue, although Thomas quickly returned to New England for his health. See "Scope and Content," Perkins Family Papers, Boston Athenaeum, Massachusetts June 1, 2021, https://cdm.bostonathenaeum.org/digital/collection/p15482coll1/id/874/; Carl Seaburg and Stanley Paterson, *Merchant Prince of Boston: Colonel T. H. Perkins, 1764–1854* (1971; repr., Cambridge, MA: Harvard University Press, 2014), esp. 38–42.

24.　On its website, Massachusetts General Hospital (MGH) is described as "the first teaching hospital of Harvard University's new medical school" when it was established. "About Us: The Mass General Difference," Massachusetts General Hospital, accessed November 9, 2021, https://www.massgeneral.org/about/. On the work of Dr. John Collins Warren, first Dean of Harvard Medical School, to found MGH, see Edward Warren, *The Life of John Collins Warren, M. D., Compiled Chiefly from His Autobiography and Journals* (Boston, MA: Ticknor and Fields, 1860), 1:98–102, https://books.google.com/books?id=WccoAQAAMAAJ, and N. I. Bowditch, *A History of the Massachusetts General Hospital* (Boston, MA: John Wilson & Son, 1851), 3, https://books.google.com/books?id=qg8DAAAAQAAJ. Bowditch lists Harvard among the original subscribers to the fundraising effort for the hospital, see ibid.,402.

25.　Bowditch, *Massachusetts General Hospital,* esp. 417, 428.

26.　"DIED [Mousse]," *The Liberator* (Boston, MA), November 5, 1831; "[Meetings of 1823]—Memoir of James Perkins," in *Proceedings of the Massachusetts Historical Society,* vol. 1 (Boston, MA: Massachusetts Historical Society, 1791), 358.

27.　Perkins Family Papers, 1780–1882, MSS. L816, Boston Athenaeum, Massachusetts, accessed October 28, 2021, https://cdm.bostonathenaeum.org/digital/collection/p15482coll1/id/874/. The relevant material in this collection, including correspondence to and from Thomas, James, and Samuel Gardner Perkins, dates to the period when the brothers ran a mercantile business based in St. Domingue (Haiti). Many of the letters are explicit in their descriptions of the purchase and sale of enslaved people, including reports from ship captains on the profits and losses associated with such sales.

28. Bowditch, *Massachusetts General Hospital*, esp. 417, 428.

29. See note 142 above.

30. Anna Gardner Fish, "Thomas Handasyd Perkins," Founders, Perkins History Museum, Perkins School for the Blind, accessed August 13, 2021, https://www.perkins.org/founders/#TH–Perkins.

31. Bowditch, *Massachusetts General Hospital*, 428.

32. Quincy, *History of Harvard*, 2:291, 543. After an 1833 bequest by Dr. Joshua Fisher, the professorship was renamed the Fisher Professor of Natural History. See Quincy, *History of Harvard*, 2:428, 628 and "Asa Gray at 200: Harvard Professor," Harvard University Herbaria and Libraries, accessed January 21, 2022, https://huh.harvard.edu/book/harvard-professor.

See also Samuel A. Eliot, *A Sketch of the History of Harvard College and of its Present State* (Boston, MA: Charles C. Little and James Brown, 1848). Between them, the three Perkins brothers also supported the Astronomical Observatory (637), the libraries (488), a fundraising effort to build an exhibition space (401, 592–593), and students (182).

33. See note 142 above.

34. Harvard University, *Dedication of the Thomas Nelson Perkins Room in Massachusetts Hall to the Use of the President and Fellows of Harvard College* (Cambridge, MA.: Harvard University Press, 1941). For family genealogy, see Harold Clarke Durrell, "Memoirs of Deceased Members of the New England Historic Genealogical Society: Thomas Nelson Perkins," *The New England Historical and Genealogical Register* 92 (January 1938): 84–85.

Neither Perkins Hall nor the Perkin Laboratory Building on the Harvard University campus are named for direct ancestors or descendants of James, Thomas Handasyd, or Samuel Gardner Perkins. See "Perkins Hall: Site Name History," Harvard Property Information Resource Center, Harvard University, accessed January 24, 2022, https://harvardplanning.emuseum .com/sites/783/perkins-hall and "Perkin Laboratory: Site Name History," Harvard Property Information Resource Center, Harvard University, accessed January 24, 2022, https://harvardplanning.emuseum.com/sites/670/perkin -laboratory.

35. Quincy, *History of Harvard*, 2:411–413, 596–597.

36. Quincy, *History of Harvard,* 2:545–548.

37. Bowditch, *Massachusetts General Hospital,* 430.

38. See, for example, "Orders to Nicholas Thorndike from Brown & Thorndike," October 11, 1791, 18460—Correspondence, Historic Beverly, Massachusetts, https://beverlyhistory.pastperfectonline.com/archive/63CB7150-96A9 -40C7-A1E3-312313391417. "Bill between Nicholas Thorndike and Brown & Thorndike," February 10, 1792, 18483—Bill of Sale, Historic Beverly, Massachusetts, https://beverlyhistory.pastperfectonline.com/archive/E697F9A5 -C2A9-4E68-BAB9-270264606260; "Bill of sales by Brown & Thorndike in account of Nicholas Thorndike," February 28, 1792, 18484—Bill of Sale, Historic Beverly, Massachusetts, https://beverlyhistory.pastperfectonline.com /archive/86F5C109-BF6A-4F44-98B1-134304130828; "Bill by Brown & Thorndike and their account with Nicholas Thorndike which includes ther merchants commission on Sales of Slaves and deducting Doctores Charges of Slaves," April 27, 1792, 18488—Bill of Sale, Historic Beverly, Massachusetts, https://beverlyhistory.pastperfectonline.com/archive/152AFA39-F8A8-477A -AC31-654751120923; W. Woodville to Israel Thorndike and John Lovett, December 16, 1801, 12847—Document, Historic Beverly, Massachusetts, https:// beverlyhistory.pastperfectonline.com/archive/9ABCA58C-18AB-47F4-900D -950629950107.

39. Bertram Zarins, "History of the Massachusetts General Hospital Sports Medicine Service," *The Orthopaedic Journal at Harvard Medical School* 9 (2007): 110, http://www.orthojournalhms.org/volume9/manuscripts/ms13.pdf.

40. Quincy, *History of Harvard,* 2:414–415.

41. See note 157 above.

42. E.D. Merrill, "The Atkins Institution of the Arnold Arboretum, Soledad, Cienfuegos, Cuba," *Bulletin of Popular Information,* 4th ser., 8, no. 13 (December 13, 1940): 66–68, http://arnoldia.arboretum.harvard.edu/pdf/articles /1940-8—the-atkins-institution-of-the-arnold-arboretum-soledad -cienfuegos-cuba.pdf.

43. Rebecca J. Scott, "Gradual Abolition and the Dynamics of Slave Emancipation in Cuba, 1868–86," *The Hispanic American Historical Review* 63, no. 3 (1983): 449–477; Rebecca J. Scott, "A Cuban Connection: Edwin F. Atkins, Charles Francis Adams, Jr., and the Former Slaves of Soledad Plantation," *The Massachusetts Historical Review* 9 (2007): 8–9.

44. Marion D. Cahan, "The Harvard Garden in Cuba—A Brief History," *Arnoldia* 51, no. 3 (Fall 1991): 30–32, http://arnoldia.arboretum.harvard.edu/pdf /articles/1991-51-3-the-harvard-garden-in-cuba-a-brief-history.pdf. See also

Jardín Botánico Nacional Universidad de La Habana, accessed February 23, 2022, www.jardinbotanico.co.cu.

Appendix B: A Note on Process

1.   See "Initiative on Harvard and the Legacy of Slavery," Office of the President, Harvard University, accessed October 12, 2021, https://www.harvard.edu /president/news/2019/initiative-on-harvard-and-the-legacy-of-slavery/.

2.   See Drew G. Faust, "Recognizing Slavery at Harvard," *Harvard Crimson,* March 20, 2016, https://www.thecrimson.com/article/2016/3/30/faust-harvard -slavery/.

3.   The members of the committee were: Sven Beckert (cochair); Evelyn Brooks Higginbotham (cochair); Alejandro de la Fuente; Annette Gordon-Reed; Evelynn M. Hammonds; and John Stauffer.

4.   Titus and Venus were enslaved by Benjamin Wadsworth, President of Harvard University from 1725 to 1737. Juba and Bilhah were enslaved by Edward Holyoke, President of Harvard from 1737 to 1769. See Christina Pazzanese, "To Titus, Venus, Bilhah, and Juba," *Harvard Gazette,* April 6, 2016, https://news.harvard.edu/gazette/story/2016/04/to-titus-venus-bilhah-and -juba/. Titus, Venus, Juba, and Bilhah, along with many of the individuals discussed here, were brought to light in Beckert et al., *Harvard and Slavery,* and by Caitlin Galante DeAngelis Hopkins, Harvard and Slavery Research Associate, 2017–2019.

Note that all pre-1752 dates have been updated to the New Style system following the Gregorian calendar, in which the calendar year runs from January 1 to December 31. See "The 1752 Calendar Change," Colonial Records & Topics, Connecticut State Library, accessed February 17, 2022, https:// libguides.ctstatelibrary.org/hg/colonialresearch/calendar.

5.   See Lydia Lyle Gibson, "A Vast Slave Society," Research, *Harvard Magazine,* March 6, 2017, https://www.harvardmagazine.com/2017/03/a-vast-slave -society; Claire E. Parker, "Conference Encourages Reparations for Harvard's Ties to Slavery," *Harvard Crimson,* March 5, 2017, https://www.thecrimson .com/article/2017/3/5/conference-encourages-slavery-reparations/.

6.   See Samuel Eliot Morison, *The Founding of Harvard College* (Cambridge, MA: Harvard University, 1935), 232–233, 425; "The History of Harvard," Harvard University; Conrad Edick Wright, *Revolutionary Generation: Harvard Men and the Consequences of Independence* (Amherst, MA: University of Massachusetts Press in association with Massachusetts Historical Society, 2005), and Bernard Bailyn et al., *Glimpses of the Harvard Past* (Cambridge, MA: Harvard University Press, 1986).

7.   Beckert et al., *Harvard and Slavery.*

8.   Janet Halley, "My Isaac Royall Legacy," *Harvard BlackLetter Law Journal* 24 (2008), http://www.law.harvard.edu/faculty/jhalley/cv/24.Harvard.Black letter.117.pdf. On the Royalls, see also Alexandra A. Chan, *Slavery in the Age of Reason: Archeology at a New England Farm* (Knoxville, TN: University of Tennessee Press, 2007); C. S. Manegold, "The Master," part 3 in *Ten Hills Farm: The Forgotten History of Slavery in the North* (Princeton, NJ: Princeton University Press, 2010); and Daniel R. Coquillette and Bruce A. Kimball, *On the Battlefield of Merit: Harvard Law School, the First Century* (Cambridge, MA: Harvard University Press, 2015), 75, 81–88.

9.   See "Royall Must Fall: The Shield is Retired," Exhibit Addenda, Harvard Law School, accessed February 9, 2022, https://exhibits.law.harvard.edu/royall -must-fall-shield-retired. Isaac Royall Jr. (1719–1781) lived just over three miles from Harvard Yard. The Royall House and Slave Quarters, where the Royalls enslaved more than sixty people and lived off of the wealth generated by yet more enslaved people who labored on the family's sugar plantation in Antigua, has been a historic site for over a century. Since 2005, the Royall House and Slave Quarters has reoriented its programming to focus on educating the public about the lives of the people enslaved there and, more broadly, the history of slavery in New England. See Royall House & Slave Quarters, accessed October 12, 2021, https://royallhouse.org/.

10. The members of Harvard Law School's 2016 shield committee were: Bruce H. Mann (chair); Mawuse Oliver Barker-Vormawor; James E. Bowers; Tomiko Brown-Nagin; Annette Gordon-Reed; Janet Halley; Rena Karefa-Johnson; Robert J. Katz; Samuel Moyn; S. Darrick Northington; Annie Rittgers; and Yih-hsien Shen. See Harvard Law School, *Recommendation to the President and Fellows of Harvard College on the Shield Approved for the Law School,* March 2016, https://today.law.harvard.edu/wp-content/uploads/2016 /03/Shield-Committee-Report.pdf, and Annette Gordon-Reed, *A Different View,* March 2016, https://today.law.harvard.edu/wp-content/uploads/2016/03 /Shield_Committee-Different_View.pdf. The law school recently unveiled a new shield, which makes clear that "Harvard Law School stands for truth, law, and justice," see "The Harvard Law School Shield," Harvard Law School, accessed February 17, 2022, https://hls.harvard.edu/about/the-harvard-law -school-shield/.

11. Brigit Katz, "Harvard Law School Marks Ties to Slavery in New Plaque," Smart News, *Smithsonian Magazine,* September 6, 2017, https://www .smithsonianmag.com/smart-news/harvard-law-school-marks-ties-slavery -new-plaque-180964784/.

12.   See Section Four of this report.

13.   The members of the subcommittee were: Nawal Nour (cochair); Fidencio Saldaña (cochair); M. William Lensch (organizer and member); Jalen Benson; Terésa Carter; Anthony D'Amico; Marcela del Carmen; Emily Gustainis; Dominic Hall; Beth MacGillivray; Stephen Maiorisi; Alisha Nanji; Jane Neill; LaShyra Nolen; Scott Podolsky; Joan Reede; Tania Rodriguez; Raquel Sofia Sandoval; Joanna Swift; and Alana Van Dervort. See M.R.F. Buckley, "Winds of Change: Holmes Academic Society Renamed in Honor of Physician-Scientist William Augustus Hinton," *Harvard Gazette,* September 23, 2020, https://news.harvard.edu/gazette/story/2020/09/harvard-medical-schools -holmes-academic-society-renamed/. See also "Guiding Principles for Artwork and Cultural Representations," Harvard Medical School, accessed February 17, 2022, https://hms.harvard.edu/about-hms/campus-culture/diversity-inclusion /guiding-principles-artwork-cultural-representations.

14.   See, for example, Colleen Walsh, "Initiative on Legacy of Slavery at Harvard Picks Up Steam," *Harvard Gazette,* October 15, 2020, https://news.harvard .edu/gazette/story/2020/10/radcliffe-based-program-rolls-out-research -efforts/; Colleen Walsh, "A Poem for Venus," *Harvard Gazette,* April 15, 2021, https://news.harvard.edu/gazette/story/2021/04/student-poem-gives-voice -to-enslaved-woman-on-campus-in-18th-century/.

ACKNOWLEDGMENTS

The committee is grateful to President Lawrence S. Bacow for launching this effort, to his chief of staff, Patti Bellinger, for her support, and to the many other dedicated members of the Harvard community who contributed their time, energy, and expertise to this report and to the nearly three-year process that underlies it.

In particular, we wish to thank the staff of the Presidential Initiative on Harvard & the Legacy of Slavery—Courtney Howard, Cristine Hutchison-Jones, Martine Jean, Dawn Ling, and Alexandria Russell—and all the outstanding student research assistants whose names are listed in Appendix B.

The initiative was anchored at Harvard Radcliffe Institute (HRI), and nearly every part of the Institute played an important role in its success. Alexander F. Hall, chief of staff and strategic advisor to the dean, and Jane F. Huber, director of communications, were invaluable contributors to all aspects of this effort.

The HRI communications team worked long and hard to bring this work to life, and the HRI events and Academic Ventures and Engagement departments were critical partners in executing 18 public programs, including an upcoming landmark conference, that engaged a broad audience with this history and its contemporary relevance. Staff of Radcliffe's Schlesinger Library on the History of Women in America supported our research and assisted in securing rights to the many historical images that bring the report's contents to life. Other HRI departments—human resources, finance, facilities management, and of course the dean's office—

made our work possible, and several Radcliffe fellows participated in generative conversations.

There are many others to thank, both within and outside Harvard, several of whom are mentioned in Appendix B: A Note on Process. We are truly grateful to all who helped us reach this important milestone.